A SHEARWATER BOOK

Also by Thomas Y. Canby

LEGENDS OF THE WEST

OUR CHANGING EARTH

WONDROUS WORLD OF FISHES

FROM BOTSWANA
TO THE
BERING SEA

From Botswana to the Bering Sea

to the

Bering Sea

My Thirty Years with
National Geographic

Thomas Y. Canby

ISLAND PRESS / Shearwater Books
Washington, D.C. • Covelo, California

A *Shearwater Book*
published by Island Press

LIBRARY OF CONGRESS CATALOGING-IN-PUBLICATION DATA
Canby, Thomas Y.
    From Botswana to the Bering sea : my thirty years with National
Geographic / by Thomas Y. Canby.
        p.   cm.
    Includes bibliographical references and index.
    ISBN 1-55963-517-7
    1. Canby, Thomas Y. 2. National geographic—History.
3. Geography—Field work. 4. Science writers—United States-
-Biography. 5. Periodical editors—United States—Biography.
    I. Title.
G69.C28A3   1998   98-5968
910' .5—dc21   CIP

Printed on recycled, acid-free paper

Manufactured in the United States of America
10 9 8 7 6 5 4 3 2 1

To Susan

Contents

Preface

To photographer Steve Raymer and me in sweltering Niger, the official's face is as unfriendly as his holstered pistol. He sits in his pool of sweat, we stand in ours, and he ponders a letter from the American consulate. It explains that we're representatives from *National Geographic*, and asks that we be granted free movement in this famine-stricken Saharan wasteland.

A light flashes on in my disbelieving brain. The man before us has never heard of *National Geographic*. He's the first human being I've encountered who doesn't recognize and love the yellow-bordered magazine. Raymer realizes this too, and he's digging in his bag for a copy—he gives them out wholesale—when the man grunts his verdict: We can travel in Niger, but no pictures of starvation or misery, or Raymer winds up in jail. Raymer returns the magazine to his bag, and we trudge away.

A little deflating, but probably good for us. Life can be almost too good when you're on assignment for *National Geographic*. I often worried, when hosts figuratively rolled out the red carpet, and doors swung open before me, whether I was succumbing to the arrogance that such deference invited.

National Geographic has rightly been called a window on the world and a passport to adventure. Each month an estimated 40 million people in 190 countries climb aboard this colorful magic carpet and glide off to exotic realms that delight the eye and mind. It is not only those who work there who call it the greatest of magazines.

Equally exotic is the inner world of the Society, the romantic publishing empire beyond the threshold of the white marble monument on 17th Street NW in the nation's capital. This is the realm of the Grosvenor dynasty, which for three generations has dominated the National Geographic Society; of indomitable *Geographic* photographers revealing the planet's hidden corners; of Jacques-Yves Cousteau and Robert Ballard exploring the oceans and Louis and Mary Leakey probing our human origins; of skilled writers and artists who explain how Mount St. Helens erupted, how earthquakes shudder, how Harlem survives, how hummingbirds hover.

This was my world for thirty-one years, as *National Geographic* writer and science editor.

By coincidence, those were decades of explosive growth and towering prestige for the Society, an era that could rightly be called its Golden Age. Though framed in that Golden Age, this book is by no means a history of that euphoric period. Rather it presents a partial and very personal view, as seen by a career writer and editor several rungs from the top. It is the view of one who proposed, wrote, and edited articles, who reveled in the romance of the Society, who thrilled in adventures and misadventures as a *Geographic* world traveler, and who across the decades observed the world changing before his eyes.

When I arrived at headquarters on January 2, 1961, the Society was in a foment of expansion, signing on new members by the millions, creating new products, hiring more staff to produce them. Through it all, the Society's foundation remained the *National Geographic Magazine*, known in-house as the flagship.

The flagship itself was in overhaul. Eager, new-generation artists were streamlining the venerable cover by removing its clustered acorns and framing a photograph within that yellow border. The editorial tone was changing. Long chided by critics as a journal of "bare breasts and sunsets," the magazine was hesitantly extinguishing the sunsets in favor of articles confronting social issues. The bare breasts? *Geographic* photographers took what came.

Observed Editor Wilbur E. Garrett, "We neither dress them nor undress them."

Such transitions, often basic in nature, ultimately raise a question: When has change gone far enough? Too far? Throughout my tenure the question would roil the magazine, wreck editorial careers, and never really be resolved.

These internal tensions meant little to the world beyond *Geographic* walls. The world loves the magazine, respects it, and trusts it. Being a reporter or editor for such an institution is a satisfaction beyond belief. Doors that are closed against the rest of the journalistic world open wide. Scientists, statesmen, and academicians willingly talk to us. People press hospitality on us with discomfiting generosity, from the Niger famine refugee who offers his last tea, to the corporate executives who serve drinks to flush-faced journalists from their jets' three bars.

For me, the *Geographic* was a science editor's dream. Not for the power; my diminutive command included only three writers and two assistants. Satisfaction sprang from the exhilaration of pursuing the magazine's goal of painless education. My job was to create articles conveying large amounts of accurate scientific information, to pick relevant subjects and write interestingly and excitingly about them. Each of those articles was a stimulating challenge.

But the *Geographic* offered a splendid laboratory for this editorial alchemy. Supporting the writers were the world's finest photographers, along with gifted designers, graphic artists, and cartographers. Sharp-eyed researchers verified the accuracy of every word we wrote, drawing on a library of 72,000 books, millions of news clips, and swelling electronic databases. In our catacomb basement, sophisticated carpentry and machine shops contrived unlikely apparatuses for exploring land, sea, and air. An efficient travel office landed us anywhere, and a doting medical center immunized us for everywhere. We had access to a purchasing office, a stock room, and black-capped chauffeurs. The *Geographic* was, in short, editorial heaven on Earth. With these rich resources, it's little wonder that the *Geographic* won innumerable awards for its photography, writing, and general excellence. Science articles won their share and perhaps more. Periodically the magazine polled its readers to discover how they ranked past articles. Consistently they accorded a lopsided popularity to those featuring science.

This book is drawn from the two worlds that shape the career of a *Geographic* journalist. One is the charming if somewhat eccentric world within the Society walls, as seen by one who deeply loved dwelling there. In telling this story, I chose not to submit the book to the *Geographic* in advance, or seek the Society's blessing. I wanted independence in presenting my observations, so I could present them my way—a perspective of the magazine and Society through the eyes of a former senior assistant editor. If I wanted to be critical (seldom) or poke fun, I didn't want the Society agonizing over small matters. Regardless, I am totally a Geographic man.

The other world of this book encompasses the travels and unusual destinations that fell my lot when on assignment. For thirty-one years I remained a wide-eyed and curious observer, tingling with excitement with each takeoff from Dulles International.

Whenever I set forth, as science writer or science editor, I carried as many as a dozen pocket-size spiral-bound notebooks. Into these went the observations from people I interviewed, along with my observations of them and descriptions of where we happened to be, whether in an MIT laboratory or inside India's fascinating Rat Temple. From these notebooks, crammed with details, would come my article. I lived in terror of losing them as I did my hats and coats; often in the field I found myself counting them to make sure they were all there, like Silas Marner with his gold. Once, while in California's earthquake country, I left a notebook at an elementary school along the San Andreas Fault. I rushed back in panic to find that a teacher had kept it safely on her desk, knowing I would return. Thereafter I always taped a business card to the back of each notebook in hope that a finder would return it.

I also enjoyed the blessing of travel insomnia, though at the time my wakefulness seemed a curse. I could seldom sleep in a plane, train, bus, or car, in which collectively I spent much time. Not thinking of a future book, I nevertheless devised a pastime that for this book has served me well. While the photographer who accompanied me made himself comfortable and dozed, I automatically reached for notebook and ballpoint pen and looked out the window or studied my fellow passengers. Whatever I saw, I described. Between observations I attempted to express what I had seen in literary terms, with a metaphor or simile. These came hard to my literal mind, and I liked working on them.

By the end of an assignment, I had a stack of ten to twenty filled notebooks; by the end of a career, twenty-one such stacks. They are my memory bank of far-flung *Geographic* trips across the decades; they are the stuff of this book.

It is gratifying to put them to use. Every *Geographic* assignment was, in a sense, high-dollar, premeditated journalistic overkill. A photographer, to ensure good coverage, brought home from each assignment an average of 500 to 700 rolls of exposed film, from which perhaps thirty frames would be chosen for an article. Similarly, we writers amassed enough notes for a book, then brought forth only a single 6,000-word manuscript. This was unspoken editorial policy. One had to range far, wide, and deep in order to be sure one's coverage was thorough and fair, and to bring the very best to the reader. Further, overkill was a lot less expensive than having to return for more coverage.

IN ADDITION to my notebooks, buttressed by my own recollections, I have drawn on many other people in writing this book. Every friend and colleague at *National Geographic* since my first day of work contributed threads to the fabric. Laurie Burnham, my editor at Shearwater, proved with countless helpful suggestions that every writer needs an editor, even if that writer is himself an editor. Deborah Clarke Grosvenor transcended her role of literary

agent to help shape the book's structure and tone. Mimi Dornack of
the Society's Image Collection zealously corralled elusive pictures.
I thank my wife, Susan, for her helpful advice, for preparing the
index, and for her charitable forbearance during my lengthy immersion in writing. And I thank the National Geographic Society
itself, for allowing me to hold what is rightly called "the best job in
the world."

Chapter 1

INSIDE THE
YELLOW BORDER

M y hip pocket bulges with traveler's checks—five thousand dollars' worth, a wad so thick my rump has lost its symmetry. Freshly stamped visas splash my passport, ink still damp on those cajoled from third-world countries suspicious about why I'm visiting them. On my desk rests a fat packet from our Travel Office, emblazoned with the gold-bordered logo of the *National Geographic* and chock full of first-class airline tickets. In one frenzied month in this winter of 1976 they will take me to a dozen countries around the world and return my spent husk to the airy architecture of Dulles International.

There's still a day before breakout, however, and here in the nation's capital Gil Grosvenor is an unhappy editor. That's nothing new; editors are born unhappy. Their authority and finances seldom match their grand schemes and expectations. And in the back of their minds they often fear the repercussions of what they soon will publish.

The latter explains Gil's sour mood. He's never really approved of my assignment, even though officially he acquiesced to it a month ago at the urging of his editorial lieutenants. He's not totally persuaded that a family magazine needs what I am set-ting off at great cost to bring him—an in-depth article on rats, on rats around the world, the rats that each year cause famine by destroying a fifth of our crops, spread plague and a host of other dis-eases, destroy a billion dollars' worth of property in just the United States. They are also among our foremost benefactors in the form of the amiable white rats of the research laboratory. In the United States alone nearly 20 million a year are used in medical and psy-chological studies that save and serve innumerable human lives.

Some 120 species of rats inhabit our planet, but I will be focusing on four that have intimately linked their destinies with humans'. These commensal rats (meaning literally that they share our table) need us as much as we hate them. They are the Norway rat, a burly burrower widely regarded as the most destructive mam-mal on Earth; the roof rat, bearer of the terror-inspiring bubonic plague, which still lurks in the world; the dainty Polynesian rat, most at home eating coconuts high in Pacific island trees; and the shaggy bandicoot, scourge of southern Asia's grain fields and gra-naries, often feasting where famine stalks.

Ample material and reasons for an article—ample to every-one except Gil. That's why he has just summoned me to his office, floating nine stories up in the glass and white-marble temple designed by Edward Durrell Stone and dedicated in 1964 by Presi-dent Lyndon Johnson on his first official public appearance after the assassination of President John F. Kennedy.

The ninth floor is no area for horseplay. Next to Gil's office sprawls that of the editor-in-chief and board chairman. He is Gil's father, Melville Bell Grosvenor. That's Bell as in Alexander, inven-tor of the telephone and Gil's great-grandfather; and Grosvenor as in Gilbert H., the editorial genius behind the success of the National Geographic Society and founder of the Grosvenor dy-nasty, who died in 1966 at age ninety-one and still is much revered.

Gil's power-secretary bestows an ambiguous smile and gestures to me to enter the lair. This involves a short hike. First I pass through a comfortable conference area furnished with beige couch and chairs and hung with Society maps and Gil's own photography, for he once worked in the field as a staff writer/photographer during his steady ascent up the editorial ladder. Next I traverse a room-size open space, paved with oriental carpets. Two functional chairs perch like penitents before the large polished desk. Facing me sits Gil, elbows planted so the fists support the chin, tight lips drawn disapprovingly across the round, spectacled face —a face not unlike mine, since we are within a year of each other in age.

The tight lips part, and the jaw drops slightly, a little like a marionette's. "Canby, your subject is disgusting. I don't know why the hell we're doing a story about rats." I fear for my plane tickets, my precious visas and traveler's checks, my carefully orchestrated itinerary. The unhappy face relents a smidgeon. "I'm letting you do this coverage, but I'm putting total faith in you to be discreet. We can't have 35 million readers all over the world vomiting from some global epidemic we've inflicted on them. I've given the same warning to Jim Stanfield about the pictures. For Christ's sake, be discreet."

Fair enough. I am the soul of discretion, an enthusiastic journalist totally infatuated with our magnificent magazine and the members who love it. Jim Stanfield's deportment matches mine. Discretion is a hallmark of *Geographic* corporate behavior, inculcated by example by genteel upper-echelon editors and business executives. Luckily, in one more day I'll be off and running.

I descend to the seventh floor, where most of my sixteen fellow writers and I occupy comfortable offices positioned around the perimeter. The size of our offices corresponds to our ranking on the magazine masthead; the higher the rank, the more space and more windows. As a junior editor/writer at the time, I rate a relatively small room with a single window. Two windows signify an assistant editor or lesser senior assistant editor. Four-window offices, at each corner of the floor, mark senior assistant editors with administrative responsibilities such as handling manuscripts from the rest of us and from nonstaff explorers and scientists. At any given time, a third of the offices are empty, their normal occupants covering distant assignments. Sometimes these quarters are temporarily occupied by a scientist or explorer whose manuscript is being worked over by one of the editors in a two- or four-window office.

My phone rings. The call is from the reception desk, down in Explorers Hall, the Society's fascinating first-floor museum. Among its displays are the sled that accompanied Robert E. Peary to the North Pole and a stuffed dog that didn't, a replica of a twenty-ton stone Olmec head from ancient Mexico, the world's biggest frog (from Cameroon, and pickled) and biggest egg (from Madagascar), the world's largest free-moving globe, and a reflecting pool whose waters have more than once been invaded by us writers during an afterwork bacchanal.

"Mr. Canby," says the receptionist, "your luncheon guest, Dr. Hamman, has arrived." Philip Hamman is the head of the National Pest Control Association. He's the last of a stream of consultants I have invited to the Society to brief me, Jim Stanfield, the picture editor, and the researchers about the complex subject—rats—that will consume nearly a year of our lives and perhaps a million dollars of Society money before it appears as thirty pages of photos and text. Today these colleagues are tied up—Jim already is out shooting our cherished rodents—so I will interview Hamman alone.

I escort the stout Ph.D. and his fat briefcase to the tenth-floor Masthead Cafeteria. This is a great place. Aromas riding the moist air announce the menu: gourmet fish, fowl, and beef concoctions piled on stainless-steel steam trays; more steamers brimful of veggies; sandwiches and burgers available on order; glass shelves laden with desserts and artful salads; ample attendants to serve this bounty; and, at the end, a cash register that removes little from the wallet. It's a company rule that staffers who bring a business guest to lunch also eat on the company tab: A toast to Dr. Hamman!

We load our trays and proceed to the gracious dining room. Floor-to-ceiling windows present views of the rooftops of lesser buildings receding far into northwest Washington. On a distant hill rises the majestic National Cathedral, nearing completion after nearly a century of toil. Underfoot is rich red carpeting; on the eight tables of various sizes, spotless white tablecloths form pristine pools around arrangements of fresh flowers.

I see Gil at a large table, bantering with a bunch of business types. I steer Hamman to a four-person table next to Gil's that bears my "reserved" sign. We unload our trays, and Hamman leans his bulging briefcase against a table leg. Sitting across from him, I feel a sense of misgiving, as if something could go wrong. I've asked him to bring interesting pictures from his files; maybe they will give ideas to the photographer. I've also warned him of Gil's skittishness—to be discreet about our subject.

A waiter removes our emptied trays. Hamman eats and speaks with equal fluency. He's obviously well informed about pest-control people and programs across the country. I struggle to snatch a bite and take notes about them all: New York City's heroic but doomed rat campaign; a company in Omaha, Presto-X, that contends with the hordes of rats infesting midwestern stockyards; the Big State Pest Control people in Houston, challenging rats at grain railyards and port facilities; the rodent-control effort right here in D.C., also doomed. Hamman is helpful, and I encourage him.

"You mentioned photos," he says. "Got some good ones for you." He wears a satisfied look; maybe these pictures are really winners. He reaches down to the briefcase and produces a thick sheaf of eight-by-ten black-and-white prints. Gag! Babies in cribs with their fingers chewed by rats, their ears notched—their eyeballs eaten! I glance sideways toward Gil. He is finished, rising from the table.

"Let's continue this in the office," I blurt to Hamman, and lean forward to scoop up the prints. Too late! Gil is already at the table—and walking safely past.

Toward sunset that evening I carry my two bags to the parking lot behind the Society building. As is customary, a staff chauffeur smoothly navigates the forty-five-minute drive to Dulles.

There I board my flight, cocoon myself in the first-class compartment, and allow the magic chemistry of the first glass of champagne to soothe stomach and mind.

I am convinced that in the everyday, work a day world, no sensation is more exhilarating than taking to the air on assignment for *National Geographic.* There are other ways to go off on assignment, of course—by train or car or foot. But the lift of the powerful jet works in concert with the buoying thrill of impending adventure to send one's spirit soaring. Not only is a *Geographic* writer or photographer made welcome wherever he or she lands. More important for a writer, one knows one is headed for experiences—their nature yet undetermined—that will be uniquely one's own, inaccessible and even unimaginable to the wealthiest tourist—experiences that will not only strengthen one's article but also enrich one's life forever.

Wait, one might say: There are other magazines; couldn't working for them be just as exhilarating? No. Often I crossed paths with journalists attached to other glamour publications, such as *Life* and *Time.* Over drinks we would talk shop. Invariably they confided their envy of those of us lucky enough to be reporting for the magazine with the yellow border. At no other publication did reporters enjoy the freedom and cooperation accorded *Geographic* writers and photographers.

I ENTERED the magical realm of *National Geographic's* yellow border on January 2, 1961. My hiring was part of a benign upheaval. The once-staid Society was growing explosively in all directions— an editorial Big Bang. The impetus came from a Grosvenor of uncommon energy, enthusiasm, and imagination: Gil's father, Melville.

Until a few years earlier, the institution had been stagnant. Melville's father, Gilbert Hovey Grosvenor, the tweedy Amherst genius who had married the daughter of Alexander Graham Bell, become the first full-time managing editor in 1900, made the camera as essential an editorial tool as the typewriter, introduced topless native women into fashionable parlors, and increased the membership a thousandfold to over 2 million—this dynamic innovator had held on to his post until 1954, long after his creative juices had evaporated. His successor was John Oliver LaGorce, GHG's sidekick for half a century, a canny promoter and builder of membership, prejudiced against Jews, blacks, and women, a portly shadow of his mentor who brought to this final task an ineffectualness that suggested senility. When LaGorce tottered from power in 1957, the Society and its magazine were as enfeebled as its recent leaders.

At age fifty-six Melville Bell Grosvenor moved into the editor's office bursting with projects planned but pent up for more than thirty years of working and waiting. He pressed them with an enthusiasm reminiscent of his grandfather Alexander Graham Bell, whose favorite he had been until the inventor's death in 1922, and whose exuberance Melville shared.

Melville plunged the Society into book publishing, creating a special division for the task. Long critical of the magazine's traditional cover, with its frame of oak leaves and acorns—"Every issue looks the same!"—he gradually uprooted the vegetation and introduced color cover photographs. Doubling the size of the Cartographic Division, he published insert maps that became the building blocks for an impressive series of world atlases, and produced a popular globe with plastic "thinking cap" for accurately measuring distances on a spherical surface. He launched the Society's awesomely popular television specials and created popular academic superstars such as paleontologist Louis Leakey and behaviorist Jane Goodall.

Melville was equally zealous about Society membership, the true foundation of the empire. The concept of membership in the Society, which went far beyond merely subscribing to the Society's magazine, was the brainchild of Alexander Bell. Membership conferred not only a subscription but also a handsome certificate, along with invitations to attend the Society's lectures and other functions. The youthful Gilbert H. Grosvenor quickly recognized the concept's advantages in inspiring loyalty and renewals of subscriptions, and enthusiastically pushed memberships. Important to future success, the Society's loyal members represented an immense reservoir of usually comfortably fixed consumers favorably disposed to buying books and other products offered at special low prices. In Melville's decade as editor, membership nearly tripled, to 5.5 million.

During these years Melville built two temples of marble, glass, and steel: the Society's handsome headquarters building in downtown D.C. and its massive Membership Center Building in suburban Maryland. Despite the hectic pace of those projects he also read everything to be published in the Society's magazine and books, scribbling accolades when pleased, dashing off criticisms when the writing dragged, hammering at favorite rules: Avoid the passive voice! Stop using the dull verb "to be"—those listless *is*'s and *was*'s.

Melville's avalanche of new products demanded increases in staff, especially in the new Book Division. Late in 1960 the Society advertised for two editor/writers. At the time I was newly married, editing a woefully understaffed weekly newspaper in suburban Maryland, and attending law school at night. The newspaper, after five years, was becoming a treadmill, and law school was failing to make a case for a career. Here was my chance to enter a lustrous new world that would combine writing and adventure. In the evenings after the law courses I struggled with the Society's writing competition, and in December I was interviewed, induced to take less pay than I'd expected, and charged to appear when the doors opened on the first working day of the new year.

I was thirty-one when I signed on to the *Geographic,* and I stayed there another thirty-one years. During those decades I changed from brown-haired book writer to gray-thatched science editor for the magazine. I also observed changes around me, both within and outside the Society.

The fiery meteor that was the Society during Melville's reign dimmed perceptibly during the tenure of son Gilbert, a well-intentioned but inconsistent leader unable to maintain the magazine's and Society's momentum. Even so, like his father and grandfather Gil left landmarks. Foremost among them was a visionary, nationwide movement to reintroduce geography into American school curriculums. In 1975 he transformed the stodgy *School Bulletin* for children into the vibrant kids' magazine *WORLD*, and a decade later he introduced a beautiful and buoyant new magazine, *Traveler*. In addition, as editor of *National Geographic* he cast off the magazine's rose-colored glasses and came to grips with real-life issues such as racism and politics. And when this departure caused alarm among a mossback minority of the Board of Trustees, Gil, backed by Melville and former editor Frederick G. Vosburgh, resolutely beat back an effort to impose a trustees' oversight committee to monitor editorial content.

But Gil's efforts after rising from editor to president in 1980 could not sustain the rate of expansion achieved by his father. Under Melville the Society had become a hydra whose many heads required constant feeding with new ideas and ever-larger markets. Gil added more heads to the hydra, but these costly innovations often did not pay their way; instead, they cannibalized the well-padded body of the Society itself. By the early 1990s, despite drastic downsizing, the bottom line for *Geographic* products had shifted from black to red. Quite possibly no one could have done better, in a time of ever-fiercer competition. However that may be, at Gil's departure in 1996, America's most-admired private institution, though still widely loved, had devolved internally from a supportive, loyal family to a diminished core of often-anxious employees heavily dependent on outside contractors. It was as if the Society were a rocket and the Grosvenor dynasty the three propulsive stages: Gilbert H. lifting off powerfully and on course as stage one; Melville as stage two, soaring sharply as if oblivious of gravity; and Gil as stage three, slowing in the climb and leveling off into orbit—with an orbit's tendency toward decay. I rode with stages two and three, the soaring climb and gradual leveling.

As the *Geographic* changed, so did the world it sent me out into. Two of the more profound changes taking place in those three decades won scant attention from the press.

One is the triumph of the English language as the common tongue of humankind. This lingual conquest began, of course, with the spread of the British empire to every inhabited continent except South America. As the empire disintegrated, the transistor radio ably took up the cause. Even in the most impoverished nations one saw headsets receiving Anglo-American pop culture; saw, inside the darkest hovels, the flicker of Hollywood television. Less visible but perhaps equally important in spreading English has been the unquestioned worldwide dominance of American science, and English as the language of that science. Today, in every nation with a scientific establishment, English continues to spread unstoppably along with American science and the new technologies developing from it. Even in China, English is taught as the mandatory primary foreign language. This profound global evolution occurred largely without the rancor and discord that have marred attempts to introduce other global conventions, such as the metric system.

The second change relates to the world's ability to feed itself. During the 1960s and early 1970s ominous food shortages afflicted the populous Indian subcontinent, and famine gripped the African Sahel. Experts eyeing the trajectory of the population curve predicted Malthusian disaster. Assigned to cover those famines and foretell our food future, I concluded that the industrialized world's enormous commitment to agricultural research, coupled with the canniness of farmers worldwide, would enable food production to keep pace with population, barring drought or war. The success of that research and those farmers is one of the most important stories of the time; and, like most successes, it goes little reported.

A new employee arriving at Society headquarters during the *Geographic*'s boomtime of the early 1960s found himself in sad straits: The staff had ballooned, but office space had not; there were no quarters to assign self-important new writers. "You'll have to drift," said Herbert Henderson, the kindly director of personnel. "The book editor will arrange for you to use the offices of staffers off on assignment."

And drift I did for three years, until Melville completed our new temple in 1964. Staying mobile with only a portable typewriter and a few desktop supplies, I would move into an office just vacated, slip invisibly away before the owner returned, and migrate to squat anew where another had departed. Dignity suffered, but other senses thrived. I found myself occupying walnut-paneled, curio-cluttered offices of the great *Geographic* writers—legendary men who had traveled the world round and round, dodged death in miraculous ways, and consorted with kings and knaves with equal gusto. Looking wistfully at their museumlike collections of tribal blowguns, poisoned arrows, and shrunken heads, I wondered if I would ever visit those exotic places.

It was a quaint place to work, the National Geographic Society of 1961. Men ran the show—mannerly white men, seemingly above tantrums and disorder, usually decorous but occasionally excessive in their wining and dining; men who despite their personal peculiarities zealously guarded the accuracy and integrity of the magazine they published. Unlike today, with the Society's ranks enriched by women and minorities, in this male world women largely tended the phones and typed the correspondence. Dark-skinned men in uniforms pushed mail carts and sat outside the higher editors' offices waiting to deliver an important document or an editor himself.

The quaintest anachronism was the cafeteria. In those days it occupied the basement of an old building at 16th and M Streets. Its distinction lay not in elegance, of which it had little, but in the peculiar rules controlling who ate where. A large, tile-floored room accommodated men beneath the professional level, plus all women. A smaller room, also tiled, was the exclusive sanctuary of the male professionals. Sometimes these professionals would sit out with the women and lesser men, but never the reverse. Most good-naturedly accepted this partitioning for what it was—a vestigial social relic teetering on the brink of extinction.

Easy to caricature, yes. But the Society of the 1960s also was a formidable publishing machine, geared to fulfill its unique editorial role in American life and worldwide. This role was to educate—in particular to educate painlessly, even pleasurably, so that Society members looked forward monthly to being taught. Geographic pictures and words did much to shape Americans' understanding of peoples beyond their shores. They also shaped individual lives. For three decades I would meet men and women who had been inspired by Geographic articles to pursue their careers—in geology, anthropology, archaeology, ecology, space.

A primary teaching aid was, of course, the camera; in artful hands it captured images whose value far transcended the proverbial thousand words. With each superb picture came the caption— what we called the legend, and all-important. By Melville's time these few lines were evolving into a literary form. A special corps of writers sweated out these miniaturized masterworks, ingeniously designed to whet the reader's interest in the accompanying article and to convey as much of that article as limited space allowed. Every article writer lived with the humbling knowledge that, despite the immense time, expense, and effort he had invested, far more people read the legends than his text.

The magazine article itself was an unusual creature, a sort of literary duckbilled platypus—warm-blooded, devoid of fangs, largely successful, and also capable of laying the occasional egg.

Every article's strength (and potential weakness) lay in the fact that it was written in the first person, through the eyes of the beholder. This technique traced back to a discovery by Gilbert H. Grosvenor in 1900. Hired by Alexander Graham Bell to revive a then-ailing geographic journal, young Grosvenor set out to divine the secret of earlier popular geographic writing. Carefully he analyzed the works of immortals such as Herodotus and Darwin. "Each," he concluded, "was an accurate, eyewitness, firsthand account. Each contained simple, straightforward writing—writing that sought to make pictures in the reader's mind." Pictures: Of course GHG would approve of them, in words as well as on film. Firsthand: The writer observed things himself or, better yet, *did* them, then described them and his reactions in ways that bore the reader with him.

In the hands of a good writer, the first-person account lures the reader almost effortlessly from one page to the next. But this genre, so blissfully easy for the reader, is devilishly difficult for the writer. Let him become lax and intrude himself clumsily, and the reader grows not only restless but also resentful—feels patronized, written down to. At times the editors allowed such an article to slip into the magazine, and its taint would linger long among discriminating readers.

Three other traits were common to most articles. They were fact-filled, loaded with statistics such as population size, economic output, and demographic alignment, all fed to the reader so obliquely, so painlessly that he or she was scarcely aware of being taught. A handy device for delivering all this information, especially in science articles, was to make comparisons; in a story about the universe, for example, my predecessor as science editor, Kenneth F. Weaver, illustrated the density of matter in a black hole by noting that a teaspoonful "weighs as much as 200 million elephants."

Second, the articles were accurate, probably the most accurate writings on Earth. This was so not because we writers were infallible—far from it—but rather because a staff of researchers, well educated and trained, pored over every paragraph, sentence, and word, searching for errors and ambiguities. Yes, a few inaccuracies sneaked through, but so few as to be talked about by the staff as disgraceful exceptions.

This rigorous fact-checking and the researchers' many quibbles often provoked exasperated writers into charges of nitpicking. Most researchers, almost all of whom were female, showed enormous tact in their delicate task. But at times those researchers who most relentlessly pursued pure truth were also the least diplomatic. One writer, taxed beyond endurance by such a zealot, howled, "I'm being nibbled to death by rabbits!" I never enjoyed learning I was in error (and was astonished at how often this happened), but I warmly welcomed the researchers' corrections. My greatest dread was to bring blame to the *Geographic* and myself for a mistake in an article.

The third distinguishing trait of *Geographic* articles was their considerable length. No other popular magazine gave such exhaustive coverage—told the reader so much more than he or she usually wanted. We were aware of this—and approved. *Geographic* articles were to be comprehensive, to possess lasting reference value. "Travel wherever you must to get the story," admonished our editors. "Stay out in the field as long as you need." Unbelievable advice. And probably the last words of advice we would receive. The instant we departed on assignment, the editor gratefully turned back to his cluttered desk, and left us in glorious neglect to do our job. How could I not love such an institution?

Chapter 2

RAT PATROL

And so I am airborne, heading westward on what will be a globe-girdling immersion in the unlikely subject of rats.

My first hop is a short one, to Denver, to the laboratory of the U.S. Fish and Wildlife Service, a key combatant in the global war on rats. Its staff includes scientists who have spent a major part of their lives observing rodents, on Baltimore streets, in Indian granaries, on English farmsteads. Others are technical experts—men and women skilled in the deadliest traps, chemicals, and electrical devices designed to destroy rats. From their combined efforts came the armaments and strategies of the U.S. effort to defeat rats, particularly in tropical countries, where their depredations are the worst. My visit is brief—only one day—but important, for during much of my trip I will be observing Fish and Wildlife personnel and their rat-control techniques in foreign cities, villages, and fields.

The scientists face a worthy and wary adversary. The rat is paranoically suspicious, its every sense tuned to an awesome acuteness. Disturb its world ever so little—place a brick where it roams—and it may shy away for days. This suspicion applies especially to a finickiness about food, and for good reason: The rat cannot regurgitate. What it eats becomes irrevocable, so its caution must be absolute. This does not simplify the task of scientists who seek to conquer with poison.

The task of the Fish and Wildlife Service is an old one. Since ancient times, when Egyptians put out the first rodenticide, humans have waged war unremittingly against rats. We have baited them with deadly poisons, stalked them with clever traps and snares, assaulted their burrows with fire and floods, and attempted sterilization, electrocution, and breeding a better cat. Yet rats flourish almost everywhere, in part because of their extraordinary physical prowess. An everyday rat can wriggle through a hole the size of a quarter, gnaw through cinder blocks and lead pipes, tread water for three days and swim half a mile, enter buildings by way of the toilet and survive being flushed, scale a sheer brick wall, and, if dislodged, plummet five stories to the ground unharmed.

From Denver I move on to Hawaii, to the Big Island, where rats maraud virtually every crop—coffee, orchids, macadamia nuts, and, worst of all, sugarcane. While I tour the cane fields biplanes roar overhead, dropping rodenticides to halt losses amounting to millions of dollars a year. Spraying beats an earlier "solution": In 1883 planters introduced mongooses to kill the rats. But the rats fed by night, the mongooses by day, and the introduced species turned instead to the island's ground-nesting petrels, rails, and shearwaters, bringing on an ecological holocaust.

A few days later I'm off to the Philippines. Rats are destroying crops throughout the archipelago, and the Filipinos have mounted an energetic campaign to poison the rodents in the fields. They are receiving powerful assistance from Uncle Sam, with money and expertise funneled through the Agency for International Development. In Manila I rendezvous with photographer Jim Stanfield, and we join the AID and Filipino combatants in the battle zone.

I'm fortunate to be working with James L. Stanfield. He's at midpoint in a career that will distinguish him as one of the world's most gifted photographers. His artistry bodes well for my article: The better the pictures, the more pages on rats the editor will publish, and therefore the more room for my text. Since every writer brings home vastly more material than the article space gives room for, the writing of a story entails painful omissions. Writers always want more pages, and Stanfield means pages.

Vastly more important, he is also the ideal companion for our rigorous assignment: likable, cheerful, a team player, and, in his forties, still the good-looking all-American boy. In the field, Stanfield works with a winning combination of goodwill, patience, and intensity. Eventually our paths will diverge—always the case with writer and photographer. A writer travels fast—takes notes and moves on—while a photographer often must wait, and wait longer, for an event to occur in the proper place (in front of his camera) in proper conditions of lighting (usually sunrise or sunset). During our coverage, for example, Jim will spend a week in the rat-infested sewers of the Vatican (I will cover them in hours) and a week in a rat-haunted Michigan chicken coop, in each case knowing that at best he will produce a single picture for our article.

Stanfield and I haven't told Gil Grosvenor that in the Philippines we will see human beings eat rats—and, if possible, will eat some ourselves. These are not urban rats, the universally loathed carriers of diseases and parasites. The Filipinos sensibly eat rural rats, which live by the billions in their rice paddies. Tasty country rat meat was once canned and marketed in Manila and other cities under the label "STAR," "rats" spelled backward. For an itinerant rat writer and photographer, this is the promised land.

IT IS TWO in the morning, and we are driving in the dark toward a rice harvest. With us is Russell F. Reidinger, a youthful Kansas-born biologist with the Fish and Wildlife Service now on loan to the Rodent Research Center (RRC) at Los Baños, south of Manila. Los

Baños ranks as a shrine among those who fight world hunger, for it is the home of the famed International Rice Research Institute (IRRI), which developed the miracle rices of the Green Revolution. The RRC and IRRI have attracted a good-size Western community, and it is there that Russ and his wife, Carol, are stationed for two years.

The RRC, jointly run by AID and the Philippine government, develops field methods for controlling rats where they compete with humans for food—methods designed to be simple, cheap, and effective, and thus credible and affordable for peasant farmers. The farmers naturally are skeptical of government help, but they know they have a rat problem: The rodents devour perhaps half their crop each year; throughout Asia rats consume about 50 million tons of rice annually, enough to feed a quarter of a billion people.

We drive north past Manila. To our left roils the South China Sea; to our right the interior of Luzon takes shape in a luminous gray hint of dawn. Stately palms emerge alongside the road. In their crowns dwell rats that live on the leaf shoots, flowers, and coconuts—destructive rats that in their lifetimes may never descend to ground.

We reach the outskirts of the small city of San Antonio, in marshland north of Bataan, and park outside a simple but large concrete structure. This is the rice-storage house of Mrs. Eufemia Perez, a major landowner and rice planter.

Two figures emerge from the rice house—a perky Mrs. Perez, and a middle-aged Filipino of martial air introduced as Mr. Liboy. Mr. Liboy works with Russ at the RRC and will orchestrate our day.

We peer into the storage building. There's no rice, only a shiny new rice-polishing machine that obviously has seen little use. "Rats destroyed most of last year's crop," explains Mrs. Perez. "Thank goodness my husband has a business in Manila."

Mr. Liboy takes the lead, and we set out single file in the growing light, balancing along the tops of rice paddy dikes. Burdened only with a small notebook and ballpoint pen, I carry Stanfield's film bag, while he carries a camera around his neck, two more with assorted lenses in a shoulder bag, and a tripod. A mile distant we see the knot of harvesters we will join.

Russ Reidinger slows, scans the dikes, and points to an array of holes: "Rat burrows." Every embankment, we discover, is perforated with burrows. A lacework of runways branches out from them into the paddies—rat highways, crossroads, interchanges. In these paddies virtually all the grain is gone, along with most of the stalks.

Mr. Liboy stops at a dike with an overhang and a ledge beneath. The ledge surface is piled with chewed stalks and leaves. "Rats feed mainly at night. For safety from predators they carry food there to eat in the shadows, out of the moonlight."

Ahead, two men are digging into a dike while a boy watches. Suddenly a digger wields his hoe like a baseball bat, then stoops to pick up a dead rat. He tosses it to the boy, who skins and guts it and puts it in a bag. Inside I count fourteen rats for the table. Looking around, I see a dozen other teams grubbing for rodents. Stanfield's motor drive whirs as he shoots a few rolls of film.

The sun climbs out of the marsh, pumping the day's first heat into the hazy morning sky. We approach the group of rice harvesters, twenty men and women, the two sexes dressed almost indistinguishably in loose trousers and straw hats. A dozen children mill around. Sickles in hand, the harvesters deploy in a loose circle around a paddy of uncut rice the size of a basketball court. "Now they'll tighten the noose," says Russ.

The harvesters bend to their timeless task. Sickles flashing, they cut handfuls of stalks until they hold a sheaf the size of a fireplace broom, then tie it with other stalks. Gradually the uncut area shrinks to an irregular circle only twenty feet across.

Now the children move in behind the harvesters, many holding sticks. In the small circle of standing rice, the stalks begin quivering, vibrating. Rats have been concentrated by the cordon of sicklers and are panicking, barging into the stalks and each other.

A rat bursts from the rice, a sickler swings and misses, and a boy behind pinions it with a bare foot. Rats explode from the tiny island of rice, sickles flail, and harvesters and children whoop with glee and occasional pain as a rodent bites hand or foot. Small children place the bodies on rice sheaves in growing piles.

A rat breaks through the cordon, dodges the children, and reaches me. Hoping I look as though I'm trying to stomp it, I dance out of its way. Quick as a cat a boy dives on it with bare hands and raps its head with a stick.

With the last stalks cut, the last rats killed, I take a body count: ninety-three gray-brown rats, now being skinned by the children and set on sheaves to dry in the sun. "We teach this method of cutting," says Russ. "It's a way to harvest rats as well as rice."

The harvesters move to another plot and form another noose. Stanfield shoots with quiet exultation: The day is a photographer's dream. Hundreds of exposures record the harvest, the killing, the skinning, the carcasses drying in the sun. We too are drying; long before noon we have consumed every drop of water we brought to last the day. It will be a desiccating experience.

At noon the harvesters stop and drink from their bottles. The men locate dry sheaves and light them afire, and the women place about fifty rats on the flames. Soon they are cooked on both sides, and the workers have their lunch.

Afternoon brings a rerun of the morning, though at a slowed pace under the searing sun. Now, after each noose is tightened and each kill completed, a family collects its share of the rats, arranges the catch tails-together, and binds them with rice straw for carrying home or to market.

Like Jim, I'm elated by this rat-rich revel. Since dawn I've been recording facts and visual descriptions of the harvest so that months later in Washington I'll be able to recreate the scene in my article. By late afternoon my notes fill sixteen pages, and Jim has dozens of rolls of exposed film.

Both of us definitely are slowing. Jim's face is crimson from sun and drawn with heat, fatigue, and desiccation. I feel the way he looks. Mercifully, the sun dips toward the China Sea. Mr. Liboy, still martial, lines us up for the homeward march along the paddy dikes. I add up the body-count figures sprinkled through my notebook: about a thousand for the day.

"You'd think it would take years for rats to recover from such a slaughter," says Russ, as we follow a harvester carrying rats to sell at market in San Antonio. "But the survivors will easily rebuild the population before the next planting. Theoretically a pair can leave 15,000 descendants in a year. Anyway, there are countless more in neighboring fields, ready to move in."

As we approach the town, a stranger stops the harvester in front of us and purchases two rats for five centavos each, the equivalent of a few pennies. We advance a little farther and watch the sale of more rats. Long before he reaches market his inventory is exhausted.

We reassemble in the welcome coolness of Mrs. Perez's rice storehouse. Stanfield stows his equipment, I talk with Russ and Mrs. Perez, and Mr. Liboy works busily with various pots and a portable cookstove. I sense the moment of truth.

The storehouse door opens, and a young man enters with a box and sets it on the table before us. San Miguel beer! *Cold!* We open bottles and guzzle their contents with unsocial haste. Thirst assuaged, everybody but Mr. Liboy opens a second bottle, and we expansively review the day: the ubiquity of the rats, the damage to the staple rice, the spirited work of the harvesters. More beer flows. The storehouse door opens again, and another case of San Miguel graces the table. Stanfield, who normally drinks little and keeps a lid on himself, is doubling over with laughter; we both are slapping backs and whooping like country boys. It is a far cry from my boyhood days on the Maryland family farm, where even in the hardest years my mother set a formal dinner table with the silver she received as wedding gifts.

The door opens yet again, and a tray appears, heaped with dressed rat carcasses. Mr. Liboy removes the lid of a large egg-shaped cooker, and it erupts with the steam of hot coconut oil. In go a dozen rats.

The hilarity subsides, but only momentarily. We are ravenous, and appetite plus alcohol easily vanquish apprehension. We hold out our paper plates, and Mr. Liboy lifts out two apiece of the specialty of the house.

Quiet descends again, but only because our mouths are full. The rats are tender and sweet, better than their bushy-tailed cousin the squirrel, of which I have shot and eaten hundreds. I look sideways and see Jim tearing into his first rat, and Russ enjoying his. Soon we are asking for seconds. At last I remember my manners and offer a San Miguel toast to Mrs. Perez and the indefatigable Mr. Liboy.

THE NEXT MORNING—with my notes, Stanfield with his many cameras, and both of us with minor hangovers—we board a flight to New Delhi, where visits to India usually begin. From there we will head to remoter sites—to the bizarre Rat Temple in the desert state of Rajasthan, to rat-infested villages in Gujarat, and finally to the plague-prone metropolis of Bombay.

One doesn't have to venture far afield in India to feel the exotic. It's palpable even here at New Delhi's four-star President Hotel as we take breakfast on the poolside veranda. Already it is warm, and wealthy Sikh men are in swimming, carefully not dunking their turbaned heads. From a bough near our table, a crow with a black body but a gray head watches us eat papaya. Across the patio scampers a cat, much leaner and rangier than American cats, as though there weren't enough rats to eat.

Rats are our business, so Jim and I set off with Mohan Rao, scion of a wealthy family that owns one of India's largest pest-control firms, now working with AID and the Indian government to fight rats. Mohan drives our rented Soviet-made car. During these decades of the Cold War, when India and the Soviet Union are informally allied against China and Pakistan, the nation swarms with Soviet cars, trucks, and tractors.

We're glad to be moving out. To a westerner, Delhi, like other large Indian cities, is congenial but wearing—a congested chaos of vehicles, animals, and humans, of pulsating noise and heat and pungent odors.

In rural India chaos gives way to serenity, to men rhythmically wielding hoes in the rice paddies, to women filing to the fields

at noontime balancing brass lunch pots on their heads, to old men
and youths watching over the humped cattle that graze along the
roadside. Here India is defined by the village: Homes are not scattered on individual farms or in suburbs, as in the United States;
instead families dwell in tight clusters, bound by ancient, inter-
twined traditions that weave a strong social fabric. Six hundred
thousand villages dot the land in a seemingly random pattern, closest together where soil and water favor agriculture. Each day in
each village men radiate out on foot to till their tiny farms; at night
they fuel the relentless population engine that will soon give the
nation a billion Indians.

The potholed two-lane road that bears us into the desert
is paved, but the earthen shoulders have been turned to mud by
rare rains, setting a cruel trap for aggressive Indian drivers. Truck
after speeding truck has strayed from the asphalt, dropped a tire
into the soft shoulder, and overturned; their hulks litter the roadside like the carcasses of animals that have been shot. Most numerous are the inexpensive but inherently unstable tricycle trucks,
manufactured with a single, central front wheel. As Jim and I crane
our necks to gawk, Mohan drives on impassively: He's seen it all
before.

We push into the desert, and trees grow fewer and noticeably
smaller. Many stand strangely leafless, shorn of their branches,
sculpted into angular silhouettes resembling saguaro cacti. Soon
we see why: a man swaying in the boughs, sawing off the leafy
branches, a small boy gathering them below. Man and boy will carry
their forage home to provide fodder for the family livestock—cattle, goats, buffalo, camels. Probably that tree will leaf no more, and
the desert will grow a little larger and more profound.

Small mountains wedge up around us, bleak and hazy blue,
reminiscent of our own Southwest. Motor vehicles grow sparse;
camel carts rule the road. The camels are two-humpers, Asian
Bactrians, grotesque and powerfully hypnotizing, their spindly legs
swinging through long strides, their cushion-feet spreading over
the sand on impact, their bodies and heads gliding with the exag-
gerated dignity of a mother of the bride approaching the church

altar. Nothing surpasses the sight of working camels in transporting a visiting westerner into the romance of the East.

The land grows drier, the potholes fewer, and now Mohan drives faster toward the Rat Temple at Deshnoke. Most village houses are flanked by a small, brightly painted cylindrical structure with a decorative roof. "For protecting stored crops from rats," explains Mohan. "Rats eat everything the villagers harvest. If the farmer can't store safely, he starves. The well-off build with brick and mortar, the poor with donkey dung."

The parched land grows ever flatter, as if the moisture has been squeezed from it by a giant press. Ahead, a miragelike structure slowly rises out of the shimmering wasteland. Turrets and columns take shape, hewn from white marble, like a desert fairy castle. We have reached the temple of the Hindu goddess Bhagwati Karniji, known to the profane as the Rat Temple.

We park and approach a stone terrace in front of the temple where men sit cross-legged, swaying back and forth as if in a trance. Pigeons flutter in and out of niches in the sculptured eaves, their cooing floating down like feathers of sound.

At Mohan's signal the three of us remove our shoes; they must not be worn inside the temple. At the ornate portal we pause to admire carved images of rats on the large iron grillwork door and the marble archway encasing it. A worshipper approaches from behind us, prostrates himself at the door, then enters and falls prostrate again.

Stepping around him, we find ourselves in a building of fine proportions, of large chambers and high ceilings, a structure built to a harmonious plan and with lavish outlays of money and craftsmanship. Like many old monuments, it wears the grime of time; like long-used houses of worship everywhere, its walls and flat surfaces support a clutter of sacred objects presumably donated by those it has solaced.

Slowly we focus on the rats. Thousands upon thousands of them wander about the floors, climb the friezes depicting themselves, scramble over the many small shrines and other votive objects. As I adjust to the temple's visual affect, I grow aware of its subtle but powerful audio accompaniment: the gentle squeaking of 10,000 rats, not unlike the soft mewing of newborn kittens.

A tickling of my right foot draws my eyes down . . . *a goddam rat is sitting on my stockinged toes!* A good kick will send him flying! But then the priest in charge—the *pujari boy*—will throw us out, and there goes our story. I wriggle a toe, and the rodent dismounts.

Now I'm aware of a cold, clammy, disagreeable dampness on the soles of my feet. I realize the floor is awash with rat urine. We Canbys are a squeamish people, and genetically I do not like this. But my journalism gene signals persuasively that this is as good as it gets.

Mohan confers with the *pujari boy*, then beckons to Jim, who fetches cameras, tripod, and lights. We advance into the temple's inner sanctum. Here a marble niche the size of a fireplace frames a golden image of the goddess Bhagwati Karniji. A handful of worshippers are bowing before her, not as a congregation responding to a liturgy, but in the Hindu way, individually, each with his own thoughts. At their feet, a capacity clientele of twenty-plus rats dine on a bowlful of *laddu*—mixed sweets, grain, and milk.

Our advance through the temple is slow, hindered by the realities of rats underfoot. Lift our feet for normal walking and we risk putting them down on a rat and inviting a bite. That means sliding, shuffling along, through the urine and numerous pellets. Soon it doesn't matter; our socks are drenched and revolting. Mentally I review my limited knowledge of foot diseases—athlete's foot, trench foot, foot-and-mouth disease . . . Then I observe that several worshippers bowing before the goddess are barefoot, one even prostrate in the puddle, and I resolve to call up greater fortitude.

I stand out of the way, against an ornately carved marble column, and take notes. Something brown moves, just beyond my ear, and there on the filigree perches brother rat, seemingly reading over my shoulder. I watch Stanfield setting up to shoot—he's having real troubles. He can't emplace equipment without displacing a few rats.

As he works with tripod and lights, rats crawl into his camera bag; another is gnawing its way in. Stanfield knows he must work fast, and not only against the rats: The priest does not seem entirely persuaded of the spirituality of our interest in his temple.

I have time to study the rats' behavior. Some are drinking water from troughs on the floor. Many are grooming, a task at which they may spend hours each day. I know they were fed millet and barley at ten o'clock this morning and will be fed again at four, in addition to enjoying the sweets brought by devotees.

Laboratory studies in the United States have shown that rats breeding to vast populations and confined to crowded quarters turn snarly, vicious, even murderous, genocidal. These findings have been extrapolated to predict similar behavior in human beings when population growth similarly compresses our living space. But the temple rats, existing in numbers never approached by the laboratory studies, belie such dire predictions. Their tranquil grooming, mannerly eating, and soft chorus of gentle squeaking seem clear signs of contentment, a contentment perhaps imparted to those who come to worship among them.

Periodically, flashes like lightning illumine the temple. Jim and his strobes are finally doing their stuff. The trick is to get his shots without disturbing the worshippers or stepping on a rat. He's good; no one could misread the apology in his smile as he intrudes himself and his equipment, then detonates his lights. But it's not going to work for long. Even the innate patience of the village Indian has limits, and the lean faces of the worshippers show mounting discomfort. Not good.

A prolonged lull follows the flashes. I see Jim taping a strobe cord, its insulation already gnawed through by a rat. Now the *pujari boy* approaches, emanating disapproval and authority. Obviously he anticipated only a few minutes' disruption of temple decorum. Little does he realize as he ushers us out that after an hour and a half, Stanfield was just warming up.

Outside in the cleansing desert sunlight, Jim and I peel off our sodden socks and place them in a plastic film bag for consignment

to oblivion. Then Jim turns to his abused equipment. Just as a combat infantryman checks and rechecks his rifle, a field photographer
frets constantly about his cameras and lights, cleaning them,
testing their drives and wires. Stanfield travels heavy, carrying gear
of enormous value that must not fail him. And the Rat Temple has
sorely tested it.

As Jim works in the afternoon sunlight, I mentally sort
my garbled understanding of Hinduism to understand a temple
given over to rats. For the Hindu, I know, every animal possesses
a soul that never dies, which upon the death of the body is reborn
in another, living body—the phenomenon of reincarnation. Entwined with reincarnation is the Hindu law of karma, by which
one's conduct during this life determines the level at which the soul
will be reborn. A human soul may be reincarnated in another
human being, or in an animal, including a rat. Given such beliefs,
there is no reason why rats should not be respected in a temple.

Could a nation with such a temple, with a population 83 percent Hindu, dream seriously of ridding itself of the scourge of rats?
But now Indians were awakening to the role played by rats in
spreading disease and destroying food desperately needed by a
soaring human population.

Indians had become conscious of rats as a health menace in
the 1890s when plague struck the subcontinent. That awareness
had sharpened in the 1950s, when a quirk of evolution wrought an
unwelcome change in the behavior of the burly bandicoot, India's
premier rat. Long content to live in the fields and feed on crops, the
shaggy rodent inexplicably began moving into Indian homes and
feeding in pantries. Since the bandicoot reproduces at a staggering
rate—a litter a month for each female, seven pups per litter, so a
pair can explode into tens of thousands in a year—the incidence
of rat bites soared, particularly among infants and the old. At
night rats rustled unnervingly in thatched roofs and rattled pots and
pans. The threatening noise and constant fear brought on an epidemic of sleep loss and attendant ills. Acceptance of the rodents
wore thinner.

Now the early 1970s had brought regional famines, and Indians had awakened to the fact that they were attempting to feed not only their own ballooning population but also a rat population perhaps six times as large: Food lost annually to India's rats would fill a railroad train stretching for 3,000 miles, more than long enough to span the nation. As shiploads of grain flowed in from America, U.S. senators complained that the aid merely made up for what the rodents ate. Calculations showed that the need for imports would vanish if rats no longer claimed their share, and that control would cost only a tiny fraction as much as food imports.

Psychologically as well as on humanitarian grounds, the time was ripe to strike against the rodent hordes. The usually pacifist Indian government was rattling its traps and poison tins, taking up arms against the rat. It was this war between two species contending over a single territory that brought Stanfield and me to India.

MOHAN RAO drops us—two pairs of socks lighter—at the train station in Jaipur. Abandoning Stanfield to cope with a swarm of porters, I wait in line to purchase our tickets for Ahmadabad, in Gujarat, near the Indian Ocean. Outside that city the Indian government has designated eighty-four villages as the battle zone in its war of extermination against rats.

The train's rhythmic clicking over the rails, the views of the desert unfolding through its windows, bring the benediction of calm. Now is the time to review my notes about the temple, to find the gaps in my rushed observations and fill in with still-fresh recollections, to complete this portion of my notebook.

"Gracious living!" gasps Jim Stanfield, newly arrived in Ahmadabad. He's staring at his room, which is nearly the size of my house in Maryland. Rich oriental rugs soften its marble floor, fine tapestries drape its towering walls. My adjoining room is equally opulent. Feeling as if we've been borne on flying carpets back to the time of the sultanate, we mentally toast the Society's Travel Office. "Richly deserved," concludes Stanfield, recalling our bizarre experiences in the Rat Temple.

We are now two weeks into our trip, and over dinner and Indian beer we take stock. Admittedly we are a little frayed—the price paid for seldom staying two nights in one place, for working by day and often traveling by night. Equally taxing is the need to be constantly the diplomat, always polite and attentive, while successions of interviewees explain their work with numbing intensity and detail. Miraculously, our jam-packed schedule of appointments, arranged weeks earlier from the other side of the world, has unfolded precisely as programmed—a tribute to the character of the people we've contacted, and fresh evidence of officials' eagerness to tell their story through the pages of National Geographic.

According to our clockwork schedule, we are to emerge from our palace chambers at seven-thirty in the morning and meet the man in charge of the Gujarat rat campaign, which is supported by AID. And here he is, right on time before our palace, as if our arrangements had been made minutes instead of months ago. Dr. G. C. Chaturvedi is a field-working academic who wrote his doctoral treatise on rats at Bombay's renowned Haffkine Institute. Tall, spectacled, and very serious, he exudes humorless efficiency. He sets to work the moment his assistant points our car toward the locales where they kill rats.

"Our official target area is the eighty-four villages," Chaturvedi reminds us. "But our purpose is far broader than to vanquish rats from a small part of India. The project must persuade the government itself that rats can be successfully controlled, so our work can be expanded.

"Our greatest problem, of course, is Hindu religious beliefs. One of the important Hindu deities is the elephant-headed god Ganesh, symbol of prosperity. In religious art, Ganesh traditionally is borne on the backs of four rats. Further, the Hindu reluctance to kill is very strong—that is why so many of us are vegetarian. Women feel this especially strongly; if someone in the family takes ill, the wife may blame it on the husband's killing rats." I know that Jim, like me, is reflecting back to three days ago, and our orgy of rat killing and eating in the Philippines.

"Muslim beliefs pose no problem to killing rats," says Chaturvedi, "and Muslims dominate the northern part of the

district. We began there. In each village our workers went in and
showed films of how rats spread disease and damage crops and
stored foods. They offered free bait. In a few weeks the rats would
disappear, and the people would become accustomed to an
improved life without them. Then we would leave. In most villages
the rats would soon reappear, and the villagers would return to the
project for help. But now we would say, 'No. If you would rid your
village of rats, organize yourselves. We will give you the poisons.'
And most of them organized.

"Seeing the success in the Muslim villages—the reductions in
losses of crops and stored grain, the relief from rat bites and dis-
rupted sleeping—most of the Hindu villages accepted us too."

We enter the Hindu village of Karli, a knot of 878 small
houses drenched in slanting morning sun. We walk to the small village common, surrounded by a growing crowd of delighted Karlians
who show a smothering interest in Stanfield and his equipment. An
explosion of rats has terrorized Karli, destroying food, biting sleep-
ers, even eating the mayor's rupees hidden in a grain bin. The villagers have at last organized and come to Chaturvedi for poisons.

I see the results. A street cleaner approaches, filthy and in
rags. In one hand he carries a pair of tongs for picking up rats, in the
other a reeking five-gallon kerosene can half full of dead and dying
rodents.

An old woman breaks through the crowd around us, breath-
less from exertion. She has a story we must hear: Two nights ago
a rat rattled menacingly in her bedroom wall. She clapped her
hands, trying to scare it off. All night she lay in fear. Then she
dozed, and the rat bit her head. She leaned forward—here!—I must
feel the welt.

Chaturvedi takes us to more villages, each with stories of vic-
tories and occasional defeats in the rat war. Meanwhile I notice that
his polite young assistant is wearing in his lapel a Lions Club pin,
exactly like those back in the States. Now, with our day's work officially done, the last village inspected, the assistant steps forward
and a little shyly asks if we'd like to see their Lions Club eye clinic,

which has been set up for the week. I already know about U.S. Lions' involvement with vision; I've heard it discussed at my hometown club when invited to speak. But an eye clinic here in the Great Indian Desert, performing the sophisticated procedures of eye surgery? So off we go toward the village of Unjha.

Our approach buttresses my skepticism. Two tents, one large and white, the other smaller and tan, stand in a pasture. Dirt paths lead to their shadowy interiors. Silently I rehearse some polite words of praise for a valiant but surely inadequate undertaking.

We enter the white canvas structure, a hundred feet long and fifty wide. Light pours through the fabric, and cool breezes waft through the open sides. Muzak floats softly from two speakers. The 240 beds appear spotless, and the air bears a clean smell.

Almost all the beds are filled, the occupants wearing a patch over one eye or both. We stop beside a tiny patient with bandages on both eyes. "Four-month-old girl with cataracts," a male nurse explains to the assistant. "Doing fine. The operations are performed in the other tent." The assistant makes his pitch: "Your village club back in the States contributes, through Lions International."

That evening Stanfield and I dine in Chaturvedi's home in Siddhipur, the largest town in the area. As is the custom, we men eat, and the woman of the house, his mother, serves us. We discover that India's leading rat killer is indeed a vegetarian. We also discover that religion is still strong: Between servings Mrs. Chaturvedi fussily dusts off a small shrine holding a golden Ganesh borne by four golden rats.

Now Bombay beckons us, with the mirthless smile of a whitened skull. In the 1890s rat-borne plague, centered in Bombay, took the lives of 12.5 million Indians. The irruption was part of a global pandemic, one of many to scourge the planet since 1347, when shipborne rats coming ashore in Genoa, Italy, brought the Black Death of bubonic plague.

The pandemic of the 1890s galvanized medical scientists to seek out its cause. In 1894 two doctors, one from France's Pasteur Institute, independently discovered the plague bacillus. But how was it transmitted to people? To find out, the Pasteur Institute sent Paul-Louis Simond to Bombay. Day after day he walked the filthy neighborhoods hardest hit by plague, down streets littered with dead rats. He observed that humans picking up the rats soon fell ill themselves, and that the dead, plague-afflicted rats carried far more fleas than did healthy rats. In 1898 he fitted together all the pieces of the puzzle—dead rats, abundant fleas, the bacillus: The flea carried the bacillus, the rat carried the flea, and when the infected rat died, the flea went to another rat—or to man. Rats were the carrier of man's greatest misery.

Bombay has never relaxed its guard against yet another outbreak. No day passes that India's largest city does not test the health of some of its many rats and identify the bacteria carried by their fleas. "Our last plague victim was in 1952, but we cannot take chances," explains P. B. Deobanker, rodent-control officer for the Municipal Corporation of Greater Bombay. For two days this courteous public servant takes Stanfield and me under his wing.

"As part of my program, we kill three or four thousand rats a day from different neighborhoods. This is a drop in the bucket of the city's rat population, of course. But it will permit us to detect plague if it returns. If it does, my small program can serve as the nucleus for a crash, citywide control campaign.

"Tonight," he promises, "we will go forth with the night killers."

Night has long since fallen when we thread our way to the Bora Bazar, one of the city's oldest areas. We pause, and twenty feet ahead I make out the dark shapes of four-story apartment buildings, ornate and once imposing but now decrepit. Each structure is separated from its neighbor by an alleyway about a yard wide—our goal.

Between us and this goal lie hundreds of sleeping men, wrapped in blankets and aligned shoulder to shoulder on the street and sidewalk. Deobonker steps nimbly between the bodies, and I follow. He trains his light in one of the narrow alleyways.

"We call these 'gullies,'" he explains. "They're alive with rats. People throw their garbage out the windows, and the rats wait below. This is one reason why Bombay suffers 20,000 cases of rat-bite fever a year."

Soon I see them, scores of rats, eating at mounds of garbage and milling between piles. A white-and-yellow cat prowls among them. Deobonker anticipates my question. "The cat isn't interested in the rats. It's waiting for choice garbage from above." Soon some arrives, and the cat chews peaceably on its morsel.

Quiet as shadows, two figures armed with wooden sticks materialize beside us—a tallish, lean youth and a short, grizzled man in middle age. These are the night killers, two of eighty-five in Deobonker's little army.

They go right to work. Entering the gully a few feet, the grizzled veteran turns on his flashlight and transfixes a rat in the beam. He raises his cane and strikes. Then he moves a bare foot forward, picks up the corpse with his toes, and drops it into a burlap sack. Twenty-four more to go to meet his nightly quota.

I step to the side for a better view, and my foot brushes a street sleeper. He awakens, rises onto an elbow, and eyes the night killers. "That's why I'm sleeping out here," he volunteers; "rats would chew me up indoors."

The killer backs out of the gully rather than advance into the rain of garbage, and moves toward another alleyway. Scavenging dogs, seeing his stick, snarl and bark. A band of half-drunk revelers shouts jibes that the night killers take good-naturedly.

We enter an apartment building and climb to the second floor. Five families live on this level, says Deobonker, eight and nine to the family. Rat bites are common; two women show us fresh wounds, one from the night before. Here, as in the villages, the bites are more bearable than the nerve-wracking disturbance at night as rats rattle in walls and ceiling.

I stick my head out an open window to look down on the night killers. Mistake. Garbage from the floors above swishes past my ear. I duck back inside like a turtle into its shell.

Next day we follow the night's kill to the Haffkine Institute, to a large sunken room located in the Rat Destruction Unit. It is not a scene for *House and Garden*. Some 4,000 dead rats repose in piles, according to their point of origin in the city. Sweating workers shovel bodies from each pile onto an examination table where technicians check the rodents' glands for the plague infection, count the flea population per rat, and classify each rat by species. In a year, nearly a million rats will pass through this unlovely chamber.

Deobonker has one more destination. "Let me take you to the godowns—our warehouses. There you will see some pampered rats."

We approach a large block of hoary stone structures next to a railroad siding—Bombay's largest godown. Here city merchants store and trade in a large menu of farm commodities: wheat, maize, millet, peanuts, and much more.

We enter one structure partly shaded by a huge, multitrunked banyan tree, and I savor an acrid aroma pleasingly reminiscent of feed stores back home. This godown is devoted to peanuts, and they are there in prodigious quantity, stored in mountainous stacks of 200-pound bags.

Deobonker steers Stanfield and me toward one of the peanut mountains. He points to a bag that has been chewed open by rats. Peanuts spill onto the concrete floor—peanuts mixed with rat pellets. A glance around shows that countless other bags have been breached. Beside one sits an old woman with a large pan. As we stare she fills it with peanuts, shakes it so the light rat pellets rise to the surface, and tosses them out, much as if panning gold. The salvaged peanuts are hers, nuggets of food to take home.

We follow Deobonker to one of the godown's fourteen stalls. Behind a counter three businessmen, garbed spotlessly in white, banter with customers as they conduct sales and keep accounts. The merchants wear the sleek look of success. These are Jains, members of an Indian religion whose absolute reverence for the soul residing in every life-form utterly forbids the taking of any life; a Jain priest not only sweeps away insects from where his feet will fall but also may wear a mask to filter out bugs he might inadvertently breathe in and kill. For the Jain laity, this taboo often leads them into commerce, which does not directly involve killing. Thus the one-half of one percent of Indians who are Jains play a disproportionate role in business affairs, including trading in peanuts at the godown.

Does the taboo against killing extend to rats—the rats so brazenly plundering their peanuts? The answer is nearby. Nodding pleasantly to the Jains, Deobonker leads us to the end of the counter so we can see behind. Three feet from the nearest merchant sits a low-sided aluminum pan of water. Drinking shoulder to shoulder are six chubby bandicoots, washing down their peanut breakfast. "You should come here at night when they're feeding," says Deobonker. "The chewing sounds like a room full of clacking typewriters." The godown's acrid smell, the profusion of rats—I recall a statistic I've absorbed during earlier reading: In six months a rat may shed a million hairs, void six quarts of urine, deposit 25,000 droppings. Not information to be welcomed by Gil Grosvenor, back at the *Geographic*.

I ask the obvious: "Don't the merchants do *anything?*" Deobonker speaks to the Jain nearest the drinking rats. Gold buttons studded with diamonds shine on his white tunic. Yes, he acknowledges, the loss to rats is great, "but our most valued profit is our religion." Yes, he knows they spread disease, but to kill them would be a sin. Well, yes, sometimes they do become too much. Then the merchants trap them, carry them outside, and set them free. Says Deobonker: "When you reenter the godown, they walk right back in behind you," and both enjoy a laugh.

Few other human beings share the Jains' tender feelings for rats. Except for those who deplore the use of animals in medical experiments, no defenders rally to demand "rights for rats" as they do for furbearing mammals and laboratory primates. Good reasons explain this universal opprobrium. Rats are scary, dangerous, furtive, loathsome. And they are far from endangered species. Rats flourish because we ourselves create their niche. Though we sometimes take up arms against them, we are the best and only friends they have ever had. And that probably explains our hatred of rats: Their presence is a reproach, a reminder of failures in cleanliness and sanitation that we would rather ignore.

Stanfield and I part. He has much to shoot in India, and my little notebooks hold enough. There is a sadness in this. Stanfield's easy manner, his extraordinary competence, his tact and diplomacy have helped immensely in our work with our many hosts. And we have been able to lean on each other. Working as a journalist in the field is astonishingly fatiguing, and not only because of the fast pace or the exposures in your camera. Fatigue is cumulative. You become seized by your subject and pursue it relentlessly, fearful you will miss something of factual importance or human interest, tormented by knowing you cannot return, that your story can be only as good as your scribblings in your notebook or the exposures in your camera. Fatigue also grows from the unceasing stimulation that bombards you every minute of every interview and with each exhilarating new experience. Bang! Bang!—new discovery! An intense interviewee! Sure, that is why I came, why I spent a lot of *Geographic* money to get here, and I'd have it no other way. But twelve hours a day, every day . . . Stanfield and I have been glad to have each other's support.

HALF A WORLD lies ahead of me, and I take it in leapfrog hops.

To Karachi in Pakistan, where a teeming rat population and its accompaniment of deadly and debilitating diseases have prompted the World Health Organization to open a busy research center.

On to Rome, where the Eternal City wages war against the eternal foe. An estimated 15 million rats are destroying food and gnawing electrical insulation, causing vast blackouts, and the outraged citizenry is waging a campaign of extermination. I join the exterminators in the great vaulted sewers beneath the Vatican, tossing out packets of poison. Then a quick visit to the Food and Agriculture Organization of the United Nations in Rome, to hear alarming reports tell of explosions of rat populations in half a dozen tropical countries, threatening local famines and epidemics.

To northern Germany—to medieval Hamelin, a storybook town that feels a rare affection for the rat. Shops sell rat-shaped pastries and liqueur bottles, and each noon the world's most famous

Glockenspiel reenacts the immortal fable of the Pied Piper: First the piping figure leads out the rats; then, when the town burghers refuse to pay, he leads away the children. Hamelin still hires a *Schadlings-bekampfermeister*—master pest fighter—and boasts the official status of *praktish rattenfrei*—practically rat free. (At last a chapter of the story that Gil Grosvenor will genuinely like.)

To tidy Britain, where rigorous rat control wrought a cruel irony, the emergence of the first known "super rats." For years a diligent Scottish farmer had dutifully set out poison for his rats. In 1960 he discovered the anticoagulant had lost its effectiveness—the creatures ate all he put out. The event told shaken rodentologists that the rats could inherit a genetic resistance to poisons—that a vaunted silver bullet could mutate into lead. Today pockets of super rats exist worldwide, so laboratories must constantly develop substitute poisons.

Then across the Atlantic, to New York City. Shades of Bombay! I visit a vast wasteland in North Harlem and the South Bronx: hundreds of blocks of apartment buildings, abandoned by owners because of rent controls, now occupied by renters and squatters living in squalor and misery.

To dispose of their garbage, many occupants drop it from their windows, Bombay style. I see it happen on Harlem's 119th Street—a window opens, trash flies out, and a gusting wind scatters it like confetti. It's known as airmailing. The culprits fear to descend to the basement incinerator, or lack an elevator, or are transients and don't care. "Whatever the reason," says my guide, "the rats make out like bandits: trash to live in, garbage to eat." A mighty cleanup campaign accompanied by liberal poisoning is paying off in fewer reported rat bites, but the number remains woefully high.

And finally, home to Maryland, to the hugs of wife, Jes, and teenage sons, and the passing out of exotic acquisitions such as unusual rat traps obtained in Karachi's Empress Market. I have been away exactly a month, the limit I set years ago as the maximum time I would be separated from my family by travel.

A few nights later we four go out to dinner, and I am describing the rice harvest in the Philippines and the repast that ensued. From the next table comes an injured voice: "We're eating—would you please stop that disgusting talk about rats?" Maybe Gil Grosvenor had a point . . .

Back at headquarters, my office is not as I left it: An unnatural neatness has replaced its usual lived-in look. I quickly realize that visiting writers have camped here while I've been gone and have overly tidied up for my return.

My admirable assistant, Rebecca Beall, thoughtfully gives me space; she knows that a writer returning from the whirlwind of field work needs time to sort the accumulated mail on the desk, the scores of papers picked up during the trip. Nor will my colleagues intrude, if past behavior can serve as a guide. Only once, on return from my very first foreign assignment, did I expect to be welcomed with brass band and red carpet—to be eagerly asked what I had seen and done. Instead, only one colleague even noticed, with the inquiry, "Been away?" On the seventh floor, everyone was always coming and going. Returning from Novosobirsk or Antarctica or Timbuktu was more or less routine.

As I sort and stack, footsteps approach, and a colleague fills the door and leans against the jamb. "How did it go?" asks Noel Grove, a bearded Iowan with a rollicking writing style, father of a daughter whom my younger son will marry in a decade. "Did you really eat those rats?" Not a brass band or red carpet, but nonetheless a hearty welcome, comparatively speaking.

Rebecca Beall decides I have had enough space, and there she is at my side, grasping a box that obviously holds a movie reel. "Remember we requested the film *Willard?* The one where that weird kid trains all those rats to murder Ernest Borgnine?" Soon we are in the Society auditorium, reveling in that lurid saga. We scan the credits, and there he is, the rat trainer, Mo DiSesso. A few phone calls track him down in Antelope Valley, east of Los Angeles. I'm off, on the final leg of rat coverage.

No wonder Mo and Nora DiSesso live beyond the city, at the edge of the Mojave Desert. In pens and cages about the grounds they pamper a small zoo of animals kept in readiness for the whims of Hollywood.

"I had trained a rat to play the piano," Mo recalls about winning the *Willard* contract. "The rat played with his two front feet. When he hit the right key, I rewarded him with peanut butter. I taught him to play duets, with a cat.

"The producer of *Willard* called, and asked if I could train rats. I said, 'Sure; come on out and watch my rat play the piano.' He came, and I showed him the rat and the cat . . . "

Mo and Nora learned much about rats during the filming of *Willard*. If trained from puphood, they made affectionate pets— "almost worshipful." The rats learned astoundingly quickly. But constant repetition, as required for filming, brought on "combat fatigue," and the rats became cranky. This called for a ready supply of substitutes, a task assigned to eighty mother rats dedicated to turning out litters. During the filming, the role of the lead rat, Ben, was played by a procession of thirteen different superstars.

Coached by the DiSessos and led by the Ben du jour, Willard's rats performed wonders: retrieving his toy cannon, ringing bells, standing and begging, kissing. The script called for rats to chew through a door to reach the hated Borgnine. Mo coated a soft balsam door with peanut butter, and they tore through it like buzz saws.

How did he train the killer horde to leap upon Borgnine? How did he train Ernest Borgnine? "At first he was as leery of rats as everyone else. So Nora lay down and let them swarm over her. That was all Borgnine needed. He didn't hesitate to coat his upper body with peanut butter and let the rats go after him. And he never got bitten."

ENOUGH ABOUT RATS; I've filled eleven notebooks, enough for a tome. The fun time—the learning and traveling—is over. Now I must pay for it—pay by having to write, the hardest work known to man, or at least to this man. What a lark to be a photographer—to return from the wars with your work all done, sit at ease beside the picture editor as he or she flicks through your pretty slides, and revel in the editor's praises. Then I think of Stanfield's week in the Vatican sewers . . .

I close my office door and sit at my typewriter, surrounded by my little notebooks and reams of documents. With a mighty effort I force aside the distaste for starting that we glorify as writer's block. I've outlined this article, more or less, and now I've got to write the first word: "For . . ." That didn't hurt so much; only about 31,999 more to go, only about a month of misery—if I bear down as I should.

But it's a rough month. Ideally, every sentence should excite and titillate to keep the reader coming. And if a writer finds his task becoming easy, it means he's probably not trying hard enough to be interesting. In short, it's hard to be a happy writer.

At last, there it is, the final sacred manuscript, a text filling thirty-four "green sheets." These tinted pages on which we write hold twenty-seven lines each, typed to the width of the columns in the magazine. Two "greens" make up a full column of text, four a full page. I hand in two more pages than the text editor wants, but that's standard operating practice; all of us figure that once the editor gets into our masterworks, he'll want all he can get.

Now I can tidy my office, collect my notebooks and those reams of documents, and dump them in someone else's office. That someone is the researcher, who will check the accuracy of every fact and figure, every quote and concept and conclusion.

Arms loaded with materials, I make my way to the office of Judith Brown and veer in. Just as luck has linked me with Stanfield on this article, so am I fortunate in the assignment of Judith. She's experienced, very smart, and mentally tough: essential qualities for an effective researcher. Like other *Geographic* articles, mine contains hundreds upon hundreds of facts—or what I believe to be facts. Experts whom she consults will disagree with some of what I've written and will also disagree among themselves—often bitterly. Judith must know the right questions to ask, determine who and what is correct, and mollify whoever is in error—me or the disagreeing expert. Not all of us possess such skills.

A few days pass, and a special rite marks a milestone in the article's progress: The illustrations editor sends out word that this coming Tuesday Gil Grosvenor will attend the projection session on rats.

The all-important projection session is conducted by the article's picture editor, in this case W. Allan Royce, a savvy veteran journalist from the upper Midwest and destined for higher things. Since the story's inception as a working title nearly a year ago, Al Royce in his office has supported Jim Stanfield in the field, advising him in his coverage, carefully reviewing his shipments of exposed film to ensure that the photographs are technically sharp and editorially comprehensive. A few weeks ago it was Al Royce who decided that the subject of rats had been covered sufficiently and suggested to the chief of photography that Stanfield be brought in.

For days Royce and Stanfield have pored over Jim's thousands of exposures, ruthlessly cutting to thirty-six "selects" and thirty "seconds," or alternative. They have read my manuscript, so they can relate the pictures to the text and fill in with pictures where the text is lacking. A design team has laid out the article, using the selects, a painting of the four commensal rat species, and a map showing plague areas. At the projection session, Royce will present this package to Gil Grosvenor and hear his judgment.

Fifteen minutes before session time, Royce is completing preparations in the Projection Room, a dark chamber tucked between Gil's office and that of Melville Grosvenor and crammed wall to wall with chairs. Royce conducts a final test of lights and slides; this is no time for a technical glitch.

I arrive early, on edge myself; Gil hasn't yet commented on my manuscript, and now we're meeting face to face. Stanfield comes in, dressed to the nines for this day of judgment.

In driblets others file in and take seats: Judith Brown and the research director; the mapmaker and chief of cartography; the working artist and art director; the head of layout; science editor Ken Weaver—my boss; the head of engraving and printing; the director of photography and an assistant; the caption writer and head of legends; and a squadron of Gil's top editors. All will listen for remarks from the editor affecting his or her area of responsibility. Because the subject is unusual, more editors than usual attend, and the room is packed, the air already thick.

Al Royce, who will explain the pictures, settles into one of three front chairs, Stanfield behind him. The other two front seats are for Gil and associate editor John Scofield.

The door from Gil's office opens punctually, and he and Scofield maneuver past the packed seats to the projector. Gil takes the chair by the controls. He scans the group, and his eyes lock onto mine: "Good manuscript, Tom. You did better with the subject than I thought you could." I feel a pat on the shoulder; it comes from Judith Brown.

Lights dim, slides click, and the first image flashes—a close-up mug shot of a roof rat glowering at the world through Jim's lens, a beautiful portrait of a worthy adversary. Gil pauses thoughtfully, then clicks the controls: to Hamelin's ratcatcher, to trained rats performing tricks, to the unforgettable Rat Temple, the Bombay rat killers, the Jain merchants, and beyond. All reflect awesome technical skill and Stanfield's ability to distill beauty from life's seamy side.

Gil clicks dutifully on. Occasionally he asks a question or makes a comment, at which half the audience scribbles notes. But he is far less inquiring than usual, less chatty; his lone attempt at humor is forced. With the selects finished, Royce brings on the seconds, and Gil riffles through them quickly.

The editor sits quietly for a moment, then speaks measuredly: "Jim, those are great pictures. You did well. Let me think on this." And the Projection Room empties, everyone aware that something is not right, no one sure what.

The answer comes first to Jim Stanfield, and it comes from Gil Grosvenor, to this effect: "Jim, I've got to let you down, cut some of those pictures from the rats article. It has nothing to do with the pictures—they're brilliant. But I'm catching hell from the Board of

Trustees about four controversial articles we're running this year—
Cuba, Harlem, Quebec, and South Africa. The mossbacks on the
board are trying to control editorial policy, maybe even create an
editorial oversight committee. Giving too much play to a disagreeable subject like rats could tip the balance, and bring permanent
harm to the magazine. I'm leveling with you, Jim, and I'm really
sorry." He was leveling, and he was sorry; and so was Stanfield, and
so was I, for Jim's sake and mine. But eventually Gil Grosvenor
would win that important war over editorial independence. Rats
were a minor sacrifice for a far larger victory.

RODENT POSTSCRIPT: It's Sunday evening, not many months after
the publication of our rat story. I rise from my chair in disgust at
what I've seen on television and switch off the set.

The phone rings. It is Bill Ellis, a Geographic colleague and
good friend. And he is steaming.

"Tom! Did you watch '60 Minutes'?"

"I sure did."

"You ought to sue the bastards! I never saw anything so de-
spicable."

Bill is right. Mike Wallace of the "60 Minutes" team has presented a feature on rats. The series of scenarios bears an uncanny
resemblance to those in the rat article, as does his punch line about
rats inheriting the Earth. No one called for information during
preparation of the show, and he gives no credit to National Geographic. No, I do not sue, nor do I even consider it. But even today,
when I watch the complacent hosts of "60 Minutes," I wonder
about the origin of their stories and think of rats.

At the end of 1977, the magazine's editorial staff votes on the
best staff article of the year, and rats scurry off with first place. It is
the highest compliment I could hope for—approval by my peers.

Chapter 3

AT LARGE IN
INUIT LAND

Until a few days ago I've been an office-bound *Geographic* captions writer, yearning to roam free like so many of my colleagues. Now I'm in the high Arctic, seated on a dogsled jolting across the rough sea ice north of Canada's Baffin Island. Ahead perches Arnakadlak, a squat Inuit of about middle age. His walrus-hide whip is busy with the dogs, and he wields it with exquisite accuracy.

Flick!—the tip stings the rump of a shirker. The dog is instantly energized. Flick!—the whip nicely turns a husky that has stepped across another dog's harness. "*Oot!*—Faster!" exhorts Arnakadlak, stinging another shirker.

Behind me on the sled sits Ham, nineteen, Arnakadlak's nephew. Ham speaks a few words of English, but I have yet to discover which words.

The scene around us is beautiful beyond belief. Ahead and behind unfurls the broad ice-paved channel known as Pond Inlet, named after an English explorer of this remote realm. On each side rise jagged mountain walls—to the south the glaciated peaks of northern Baffinland, to the north the glacier-clad ramparts of Bylot Island. Our goal lies some eighty miles eastward, an area known to local hunters for its abundance of seals, for centuries the staple food in the eastern Arctic. Arnakadlak and Ham hope to shoot a ringed seal for meat to feed the sled dogs. I am along for the ride, biding time while a reluctant author back in the Inuit village of Pond Inlet overcomes writer's block and grinds out a *Geographic* article.

The terrain's striking beauty is accented by the remarkable clarity of the May air. In a setting less pristine, the bare rocks on the windswept mountains would appear drab. In our dazzling spring sunshine they vibrate with color, like lighted gemstones on display. Snowfields and glaciers glow with the whiteness of bridal gowns. The sky is a vast inverted bowl, cast in flawless blue porcelain. Seemingly this bowl has trapped the sun, which rolls inside twenty-four hours a day, unable to escape beneath the rim and duck below the horizon.

Air this pure makes distant objects appear close, so it's diffi-cult to estimate distance. Arnakadlak's whip encourages the dogs to pull us at a good clip, yet we seem to be making almost no forward progress. This is because mountains that I thought were just ahead, and which we now should be passing, were actually thirty and forty miles away and seem to grow little closer with time.

Pure air to the eye, but not to the nose: A stench rides with our threesome. I cannot detect its source. A prime suspect is the untanned sealskin that Arnakadlak and Ham lashed over our mounded cargo of food and other supplies, and on which we sit. Trying not to insult my hosts, I furtively examine the hide for bits of flesh that may be mellowing in the sunlight, or in the warmth of our seated bodies.

I DIDN'T ANTICIPATE such a problem when I set out three days ago. In fact I had little idea of what lay ahead. It is 1970, and this is my maiden *Geographic* field assignment. By chance it is a plum.

To the nonjournalist, every *Geographic* assignment sounds like a plum; we wouldn't be going there if "there" weren't interesting, alluring, important, exotic. By and large that is true. But then there's the terrible downside: After you get back you've got to write an article—pain and suffering.

This trip is different, in that it carries a minimal writing penalty: I won't have to grind out an article. I've lucked into it because of my current lowly position in the *Geographic* hierarchy, and because I've been in the right place at the right time.

Two years earlier a Roman Catholic missionary to the Inuit had submitted photographs made during a quarter-century spent in the wilds of the eastern Canadian Arctic. As often happens at the *Geographic*, they arrived unsolicited—"over the transom," in journalese. Precious few of the offerings that flow over the *Geographic* transom ever pan out, often because they are of inferior quality, more often because they fail to present a coherent story as required for photojournalism. But right from the beginning the missionary's pictures were irresistible. Not only were they technically excellent; the story they told was priceless. Through the lens of his camera, Father Guy Mary-Rousseliere had recorded a unique and poignant chapter of Inuit history: the closing moments of their traditional life as subsistence hunters and fishermen, and their irreversible transition to a new, settled life shaped by a well-intentioned but not infallible government to the south.

Father Mary-Rousseliere had arrived in Pond Inlet from France in 1944, a young Oblate missionary sent to the world's northernmost Catholic mission. Foraying far from pulpit and confessional, he lived the Inuits' life, learned their guttural language, ate what they ate, traveled by dogsled to families in their igloos to serve as doctor and teacher as well as priest. The Inuits called this concerned and kindly white man *Ataata Mari*—Father Mary.

In 1944 Pond Inlet contained only twenty-nine Inuits and whites; virtually all Canadian Inuits then lived as seminomads, moving with the seasons to hunt seals and caribou and to fish for arctic char, a cousin of the trout. During this period Father Mary watched with concern as the Canadian government coaxed the native people to congregate in large, permanent settlements where they would have access to medical facilities and schools. Periodically he visited Ottawa, the capital, vainly urging the government to moderate a policy that uprooted the Inuits from their traditional livelihood with little prospect of work in the new settlements.

By the time Father Mary submitted his photographs, the relocation of Canadian Inuits into large settlements was complete. Pond Inlet's population had soared to 390 Inuits and 40 white administrators and support staff, all residing in government-built prefabricated frame houses. So large a population quickly exhausted the game and furbearing animals within range of snowmobiles, and few jobs existed to provide salaries. As a result, joblessness was endemic, and many depended heavily on government allowances.

Realizing the worth of Father Mary-Rousseliere's photographs, the *Geographic* had asked him to write an article about his experiences and observations in Inuit land. He accepted the invitation. But no article materialized. Father Mary was by nature busy, and high latitudes offer no immunity to writer's block. Another magazine might have sent a staff writer to tell Father Mary's story. Not the *Geographic*: The subject always tells his or her own story directly to the reader.

The editors devised a plan. They had pictures in hand; they would dispatch a caption writer to Pond Inlet, to obtain detailed information about what each picture showed. While there, the caption writer would persuade Father Mary to begin his manuscript.

That caption writer would be me. Elation! A great assignment after nearly a decade of being largely deskbound as book writer, writer for a Society children's publication, and now a caption writer. One question: How was I to persuade Ataata Mari to begin writing? "Just get him to sit and start typing," responded John Scofield, an able and amiable (but not always specific) associate editor.

The year 1970 was an interim time at the *Geographic*, a time when the editor was not a Grosvenor but the trusted regent Frederick G. Vosburgh, when Gil Grosvenor was an associate editor expectantly waiting in the wings, and when I was one of the magazine's half-dozen caption writers, a niche well down the editorial ladder but nevertheless a very happy one.

The unexalted status of caption writers bears no relationship to the captions' huge significance to the magazine, or so we assured ourselves. Every editor readily concedes that an average *Geographic* reader compulsively looks at the superb photographs, reads the captions of compelling pictures, and *maybe* reads the article, *if* the subject interests him. Obviously, caption writers should outrank article writers. The reverse of course prevails. Article writers enjoy higher status, earn more money, and traditionally occupy the top editorial jobs. A rationale for this is that while captions require cleverness, articles require far more: firm grasp of a broad subject, organizational ability, a capacity for literary synthesis, and sustained discipline.

Then as now, captions at the *Geographic* were known as legends; this nomenclature derived from the Society's long history of producing maps enriched with factual notations, or legends. Picture legends fell under sharp scrutiny during the editorship of Melville Grosvenor. His scribbled admonishments filled the margins of proofs like scrollwork. Legends must sing! Legends must soar!

For those of us toiling in the legends mill and fearful of eternal editorial anonymity, attention from the top—even negative attention—came as welcome recognition. The Legends Department also meant opportunity. We were younger writers aiming upward, and Legends was the doorway to article writing; when one of those guys moved up or out, one of us stood a fair chance of moving in.

Best of all, legends were challenging and fun to write. You'd study a picture for perhaps an hour, staring at it, seeking to identify what the image was "saying"; then you'd capture this thought in the three or four boldface words that open each legend blurb. You packed the rest of the legend with information, paralleling the article but not repeating it, making it as interesting as humanly possible. Not all writers could write legends, could decipher the photo's message and convey it excitingly and engagingly. We legends writers were proud of our shining nuggets.

Another charm of Legends was that the writers were young and energetic souls who hugely enjoyed partying. Multimartini lunches erupted at least weekly; afterwork gatherings with a few researchers could evolve into transcendent orgies that generated days of incredulous postmortem comment by participants and innocent observers.

This strenuous blend of hard work and hard play mirrored the powerful persona of the editor of the Legends Department, Carolyn Bennett Patterson. A Mississippi native and journalism graduate of Louisiana State University, she was only the second woman to reach the magazine's higher editorial echelons. Tornadic of energy, huge of heart, gifted as editor, deeply dedicated to the *Geographic*, indefatigable crusader for rights of every sort for everyone and everything and especially for women, Carolyn Patterson benignly looked after her subjects' welfare and asked only that we write good legends and be kind to one another. When one of her writers turned in a weak set of legends, Carolyn patiently worked with him or her to improve them. When legends sang, Carolyn heaped on the praise. Loved by her troops, she provided living proof that motivation from above can tap skills and productive capacities often unknown to their possessors.

AND SO, WITH A LAYOUT for Father Mary's article in hand, I am winging north—a stop in Montreal, then over the wooded and lake-strewn wilderness of enormous Quebec Province. Soon the forests thin, the lakes acquire a hide of ice. Off to the west I see the widening ice wedge of James Bay, then the immensity of Hudson Bay. Second only to the Mediterranean among inland seas, Hudson Bay, scooped from the Canadian Shield by a million years of glaciation, is still locked in ice that will relax its grip only for six weeks in late summer.

We cross north of the tree line and overfly the tundra. A twentieth of Earth's land surface exists as tundra, underlain by permafrost that in northern latitudes extends a mile deep. In summer the top few inches of surface will thaw, creating the "active zone" that sustains arctic life. Plants hurriedly blossom and fruit; animals frenziedly feed, breed, nurture, and store fat as fuel, either for migrating south or for enduring the grim winter in situ.

In crossing the tree line we cross the boundary between North America's two native peoples. Historically, the people we call Indians ventured northward no farther than the forest fringe; they lived in fear of the short, mysterious ice dwellers to the north. For their part, the people we used to call Eskimos lived in mortal fear of the forest dwellers and did not stray from the tundra. Inhabiting a world with little wood, these people did not cook their food, so the more southerly-dwelling people called them Eskimo, "eaters of raw meat." Today the arctic dwellers have reestablished their own name for themselves, Inuit, "the people." And in 1999 they will accede to local self-government when Canada hands over control of 772,000 square miles of tundra to be known as Nunavut.

At the top of Hudson Bay sprawls Baffin Island, my ultimate destination, stretching for nearly a thousand miles alongside Greenland to the east. The island is the easternmost reach of Canada's Northwest Territories, extending west to the Yukon. On my map Baffinland resembles a giant lobster, with northerly Cape York as its curved claw. There the explorer John Ross discovered Inuits, who greeted him in astonishment, having thought themselves the only human beings in the world.

We land briefly at Frobisher Bay, unofficial capital of the eastern Arctic. It's 10:00 P.M. when we take off again, but we see no nightfall, only twilight; there'll be no more darkness on this trip. Soon we fly over the invisible line that on maps marks the Arctic Circle, southernmost advance of the midnight sun. A person standing on this line at sea level at the summer solstice, usually June 21, will bask in twenty-four hours of sunshine. Each mile traveled northward turns on more midnight sun.

The jet drones northward over an immense wilderness of snow and ice. Now we pass over a man-made line, a defensive feature that spans the continent like a techy Great Wall of China. It is the

Distant Early Warning Line, a chain of radar stations built in the 1950s across arctic Canada and Alaska and operated jointly by the two nations in order to detect Soviet aircraft and missiles. Many Inuits helped build the DEW Line. The experience gave them a familiarity and taste for modern ways that accelerated their transition from seminomadism.

Our plane flies right over Pond Inlet, whose postage-stamp airfield scarcely accommodates even small propeller craft. We press 300 miles farther toward the Pole, pick up Cornwallis Island, and slant down at Resolute Bay, the world's northernmost jetport. Exhilaration sweeps over me: I really am representing the *Geographic* in an exotic world—living the dreams stirred years earlier while temporarily occupying the offices of veteran writers.

At the moment Resolute is exploding as a frontier boomtown. All of arctic North America is swarming with prospectors searching for minerals and petroleum, and with workmen struggling to wrench them from a reluctant environment. Resolute is the high-arctic hub for this frenzied urge to exploit. Atop the snow-crusted permafrost has grown a raw assemblage of equipment storage depots, fuel facilities, and prefabricated offices and barracks. Not pretty, but hopping.

On this Saturday night a party is under way at the satellite tracking station four miles out of town, near the Inuit village. A genial oil field worker named George offers a ride.

The party obviously has gone on for a while. A bleak room redolent with smoke and alcohol fumes holds about thirty churning persons, including half a dozen women and as many Inuits. Some are drinking beer, the others a mix of juice and medical alcohol. At least half are drunk. A three-piece combo is blaring.

I turn back to George, but he is already out on the floor, dancing, with a bottle balanced on his head. I chat with other men, who clearly are starved for a fresh listener. They describe their fondness for frontier life, with its freedom from petty restraints, its easy acceptance of human individuality. Many have bounced between similar hubs of arctic action—Yellowknife, Frobisher Bay, Prudhoe

Bay. "Gets in your blood," they agree. Elsewhere on my travels I will meet similarly bonded men who have either found or lost themselves at society's margins—on isolated Pacific isles, in the outback, perhaps even in the astronaut and cosmonaut corps.

Early Sunday morning I check in at the airport, where a small plane will take me to Pond Inlet and Father Mary. "Looks like good flying weather," I volunteer to the pilot of the Twin Otter. He wants no such cheer. "Once you're up, clouds can roll in under you. When you go to land, you don't know whether you're setting down on snow or on the clouds. Landing at Pond Inlet, where you're headed—that's always a bitch." He'll get little help from the plane's magnetic compass. The north magnetic pole, ceaselessly wandering across the Arctic, now tarries on Bathurst Island, only 150 miles to the northwest. Compass needles can spin meaninglessly at this latitude and longitude.

Three others on the Otter are bound for Pond Inlet. An electrician will be checking on the settlement's oil-fired generators. A young English woman is returning from vacation to resume work as a nurse at the small clinic. The third, by profession a teaching consultant, has come on an unwelcome assignment. In the channel off Pond Inlet, a Canadian seaman has committed suicide on the icebreaker St. Laurent, accompanying the tanker Manhattan in its research on establishing an all-weather Northwest Passage. The consultant will conduct the inquest.

Our plane lands at Arctic Bay, a settlement 200 miles west of Pond Inlet and often visited by Father Mary. A passenger debarks; waiting Inuits manhandle two snowmobiles from our hold. Up again. I look out and down, studying the surface beneath us. Is it ground, or is it clouds? The pilot has a point.

We bank, and Pond Inlet wheels across my window. The settlement's muted geometric structures paint a cubist watercolor on the white canvas of the snow. At least there are no clouds to worry the pilot. Far down the channel I see the great tanker Manhattan and a smaller vessel that must be the St. Laurent. The consultant eyes them intently.

We circle Pond Inlet and glide down—directly toward a bluff. Just before impact the pilot noses us up, then plops us down onto the snow beside a flapping windsock. Landing here *is* a bitch. A cluster of people waits to greet the new arrivals and pick up cargo. To one side stands an individual obviously accustomed to standing alone, a slender man with grizzled hair, longish face, and steel-rimmed spectacles. Ataata Mari, just as in his pictures.

We all know people who, at first meeting, can melt one's heart with effusive warmth, then revert to a natural indifference made worse by the false greeting. Others greet people with a reserve that can easily be misinterpreted as unfriendliness, yet in time reveal a genuineness and inner warmth that lead to lasting friendship. My hope is for the latter. Father Mary is no flash-in-the-pan; we will put our faith in the long haul.

He lives beside his small frame mission church, in quarters tight but cozy. I have a tiny room. Water comes from a pitcher, and sewage goes into a plastic-lined bucket. There is no plumbing in this land of permafrost. Waste ultimately travels by tracked vehicle to a landfill.

He guides me on a walking tour of the settlement, planted on a gentle slope rising from Eclipse Sound. Past the electrical generating plant; past the government administrative office, the Royal Canadian Mounted Police headquarters, the Hudson's Bay Company store—all ubiquitous in the Arctic; past the garage sheltering tracked vehicles that distribute water and heating oil and pick up sewage and garbage.

Past the Anglican church, much larger than the Catholic. English whaling boats plied these waters, English traders bought furs, and English missionaries came to save souls, building a following vastly larger than Father Mary's sparse flock.

Past the large red schoolhouse, which offers instruction through the seventh grade. Compulsory education played a key role in ending traditional Inuit life. A decade ago the government built schools with student dormitories across the Arctic, and required attendance by young Inuits. Parents' attachment to their children drew them irresistibly away from the life they had lived for hundreds of years, into the confining settlements, away from the tundra forever. We walk among the houses, snug and boxy. Bright paint on many helps offset the total absence of trees or shrubs. An occasional snowmobile roars past, often carrying a family of three or four.

Something incongruous catches my eye. On many of the small front porches leans a rifle, sometimes two. "Keeps them from rusting," explains Ataata Mari. "Carry your gun inside, and condensation forms on the cold metal and causes corrosion. The outside air is extremely dry. Most of the arctic tundra is desert." No danger of theft? "Stealing is almost unknown in the settlements," he says. "Everybody knows everything. And where could one dispose of a stolen gun?"

An elderly Inuit approaches on foot, a rifle slung over his shoulder. "That's Qumangapik," explains Father Mary. "Eskimo dogs are dangerous; they've killed children in the villages. A law requires that they be tied up. If one breaks loose, if a stray appears, Qumangapik shoots it."

We walk down to the sound and out onto the sea ice. A score or more husky dogs are staked out in two separate groups. "These are the only two-dog teams left in the settlement," says Father Mary. "In the old days every family had sled dogs. Snowmobiles have taken over." I notice that each animal is chained to a separate pin driven into the ice, and that no chain allows one dog to reach another.

An Inuit comes out from shore, carrying a bucket. Father Mary murmurs a greeting to his trusted friend, Arnakadlak, who approaches a cluster of dogs and begins pitching chunks of meat to each. "He never goes among them," Father Mary explains. "If he slipped and fell, they would kill him."

We climb back up the hill toward the Catholic mission. At a fork in the roadway stands a mountainous pile of snow, obviously heaped by the tracked vehicles. It's eleven at night, yet the sun shines brightly well above the western horizon. Despite the hour,

Inuit children are playing on the snow pile, climbing up one side, sliding down the other, shrieking delighted whoops and whees.

Isn't it past bedtime? "It seems almost as though they sleep through the winter darkness, then play through the summer daylight," muses Father Mary.

My thoughts fly back to Maryland, to our sons, Yellott, now seven, and Mac, five. Already I miss them. Mac will celebrate a birthday two days after my scheduled return. Will the fickle arctic weather cooperate? It would hurt to miss the festivity and to put all the arrangements on Jes.

In bed that night I rehearse my strategy for launching Father Mary on his writing career—a subject we have avoided. Next morning he's ahead of me. "I have a plan," he announces. "Arnakadlak, whom we saw with the dogs, needs to shoot a seal; he's running out of dog food. You can go with him and his nephew Ham to Cape Graham Moore on Baffin Bay. You won't find many opportunities these days to hunt with Eskimos by dogsled on the sea ice."

I hesitate, uneasy about leaving without signs of progress. Father Mary sees my discomfort and points to a small table. It holds an ancient typewriter. "I'm ready to start." Still I hesitate, unsure. He breaks into a smile. "I've started!" he says, sitting down at the machine and lifting his hands to the keyboard. He types out a sentence, and I read over his shoulder: "J'avais offert à Alain Maktaq, pour le remercier de services rendus . . . " Ah, me—wrong language. But John Scofield, the amiably unspecific editor, has not specified a language. And the Society has a Translations Department. It is enough that writer's block has been banished at Pond Inlet. I will go seal hunting. Besides, I'll be gone for only two days.

And soon I am jolting across the sea ice with Arnakadlak and Ham in quest of meat for the dog team, marveling at the clearest air on the planet—and still wondering why it smells so foul.

A change is coming over the dogs. They're fighting less with those beside them, inviting less instruction from Arnakadlak's whip. Their character is not improving; rather, their work is getting harder. Warmth from the climbing sun is causing the powdery surface snow to soften slightly. The result is greater friction for the sled, meaning harder pulling for the dogs and less energy for troublemaking.

A distant object to our left catches Arnakadlak's attention. From a pocket he pulls out a small brass telescope and holds it to one eye like a sailing-ship captain. Pocketing the scope, he turns the dogs in that direction.

In using a telescope rather than binoculars, Arnakadlak is living a legacy of the early English seafarers. Whalers in particular often took on Inuits as crew members, and during their service some acquired the instruments. So strong is the telescope tradition in the eastern Arctic that those Inuits who use binoculars hold them to their face vertically, so that only one eye looks through a lens.

The speck in the distance that has caught Arnakadlak's eye slowly grows into a tiny camp, set up in grand solitude on the sea ice. A one-man tent houses the human population. A dog team is staked out to one side. Nearby rests a sled like ours, loaded with two bags of coal, a flag from the tanker *Manhattan*, a rifle, and a large ringed seal with a bullet hole in its head.

Carefully skirting the dogs, Arnakadlak trots up to the tent, flings open the flap, leans halfway inside, and starts talking. Moments later a sleep-drugged Inuit emerges.

Arnakadlak sets forth again, doubtless armed with advice about seal-hunting grounds. "Oot! Oot!" he urges, flicking his whip. I see that his efforts are directed at a single intractable shirker: The animal pulls with each sting of the whip, then at once slacks off again. At length Arnakadlak stops the sled and unhooks the dog from the harness. Head down, it shuffles to one side and waits until we've passed, then trots in disgrace behind us.

Fissures appear in the sea ice—long cracks a foot or two wide and four and five feet deep, refrozen at the bottom. The dogs have obviously encountered this problem before; cleverly they gauge each leap so they can sail across without drawing the harness line taut and being jerked down into the crack. Concern for their safety soon gives way to fascination at their performance: Here in the Arctic is the obverse of our Maryland hunt-country steeple-chases, with the jumps not raised but sunken.

A wide crevasse appears ahead. Like a fleeing herd of African impalas, the dogs gracefully leap—and one misjudges. In midleap its line draws tight, and the animal spins downward onto the floor of the crack. It scrambles to its feet and claws at the slippery ice wall, half out, half in; in a split second the heavy sled will slam across and crush it. The creature struggles, the sled smashes across—and the dog shoots out before it like a rocket. For the first time I see emotion flicker in Arnakadlak and Ham.

Though the air is well below freezing and calls for a snug parka, the softening surface snow is increasing the friction and strain on the dogs. Also, the high sun is signaling time for tea. Arnakadlak stops the sled, heats snow on a primus burner, and produces sugar cookies: high tea for three on the sea ice.

Then Arnakadlak addresses the friction problem. He and Ham turn the sled upside-down. While Ham stands so his shadow falls on a runner, lowering its temperature, Arnakadlak daubs the runner with caribou fur dipped in water. It freezes instantly. Now runners glazed with ice will speed our sled.

Throughout our dogsled journey mysterious waves of foul odor have continued floating over us. I've all but abandoned trying to explain their cause. I have a bigger problem: For endless hours we've been sitting on the mounded cargo without a backrest—murder for a writer with a bad back. Since the sled is moving at jogging speed, I decide to hop off and jog.

I spring onto the ice. The footing is good. I fix my eye on a distant mountain; maybe it will move closer as I run. I'll be able to jog until the next fissure compels me to reboard.

I speed up and come abreast of the running dogs. The mysterious odor vanishes. I hear a popping sound, then another and another. Of course! The dogs are breaking wind—just as one might expect on a diet of raw seal meat.

A black speck—a raven—appears in the sky, silhouetted against a glacier on Bylot Island. Hardy ravens, along with snow owls and ptarmigan, winter over in the Canadian Arctic. Soon the softening tundra will ring with the cries of the legions of summering arrivals: sandpipers, turnstones, yellowlegs, curlews, avocets, dowitchers, godwits, snipes, willets, phalaropes, and golden and semipalmated plovers. With most, the young will begin foraging almost the moment they hatch and in six or eight weeks will spread their virtually untested wings for the grueling migration south.

The sun sinks toward the western horizon as if to set, then changes its mind and heads eastward—the return leg of the daily solar journey hidden to those billions of us who dwell below the Arctic Circle. Meanwhile, we seem to be getting somewhere. Ahead, Baffin Island to our right and Bylot to our left are tapering to an end. The channel is opening wider, into Baffin Bay. Three hundred miles across it lie the frigid fjords of northern Greenland. Hereabouts, waters of the Arctic Ocean meet waters of the North Atlantic—junction of two of the three oceans that lap continent-spanning Canada.

Ham points ahead to the left, to the farthest cape of Bylot Island. Rounded boulders march down to the shore and disappear beneath the sea ice. Several hundred yards from the shoreline, beyond the reach of storm-driven ice and waves, stands a small, ramshackle wood cabin. This is the camp shared by Inuit seal hunters. We have arrived.

Moving carefully among the dogs, Arnakadlak stakes them out on the sea ice. With a hatchet he hacks up the last chunk of seal meat we've brought with us and feeds all except the ostracized loafer. It skulks to one side uncomplaining, obviously expecting nothing.

Seated on the boulders, we eat bread, cheese, and canned sardines. Suddenly the dogs join voices in a mournful moaning, the husky's substitute for barking. Seeing my interest, Arnakadlak points upward. High overhead, a tapering contrail leads my eye to a gnat-size jetliner plying the polar route, perhaps to Moscow. The dogs have heard engine sounds that we have not.

Near midnight we enter the cabin. Along one side runs a sleeping platform, a crude frame shelf the size of a desk top: the bed of choice for Inuits. One wall is missing a few boards, and the floor is strewn with a rich variety of unsavory debris. In the middle of the room slumps a steel bedstead, minus a mattress, its springs sagging almost to the floor: the bed of choice for whites.

Having spread blankets on the platform, Arnakadlak and Ham are soon asleep. I step into my bag and lower myself into the sagging springs. Gravity seizes control and pulls me down in a ball to the springs' lowest point. There will be no sleep for me this sun-shiny night. But sleep can wait. There are times when memories of the day just past are far better than dreams.

The Inuits stir after six hours of deep sleep, and I gratefully struggle out of my cage. Arnakadlak fetches his brass telescope, sits on a boulder, and scans the sea ice off the cape. Presently he stead-ies on a bearing and twists the scope for better clarity. He holds up two fingers: two seals basking, far out on the ice. We need only one of them.

From the mound on the sled, Arnakadlak pulls out a small white sheet and a pair of lathlike wooden slats, each four feet long. He crosses them at right angles, lashes them together with a thong, then attaches the sheet at the corners. The creation resembles a white kite. It will be our camouflage, a portable screen resembling snow to hold between us and the seals.

He hitches up the dogs, and we move across the sea ice toward the seals. Four hundred yards away and still undetected, we halt. Arnakadlak places Ham in charge of the dogs and hands him the whip. He slips his rifle from its scabbard, holds up the white screen, and motions for me to fall in close behind him.

With the screen before us, Arnakadlak and I trot briskly toward the seals; to Ham we must look like some four-legged ice animal with its legs out of synch. Periodically Arnakadlak peers around the screen. Seals sleeping on the ice awaken every minute or so to rear up and look for enemies. With each look we freeze until the animal lowers its head again.

A hundred and fifty yards from our quarry, Arnakadlak slows. Now we creep toward the seals. At a hundred yards he stops. He waits until both seals' heads are down, raises his rifle, and fires. *Thwock!* One seal leaps to the hole and disappears. The second, wounded, struggles toward the hole. *Thwock!* Still struggling, the creature is nearly there. *Thwock!* At the edge of the hole it lies still, in a widening puddle of blood.

We approach, and I wait for Arnakadlak to cut out the seal's liver, hot and bleeding, and bite into it—an Inuit tradition far older than the use of telescopes. I gird myself for the moment he will hand the dripping organ to me to share in the victory of the hunt; after all, a true *Geographic* writer seeks out the personal experience. Arnakadlak reaches into a pocket, pulls out the knife—and cuts the thong holding the white screen. Let's hear it for breaking with tradition!

Ham brings the dogs, and we roll the bulbous 200-pound seal onto the sled: food for the dogs for weeks, a fine hide to be sold. Then we turn for home down the broad channel, whose glaciers gleam like bridal gowns.

Father Mary has done nobly; when we arrive the next evening a stout pile of pages has grown on his small table. At this rate he'll finish before I leave. A brief scan of the opening paragraph assures me he's taking the correct *Geographic* approach, introducing himself and his story with an anecdote.

MY THOUGHTFUL HOST has also conceived another scheme. Tomorrow the consultant I met on the plane will fly out to the *St. Laurent* to conduct the final interviews of his inquest. I can join him in the helicopter and spend some hours on the icebreaker. The following days I can gather information about the pictures being used in the layout. Father Mary will be writing away.

The copter lands on the ship's fantail, and I make my way toward the bridge. The few crew members I pass are unquestionably subdued. In the best of times morale is tricky on board a small vessel, with its cramped quarters and cultural isolation. Stresses multiply with repetitious duty, with the sense that duty is unimportant, with unchanging scenery and a lack of ports of call. In such a climate, a suicide punctures spirits already deflated. I don't envy the men and officers of the *St. Laurent*.

The officer of the deck briskly welcomes me to the quarterdeck, then returns to training *St. Laurent*'s newer crew members icebreaking.

"Full ahead!" The ship shudders with surging power. Gaining speed, she moves toward a wall of virgin sea ice. Obviously this overzealous officer intends to sink us: Impact will rip the bow apart. But that is not the icebreaker's way. On contact her rakish bow slides up onto the ice. Momentum pushes her higher still. Suddenly her weight snaps the ice shelf, and the bow plunges down in an explosion of geysering water and flying ice chunks. "Full astern!" Then "Full ahead!" for another slide up onto the ice.

A mile or so to starboard lies the *Manhattan*, immobile in a straitjacket of ice. Her complement of scientists is out on the sea ice, collecting data on thickness and salinity and water temperatures, and drilling ice cores for later study.

Though *Manhattan* has become the first commercial vessel to make the transit of the Northwest Passage, her victory has been less than complete. Virtually unstoppable when moving forward, she can't unleash her full 43,000 horsepower when moving astern. This vulnerability has cost dearly. Attempting the most direct route, through notorious M'Clure Strait, she was pinioned by the pack ice and required the assistance of an icebreaker. Doggedly she completed her journey, but by a longer path. The Passage has not become a highway for commercial shipping.

Later, at *Manhattan*'s signal, her Canadian escort will smash a way to her stern and unzip the straitjacket. The tanker will await this assistance with mixed emotions. Mariners rightly fear collision when another ship draws near, no matter how benign her intentions; this apprehension intensifies when the visitor's duty calls for violent maneuvers in great proximity. This fear will prove well founded. A few days later, as *St. Laurent* is breaking *Manhattan* free, shifting sea ice will slam the vessels together beam to beam, damaging the icebreaker.

FATHER MARY WEARS a confident smile when I return to the mission. His mounting stack of typed pages tells why. That night, relaxed, Ataata Mari speaks of the arctic events that have filled his adult life, events he is now writing about:

Of the Inuits' frequent encounters with starvation and the occasional instances of cannibalism, such as the winter-locked family of the woman Ataguttaaluk, whose members died one by one and were eaten by the dwindling survivors, until only she clung to life and was rescued, to be known ever after as the Eater of Men.

Of the Inuits' traditional reliance on shamans—those individuals who communicate with the spirits that dwell in nature and control it, and to whom one went for help when he broke a taboo or suffered misfortune. "Man's landing on the moon held no surprise for the Eskimos," recalls Father Mary. "Their shamans had traveled there many times."

Of the scourge of lice, which in the Arctic infest all animals from the bumblebee to the narwhal to human beings and most cruelly afflict helpless infants; he had seen children virtually eaten alive by lice.

Of the Inuits' pampering of children and especially young males; he recalls observing a mother suckling a son aged six, then at his demand surrendering her pipe for him to puff.

Of the harsh abruptness with which the Inuits have been led to abandon one life and adopt another, and the many problems this left unresolved: of joblessness, alcohol, and an uncertain identity. Soon he will again be flying to Ottawa to speak for their interests as he sees them.

In a settlement as small as Pond Inlet, it takes little time to gather information about Father Mary's photos: of fishermen, of walrus and narwhal hunters, of families at traditional games and in igloos, of children at school and in health clinics, and of the drab town itself. At the newly opened craft shop I buy Jes carved soapstone figurines of a seal and a walrus, along with the skin of a ringed seal like the one bagged by Arnakadlak. From him I purchase a harpoon, an *ulu*, or crescent-shaped fleshing knife, and a *kakivak*, or fish spear—souvenirs for the office of one more *Geographic* traveler.

Carefully I pack away my caption notes and Father Mary's completed manuscript. We walk up the hill to the tiny airfield, where the Twin Otter has just bounced over the bluff. There I say farewell to a man who, at first greeting, seemed coolly aloof, and who instead has kindled a lasting warmth both in me and in the entire eastern Arctic.

For the first time I have the professional satisfaction of writing legends about a remote place I have seen firsthand. I can watch an article I have midwifed progress through translation, picture layout, text verification, and final printing in the February 1971 issue, its cover adorned with Father Mary's powerful photo of an Inuit fisherman. Within a year I will go forth to write articles on my own. One of the first will be about the threat of global famine.

Chapter 4

HOLDING FAMINE
AT BAY

Alighting silently on vulture wings, famine invaded tropical nations around the world in 1973–74, sitting at the bare tables of the planet's poorest peoples. Some it killed outright by starvation, as in the drought-ravaged sub-Saharan region known as the Sahel. More often it weakened its victims through malnutrition, and then disease finished them off. The United Nations Economic and Social Council noted with alarm that the global extent of food shortages was unprecedented in historical times.

A multitude of forces had converged to produce the famine, but foremost among them, many experts agreed, was rampant population growth. In this view they followed the dark predictions of Thomas Robert Malthus. "The power of population is so superior to the power of the earth to provide subsistence," the English clergyman/economist had written in 1798, that mankind faced "gigantic inevitable famine."

The global psyche had already been primed for impending apocalypse, first by the arms race of the Cold War, then by warnings of ecological disaster such as Rachel Carson's *Silent Spring* in 1962, and most recently by Stanford biologist Paul R. Ehrlich in *The Population Bomb*. "The race between population growth and food production has already been lost," wrote Ehrlich in 1968. "Before 1985 the world will undergo vast famines—hundreds of millions of people are going to starve to death . . . unless plague, thermonuclear war, or some other agent kills them first." Now, as the world awakened to the famine girdling the tropics, prophecies of massive human die-offs became commonplace. Some influential voices even urged a "lifeboat ethic": At some point the wealthier "have" nations must refuse help to the starving "have nots," lest the latter swamp us all.

In 1974 the deepening crisis and the public's need for reliable information persuaded Editor Gil Grosvenor that the *National Geographic* should assess the impact of the famine, look behind the agony to its causes, and, most important, forecast the world's ability to feed its people. With a worldwide membership exceeding 7 million and a readership perhaps four times that, the *Geographic* seemed the perfect forum for such a project. People trusted it. Moreover, given the magazine's conscious policy of usually avoiding social issues, its decision to tackle such a question head-on would reinforce the importance and urgency of the topic.

Because a food/famine story would touch on a medley of sciences—demographics, soils, climate, agronomy—Gil turned for an author to Science Editor Ken Weaver. And Weaver turned to me. I was flattered but also overwhelmed. At this point I was a newly hatched science writer who'd never even had a foreign reporting assignment. Suddenly I was about to explain to the world whether it would eat or starve. The editors felt a confidence in me that I couldn't say I shared.

My elevation to science writer had occurred a year earlier, when Gil created a small Science Department. Until then I had been a caption writer in the Legends Department—the work that had sent me north to Inuit land. It was in Legends that I'd discovered my fondness for science stories.

In almost every issue, the magazine tackles a subject dealing at least in part with science or technology—space exploration, energy, environment, astronomy, climate, natural history. Most caption writers—indeed, most editors—recoiled from articles so lacking in romance and so tricky to explain. It is one thing to give the flavor of a city, a people, or a journey; another thing entirely to explain accurately the science behind, say, an astronomical event. But I liked the science pieces best—liked the satisfaction of understanding a serious scientific subject and trying to explain it simply and excitingly. Carolyn Patterson, the Legends chief, gladly sent those articles my way. "Write your legends so Ah can understand them, Tawm," she admonished in her Mississippi accent. "If Ah can follow them, anyone else in the world can too." Striving to comply with Carolyn's mandate, I acquired a certain adeptness at science writing.

When Gil created the Science Department, he authorized Weaver, who had already written more than a score of science articles, to recruit two writers, and because of my legends experience he tapped me. Suddenly in 1973 I was a *National Geographic* article writer—the choicest job in the known universe. Article writing offered everything: independence in planning one's coverage, ample time in the field, a liberal expense account, travel to the ends of the Earth if required, liberty to write in one's own style, and a chance to be read by nearly 30 million people worldwide. In short, a salaried writer's nirvana.

Though the famine story would deal only partly with science and was intimidating in scope, I knew I had one advantage. A story about feeding people would be heavily involved with agriculture, and I had grown up on a Maryland farm, working beside my father in the fields. In this respect I would feel a kinship with those who strove to feed their families and the world.

Like anyone lucky enough to have an able assistant, I immediately turned to mine. Rebecca Beall had just been hired, one of those overqualified college graduates who accept positions beneath their abilities with the expectation of working into better jobs as they open. She had studied English at the University of Colorado and knew she wanted to be in publishing, somewhere. She was smart, a hard and competent worker, and an ardent team player. It was utterly impossible not to like and admire Rebecca Beall, and I did both, very much.

"I'll hit the library," said Rebecca when I'd described my assignment. In short order my shelves held piles of red manila folders filled with articles from the New York Times and eleven other newspapers, snipped and filed by our library's clipping service.

The clips told a horror story that made a good case for Malthus.

More than 100,000 people and millions of head of livestock had starved to death in the Sahel, the belt of largely pastoral nations that rim the southern edge of the Sahara: Mauritania, Senegal, Mali, Upper Volta (now Burkina Faso), Niger, Nigeria, Chad, Sudan, and Ethiopia. Some had not received meaningful rain for seven years. The expanding Sahara had pushed millions of refugees southward until stopped by the tsetse fly zone. Thirty nations had responded with food aid that in time would total more than a million tons. So ravaged was the Sahel that some relief officials advised privately to write the region off.

The articles told more—of desperate hunger afflicting India, Bangladesh, and Pakistan and the rural poor of South America. Many laid blame on imagined failings of the Green Revolution, whose "miracle" grains had held high promise in the 1960s. If global famine could strike on the heels of the revolution, could Malthus be wrong?

In reality the famine flowed from many causes, suddenly converging. Drought was a major player. In addition, the Green Revolution had caused demand for fertilizer to outstrip supply, stunting crops and raising prices. Energy costs had soared. Disastrous grain harvests had led the Soviet Union secretly to buy up U.S. grain surpluses that had shielded the world from hunger. The fuel and fertilizer shortages had drastically reduced global food production and increased prices. Thus hunger came to the world's poorest people, concentrated in the tropics.

Rebecca and I pored through the folders for leads to famine fighters. They were there in abundance. Many were headquartered in Washington, only blocks from the *Geographic*. Working by phone, I lined up interviews with key officials, scheduling the earliest for the following week. This would give me time to educate myself; busy academics and executives rightly resent talking to journalists who haven't done their homework.

By now I had two potent partners. Elie Rogers had been assigned as picture editor and Steve Raymer as photographer. Both were good friends and hard-working professionals; both would wear well during the article's yearlong gestation. A decade later Steve and I would cover the Soviet space program. Elie enjoyed enormous respect for the creativity and energy he brought to directing the picture coverage of his assignments. He and his wife, Lesley (now head of *Geographic* Research), would buy and refurbish the old Maryland farmhouse, Rose Hill, where I grew up and where my family had farmed for six generations.

Loading up with hip-pocket notebooks, I set forth to talk with people at AID, CARE, the Catholic Relief Services, the Economic Research Service, UNICEF, the Agricultural Development Council, the Food and Agriculture Organization of the United Nations, the Rockefeller and Ford Foundations, the Society for International Development, and of course the mighty World Bank. Each expert produced names of many others I should contact, in other agencies and in the field around the world. In a few weeks I had the names of hundreds of people and a picture not only of the problem but also of the massive international crusade combatting it—abundant information for planning my coverage and banishing initial apprehensions about the assignment.

Now it was time to set up appointments with these far-flung contacts, to draw up an itinerary, and to rustle up visas, traveler's checks, and plane tickets. Time, too, to bare my body for immunization shots. Descending one floor, I followed my nose to the source of the pleasantly antiseptic aromas emanating from the Society's medical dispensary. This busy facility had three nurses and a part-time doctor, three spotless bedrooms in which ailing staffers could briefly collapse, and a waiting room staffed by a receptionist and stocked, of course, with *National Geographics*.

Chief Nurse Ruby Schaeffer led me to her office. Studying my itinerary, she matched the countries I'd visit against a chart listing the vaccinations required for each one, published by the Centers for Disease Control in Atlanta. She leafed through CDC updates, sent out twice weekly to alert health practitioners to disease-causing events such as famines. Comparing her shots-needed list with my immunization history, she concluded that I needed a lot: cholera, meningitis, typhoid, hepatitis A and B, yellow fever, and tetanus. She assembled a medical kit tailored to my trip: pills and potions for dysentery, diarrhea, fever of undetermined origin, malaria, itching and insect bites, insomnia, eye infections, pain, and dehydration, along with a comforting first aid assortment of salves, bandages, and water-treatment chemicals. Leaving Ruby's office with my bulging kit, I knew that if I faltered in my travels, I could not blame my friend and protector, Ruby Schaeffer.

W EARY FROM A LONG FLIGHT, Steve Raymer and I touch down in Niamey, capital of Niger. Drought has all but crushed this immense nation wedging into the empty Sahara just north of Nigeria; crushed the farmers in the savanna in the south poking sticks into the soil to plant their millet; crushed the pastoralists whose vast herds once supplied meat to other African nations—2 million Niger cattle have starved—crushed the nomadic Berber herdsmen to the north, including the proud blue-robed Tuareg so idealized by those who write of Saharan cultures.

Aid is pouring into Niger from donor countries, 47 percent of it from the United States. The drought has broken. But the famine grinds on, and the rain impedes the relief effort; food-laden trucks have mired helplessly in the mud of Niger's dirt roads. Now a fleet of 5,000 camels carries sacks of millet and sorghum to the relief camps.

Steve and I do not find a warm welcome. Testy government officials have had enough of journalists flocking in, photographing starving children, ignoring the country's own substantial relief effort. We are free to travel, but Raymer faces jail if he photographs the relief camps or those starving elsewhere. He takes the ban seriously. Uniformed soldiers with bulging hip holsters are everywhere, and they scowlingly follow our movements.

The rains have transformed the Niger River from trickle to flood. As darkness settles in Niamey, Steve and I walk to its banks. Half the town seems to be gathered to savor the big water. As a half-moon rises, a soft hum of talk and laughter drifts like music, and people slowly walk naked into the black flood to luxuriate in a gift long deferred.

The U.S. embassy in Niamey is not surprised at the official coolness we encounter. A new government installed by a recent coup is trying to cope with the effects of long-term corruption, but negative reporting and a natural resentment of dependence on aid have aroused hostility toward outsiders. The embassy presents us with a letter certifying our bona fides and advises us to use it freely.

Bright and early we board a plane for Agadez, a market town in the north—a tiny hub of nowhere. The sun, still low in the east, is already turned on high. Our craft is an ancient and sand-scarred DC-3. Inside, a blast of vestigial body smells reminiscent of college locker rooms seems to emanate from the seats, whose worn cushions are palettes of stain and grime.

We drone northward, out of the savanna and into the desert. Before the drought, this transition zone lay a hundred miles northward. Lack of rainfall and overgrazing have invited the desert to encroach. Farms and dirt tracks vanish. This desiccated realm belongs to herdsmen adrift on the land.

Small rectangular shapes take form, resembling bales of beige cotton clustered on the desert. These are the adobes of Agadez, as thrilling to me as the igloos of Inuit land. Soon we are walking the town's gullied sand "streets." Wind lifts the sand and fires it between the mud buildings. Sand that is not in motion sends up a blinding glare from the fierce noon sun. Beside a low building, two goats equably share the remains of a cardboard box.

We check in at Agadez's hotel, an eroded mud structure that resembles an oversize termite mound. Entered from the sun-dazzled street, the interior is cave-dark and hums with flies. A ceiling fan rotates slowly above a small black table set amid four chairs. I half expect to see Humphrey Bogart as Rick in *Casablanca*.

Walking through the town, Steve and I see three European-looking types, two young women and a young man. It is a fair guess they are involved with an aid project. We introduce ourselves as reporters for the *Geographic*.

"I suppose you want to see starving children," says the man with a distaste he cannot hide. Obviously he, like the Niger officials, is tired of journalists who exploit human suffering.

"Our story is partly about the famine, partly about what's being done to prevent another one," I respond. "Where are you all from, and what's your project?"

Jean-François and Bea are from Belgium; Nel is from the Netherlands. They work through the European Economic Community to encourage vegetable gardening—much needed in malnourished Niger, and a potential source of exports to Europe.

Once they see that our interest is genuine, they describe their own work and that of others: the garden projects of the Frères des Hommes and the German Council of Protestant Churches; a UN well-drilling program; the construction of brush catchment dams in the wadis to capture runoff. One of these programs is run by the Père Sage, a legendary Catholic father who came twenty years ago to the desert east of Agadez.

"It's hard to believe," says Jean-François, "that 150 years ago this land was forested. Then the French came and introduced medical care. The mortality rate plunged, especially at childbirth. The population soared, and so did the herds. Over time they destroyed the forests, winds tore at the soils, and the desert invaded."

Jean-François grows thoughtful. "You'd probably like to see the relief camps," he now concedes. "I know where you can rent a

Land Rover and driver for tomorrow. We could go to Ingal." We agree to rendezvous at seven-thirty.

Steve and I return to the hotel and daub our faces at a tiny sink. Then we sit at the black table beneath the languid fan to see what will happen.

From the kitchen comes a man with a greeting, "Bon soir," and an opened bottle of red wine. We pour, clink, and sample appreciatively. The kitchen door opens again, and the man emerges carrying a steaming tray. He sets two plates of fish and rice before us. "Where do you find fish out here in the middle of the Sahara?" I wonder out loud. "Probably came up on our plane—part of the French heritage," Steve replies, his first forkful nearing his mouth.

"I'll be damned," he says with his mouth full. "Better'n Paris," one of his favorite photographic haunts. And it is—a meal worthy of Bogart's portly adversary Sidney Greenstreet.

Our Land Rover, like the DC-3, has seen its share of desert sand. The driver checks it out. He untwists some wire and raises the hood. He wipes the dipstick on a sleeve and reinserts it with a satisfied look. He unscrews the caps of the battery cells and sticks a finger into their acid to test the levels. Unorthodox, but thorough.

Tossing my quart canteen of drinking water into the back, I notice that our three friends have brought two gallons each. "You can't believe how dehydrated you get," says Jean-François. "And of course we could have a breakdown." Yes, that seems a possibility. We lurch to a start.

Ingal is a small settlement several hours' drive to the west. Minutes out of Agadez the dirt track disappears, erased by moving desert sand. The driver proceeds unperturbed. Several miles farther the road reappears, with the driver uncannily aligned. These vanishing acts and navigational feats will mark our trip to Ingal.

All around we see the drought's toll in the bleaching skeletons of herd animals—cattle, camels, goats, sheep, donkeys. Cattle have suffered most, and the loss of their milk has contributed greatly to the famine. Here in the middle of nowhere, Steve can safely take pictures, and his film drive whirs.

Jean-François points: a Tuareg family on the move, its shrunken herd drifting before it. The greening desert has lured some of the nomads from the relief camps to resume their seasonal migrations. We will see mirages that day—lakes on the horizon and trees upside-down—but nothing would be as hypnotizing as the sight of Berber families gliding in slow motion across the Sahara: men riding camels at the fore; women and servants following on donkeys; pack animals laden with tents, tent posts, beds, grain grinders, and kitchenware. In all my years of travel to come, only the Inuits of the Canadian Arctic will ever seem as exotic as the people of the desert.

En route we stop at tiny Assaouas, site of a well and hence meriting mention on Saharan maps. Here a relief camp has mushroomed; it now holds 737 Tuareg. Self-help teams from Europe have attempted to transmute the proud pastoralists into agriculturalists by teaching them to capture rainwater and to grow gardens, maybe even to irrigate. Bea and Jean-François lament that the Tuareg are difficult to motivate and appear willing just to stay here and accept relief rations. As a political science graduate from the University of Virginia, I am fascinated by this isolated experiment in welfare response.

We go on. Palm trees, green and inviting, shimmer on the horizon—surely a mirage. But these are rightside up and grow larger. We've reached the oasis of Ingal. The coolness of the shade, the magic of the springs, the sweet dates on the palms make it clear why desert peoples defend their oases to the death.

We walk Ingal's baked-earth streets. Knots of Tuareg men, tall and fair skinned, stand in shaded areas talking and sipping tea. Many wear swords; others hold ancient rifles, some of which are muzzle-loaders. Clothed in indigo robes whose dye colors their skin, swathed in veils while their women go veilless, the Tuareg are the famous "blue men" of the Sahara.

We see the toll of famine in Ingal. Emaciated mothers nurse wizened babies; children with sticklike limbs and hair discolored by lack of protein recline listlessly. Thus weakened by hunger, the children are now succumbing to diseases borne on the cold desert nights—bronchitis, colds, fatal measles. My thoughts turn irresistibly to my ten- and twelve-year-old sons back in Maryland. "Arab children suffer worst," says Bea. "The mothers eat the children's rations because husbands like them fat."

Crowds of camp people are flowing in and out of an open-front building, and we enter. It is a food distribution center, and this is the day for distributing powdered milk. One look at the scene before us tells me that Steve has his best photo-op of our whole trip.

The man distributing milk is large—almost spherical—and very black skinned. Around him crowd hungry refugees, reaching out with empty bowls and pleading faces. Energetically he scoops the powder from a canister and empties it into a recipient's container. With each scoop, powder floats into the air, then settles as a white patina on the black skin. It is a striking visualization of hunger and the benediction of outside aid. I turn to watch Steve do his magic. His camera hangs at his side, and his face is twisted with anger. I look past him and see why. An armed soldier stands nearby, his eyes fixed malevolently on Steve. A veteran of Vietnam, Steve knows when he's been ambushed.

The early afternoon air is a furnace as we walk to a Tuareg camp named Ibrik. It holds 3,000 refugees but does not feel crowded; space-loving Tuareg place their tents far apart. As we stroll, a smiling man approaches Bea. She helped his family in its struggles against malnutrition, and Mohammed Nakou remembers.

Mohammed herds us to his tent of rough matting supported by carved sticks. We crowd in beside his wife, ten children, and two chickens, and sit on the low beds covering the mat floor.

The other family furnishings consist of Mohammed's sword and knife, and kitchenware of old tin cans and a store-bought bowl. Our host adjusts the roof mats so that we all sit in the shade. In no time he pours hot, sweet tea, prepared on a tiny bed of coals before the tent.

Mohammed describes the drought's devastation. They've lost all their camels—he laughingly points to his belly, indicating that they starved—their dozen cattle, and all their goats except a black-and-white billy. Through Bea I ask if he intends to rebuild his herds and resume nomadic life. No, he will stay in the camp; how can they go back onto the desert with a single goat? As we leave, Bea voices doubts that the family will remain in Ibrik much longer. The Niger government is closing down the relief camps because they breed epidemics and because the camp dwellers are adjusting too easily to the dole.

Our driver once more untwists the wire on the Land Rover hood, checks the oil, dips a ritual finger into the battery acid, and sets off back toward Agadez. I marvel at my thirst—a result not so much of heat as of near-zero humidity. I long ago finished my quart of water and am drawing heavily on Bea's ample supply.

A long day, but a good one. A journalist in the field can never be sure what material will survive the severe distillation involved in producing an article. But I sense that Mohammed will do so, along with the three young Europeans who have shown us such kindness in their adopted desert land. We lack the golden photo of the powdered milk distributor, but we have the bone-strewn desert and the Tuareg again on the move. A good day indeed. I stash my little notebook in my hip pocket and contemplate the coming evening at our nameless hotel. Wine . . . fish and rice . . . probably in company with Bogart—and maybe Ingrid Bergman.

NIGER IS famine present. Kenya, our next destination, is famine future. Here the fuse of the population bomb is lit and hissing but has yet to explode.

Kenya doesn't convey the sensation of crowdedness that one feels in India or Bangladesh; its 21 million people inhabit an area almost as large as Texas. But much of the land is arid, infertile, or set aside as game parks; there is little room to expand. Further, the population is exploding by 3.6 percent a year and climbing—one of the highest growth rates in the world. Kenya is Malthus country.

It also is a pleasant country, relaxed and friendly to the traveler. Nairobi customs officials scarcely blink as Steve herds his eleven bags and boxes of equipment through customs. The rambling brick Norfolk Hotel smacks of colonial privilege and decadence—welcome indulgence after Niger. There is mail from the family—wife coping, boys healthy, lawn under control—and no word from the *Geographic*, a good sign. Laissez-faire—that's the *Geographic*. The journalistic freedom allowed us writers and photographers ranks high among the many blessings of working for the magazine. The only reason I might have heard from the *Geographic* is that I've just finished a piece on *Skylab*, the successful space laboratory launched in 1973 toward the close of the Apollo program. I left on the famine assignment before the *Skylab* article was put to bed, and if something has gone wrong—a quibble over a quote, a change of mind by an interviewee—I would have had an emergency call from Gil Grosvenor or Rebecca Beall. No news is good news.

Steve and I want to see the pressure of overpopulation on agricultural land. We team up with two officials from the Agriculture Ministry and drive south toward Kajiado, along the high plateau east of the Great Rift Valley.

This beautiful area of farms and bush was known as the White Highlands when Europeans farmed vast acreages; among them was Baroness Karen Blixen-Finecke, the Isak Dinesen of *Out of Africa*. With independence from Britain in 1963 the area became the Kinangop Highlands, and many of the great spreads were carved into settlements for native farm laborers. But the flavor of the old Africa persists. Thatch huts of the Kikuyu huddle on hillsides. In areas still bush, giraffes browse the tops of acacias, and ostriches feed among herds of Grant's and Thomson's gazelles. No matter that these are minor players in the great African biome; they are wandering free, and to this pilgrim on the savanna they are superb.

We reach a settlement known as Kipipiri, and our officials accost a lean, friendly farmer who is glad to chat. Kio Kimani has eight children—enough to secure his future. He owns twenty-four acres and a dozen cattle; until planting time he owned thirteen, but he sold one to pay for ten bags of costly fertilizer. As I jot notes he disappears into his mud-and-thatch hut. In a moment he emerges with a small plate holding hot sausages made of mutton and blood. Mine is delicious, and I pray that my stomach agrees.

Behind settlement huts much like his, hills rise until they vanish in the morning mist. As far upward as we can see, the red earth wears a quilt of tiny plots of corn, wheat, and gardens. I look at the many young people playing in the village, then again at the patchwork of fields. When the children's parents die—when Kimani dies—tradition dictates that family lands be divided among the sons. In a nation whose population will double in twenty years, those small plots soon will fragment into slivers.

Family planners, Steve and I are assured, are hard at work, energetically supported by AID and many other organizations. But 55 percent of the population is below fifteen years of age. A fearsome bulge of future breeders is coming on fast—the population bomb.

During our preparations in Washington, AID officials talked about Kenya's loss of pasture land to proliferating termite mounds, particularly in the Masai country, east of Nairobi. The subject could make a good photo, and Steve charters a plane.

We fly at 1,000 feet, so everything below seems very close. Soon we see rhinos, elands, wildebeest, giraffes, and male ostriches sitting on eggs. Masai huts of mud and cow dung cluster inside *manyattas*, the circular fences built to keep lions from marauding the precious cattle. Cattle graze in seeming abundance, yet the Masai owned many more before drought thinned the herds. They are among tens of millions of African pastoralists who subsist largely on milk and meat and whose lives center on cattle, much as the lives of the American Plains Indians centered on buffalo.

Below us we see a Masai armed with a spear trailing his cattle toward water. The animals walk placidly in four long columns, as disciplined as Prussians. They and their spear-bearing herdsman, casting long shadows, etch an exotic tableau on the savanna.

Steve taps the pilot's shoulder, and we swing around so he can shoot through an open window. We make another pass, and another. I see the Masai looking up in irritation. One more pass—and several cattle break ranks, disturbed by our buzzing. The Masai raises his spear and brandishes it in anger. As journalists will, we have gone too far. We admire his defiance.

We reach the escarpment of the Yatta Plateau near Tsavo National Park and fly beneath its heights. Termite mounds extend to the horizon, standing like tombstones in a boundless cemetery. Around each, the termites have stripped the ground of vegetation, leaving little forage between. Steve knows he is getting good pictures. He also knows they'll have difficulty competing with photos of more critical food subjects. But he shoots on, as all *Geographic* photographers are instructed to do: We have already spent thousands of dollars to get here, and this is no time to skimp on pennies for film.

A graver problem awaits our coverage. All across East Africa the ripening wheat crop, vital for survival, is being destroyed by the sparrow-size quelea bird. Numbering in the billions, the birds alight on the heads of the still-milky grain and peck off kernels. As they scrabble to hang on, their feet dislodge ten times what they eat, scattering the grains on the ground. Always a pest, in this year of want the birds have amassed in record numbers.

Kenyans have been fighting back with a grandiose stratagem known as the petrol blow-up. When a farmer locates a quelea roost, often frequented by millions of birds, the local agriculture office dispatches a blow-up team. The men set out fifteen or twenty barrels of fuel, each armed with a charge of nitroglycerin and all of them connected by a long fuse. When the birds gather at dusk, the men trigger a fiery cataclysm. Successful blow-ups are killing 2 and 3 million birds. Yet the officials admit they've seen little depletion of the quelea hordes.

The queleas must be photographed. Steve and I and an agriculture guide drive to a wheat farm, where we range through the fields like bird dogs, flushing clouds of queleas. Perversely the flocks flutter away from Steve. In my forays I see that much of the standing wheat holds stripped heads, and that grain litters the ground.

Whoosh! An explosion of tiny wings propels a blizzard of birds directly past Steve. He is firing away. The beautiful scene that he bags will provide a double-page zinger for our article. And a large framed print will hang in my office, already filling with mementos from the field.

Back in Nairobi that evening, with Steve engaged elsewhere, I gravitate to the Norfolk lounge. It is dead. "Try the X Bar downtown," suggests a British patron. "It's nice."

The X Bar doesn't look either nice or not nice—just guys at the bar talking and drinking and laughing, and attractive Kikuyu girls at a table doing the same. The girls are dressed in jeans and blouses. One, I notice, is especially animated. She obviously is about to break away, like a bubble lifting from boiling water.

I order a beer, edit some notes from the day's jottings, and glance again at the table of girls. Miss Steam Bubble is indeed breaking away, advancing on the bar.

She is cute—tight jeans, nice figure, saucy face. A pleasant sight.

She veers and heads my way. Arrived at my bar stool, she looks up and charmingly speaks her four words of English: "I drink, I dance, I fuck."

For the starved journalist who has had only Raymer around these past weeks, this is a rewarding event. Not since Julius Caesar and his *Veni, vidi, vici* has language been used so sparingly, so powerfully. Caesar is a helpful analogy to recall: I am a married man and must be purer than his wife. This lofty puritanism stems partly from fear of disease, even in the pre-AIDS era. An occasional field worker has returned home with VD. There are many good reasons for virtue. Back to the Norfolk.

Our coverage takes us down into the Great Rift Valley. For the geology buff, the rift is the promised land—a living diorama of 30 million years of tectonic violence. Here the ancient African plate has fractured for 3,500 miles—from the Red Sea to Mozambique—as the nascent Somali plate attempts to tear free and give birth to a new ocean. In the process Earth's crust has been stretched and thinned until the hot mantle beneath squirts up lava and roils the valley floor with volcanoes.

For the anthropologist, the rift offers even more. Its sediments and volcanic ash have preserved the fossil bones of the earliest known prehumans—*Zinjanthropus* and *Homo habilis* and the petite australopithecine nicknamed Lucy. Those ash and sediment layers are *Geographic* turf. The eminent anthropologists involved—the Leakeys, Donald Johanson, Alan Walker—were funded by the Society's Committee for Research and Exploration, and the magazine has richly documented their discoveries.

Louis S. B. Leakey, who started it all, was in many ways a Geographic Man; the Society loved him and in a sense created him. The son of British missionaries in Kenya, Leakey grew up with Kikuyu playmates, learned to throw a spear through a rolling hoop, underwent secret warrior rites, wrote a Kikuyu grammar, was called by his tribe "a black man with a white face," and in 1972 died a tribal elder. Educated at Cambridge, Leakey heeded an intuition that human origins began in East Africa. He and his wife, Mary, fixed on Tanzania's Olduvai Gorge in the Great Rift, where they found primitive tools that hinted of ancient makers. Financially strapped, they stubbornly dug for three decades. Then in 1959 Mary discovered the fragments that formed the skull the Leakeys labeled *Zinjanthropus*. The Research Committee took it from there.

The discovery of a human ancestor who lived 1.8 million years ago shook many worlds. The Leakeys became assured of Society funding and worldwide fame, though many of Louis' interpretations would later be challenged. The Society acquired a colorful, hands-on academic hero in a field of immense romance and public appeal; Leakey articles and television specials enjoyed vast popularity. Of importance to anthropologists, their search for man's origins suddenly found a focus in Africa's Great Rift Valley.

The rift rewarded those who searched. Richard Leakey, son of Louis and Mary, found startlingly old remains near Lake Turkana in northern Kenya. At Laetoli, near Olduvai, Mary discovered parallel trails of fossil footprints left by upright hominids 3.6 million years ago. Meanwhile, in 1960 Donald Johanson, then a Chicago teenager, read Louis Leakey's maiden *Geographic* article, "Finding the World's Earliest Man." Johanson resolved to join the search someday. "The name Olduvai," he would recall, "rang in my head like a struck gong." Fourteen years later and with Geographic

Society backing he was combing the scorching Afar Desert in the far northern rift. There he spied an arm bone thrusting from a gully—the arm of 3-million-year-old Lucy.

The gong that rang in Johanson's mind: How many such gongs has the *Geographic* rung? How many careers or avocations have been inspired or shaped by the stimulation of *Geographic* pictures and words? I suspect many indeed. One rang in my household. In 1968 my *Geographic* friend Sam Matthews wrote an article, "Nevada's Mountain of Invisible Gold." Then a legends writer, I wrote the captions. The story caught the eye of my younger son, Mac. He would read it seven times on his way to becoming a mining geologist in the Nevada gold country—the area of Sam Matthews' mountain of invisible gold.

It is easy to forget, when under the spell of the magazine's beguiling photos, that the National Geographic Society is first and foremost an educational institution, the largest in the world. Even before there was a magazine, the Society presented informative lectures in Washington, D.C. It entered the classroom in 1919 with the *School Bulletin*, which in 1975 evolved into *WORLD*. Books, television specials, and classroom teaching aids help fulfill the mission. In the 1980s Gil Grosvenor launched the Geography Education Program, with a nationwide network of teacher alliances. To commemorate the centennial year in 1988, the Society allocated 40 million dollars to seed an Education Foundation. Grants of the Committee for Research and Exploration steadily increase. Indeed, Raymer's and my presence in Africa on this assignment represents a costly educational effort.

Leaving Steve in Kenya, I fly to struggling Egypt, whose population of 37.5 million is the largest of any Arab country. Here the great vise of the Sahara Desert squeezes 99 percent of the people onto the gossamer thread of land watered by the Nile; Egypt's total arable land equals less than a tenth of an acre per capita. I see the effects of this crowding in the delta north of Cairo, in fields as small as a suburban living room. Yet each year scores of square miles of farmland succumb to urban sprawl and invading soil salinity

resulting from construction of the Aswan High Dam. Family planning officials with whom I talk are confident, assuring me that
Egypt will win the race between population and food. But the tradition of large families runs strong, and a quarter of the country's
families are still polygamous; and I wonder. In 1979 the United
States will financially adopt this problem-plagued nation to help
stabilize the volatile Middle East.

A DAY'S LAYOVER in Athens, with time to climb the Acropolis,
marvel at the Parthenon, and drink a glass of retsina. Then an endless flight via Air Bengali to Bangladesh. In Dacca, the capital, I
meet up with Raymer again, and we melt into a sweltering crush of
humanity unparalleled anywhere else on Earth.

For the 75 million crowding this Wisconsin-size hothouse, disasters are routine. A 1943 famine killed a million people. Monstrous typhoons regularly drown tens of thousands. The 1971 war of
independence from Pakistan drove 10 million as refugees into India
in the largest human migration known. Family incomes—seventy
dollars a year—are among the world's lowest and falling; massive
floods have destroyed crops, robbing people of jobs. Surplus food
sits in warehouses while thousands silently starve.

Why do so many souls crowd this tragic land?

"This is the richest agricultural country in the world," exults
an AID official who we initially regard as deranged. "Topsoil in the
deltas of the Ganges and Brahmaputra Rivers is 300 feet deep. You
can grow *anything*." The man has a point. Over the next decades
the canny farmers of Bangladesh will give Malthus a run for his
money. In the meantime Bangladesh is receiving an unprecedented
outpouring of assistance. Foreign governments are dispensing billions in food aid. More than a hundred private relief organizations,
from the Mennonites to Catholic Relief Services to the Ford Foundation to Planned Parenthood, are extending helping hands.

The Ford Foundation office in Dacca offers a car and driver to
show us aid projects under way in the countryside. Our survey will

take us from the capital to Chittagong, the nation's second-largest city, hard by the east coast of the Bay of Bengal.

Driving out of Dacca, we discover the stunning beauty of this land. Rice paddies of myriad shapes and sizes spread in chartreuse mosaics to the horizon, like vast water gardens. Some of the mosaic pieces are minute; one Bangladeshi in three owns an acre or less, and this may consist of scattered slivers. No litter mars the vista in this land that tosses out nothing.

Where the land rises above irrigation level, thatch huts cluster beneath palm and fruit trees. In richer agricultural areas population densities reach more than 2,500 per square mile, and villages stand nearly shoulder to shoulder. In the shadowy depths of the huts Steve and I often glimpse knots of women, peering curiously from their Muslim seclusion.

At an arm of the Ganges we halt to wait for a ferry. The river swarms with lateen-rigged dhows and high-prowed sampans powered by paired oarsmen. On the bank, a milling clot of humanity swelters in heat and humidity that hover near 100. Many of the men are holding hands in Muslim tradition. Many are lepers or blind and are begging, holding out hands or empty metal bowls. Moti, our driver, detects our impulse and discourages us; if we give we will be mobbed. He sees two small boys giggling at us, hesitates, then decides to explain their amusement: "To young Bangladeshis, white foreigners are 'red monkeys.'"

Shouting hucksters hawk their wares. One sells bananas, and I ask Moti to procure a bunch. A case of borderline hypochondria tells me that this sultry nation harbors megamicrobes of unusual variety and voracity. Bananas, equipped with natural wrappers, may offer protection. Fear of illness, our constant concern, looms menacingly here.

A tea shop stands on the riverbank, and thirst drives us toward it. As we approach we see a child filling the tea kettle—from the turbid, lumpy river. Steve and I sit tealess, enjoying the coolness while Moti drinks; he wouldn't risk it, he asserts, if the water hadn't been boiled. At last we board the ferry. Arriving at the other side of the river, I calculate that we've traveled twenty-five miles in four hours.

Moti guides us to a woven bamboo hut. Inside, the air is filled with clicking, tapping noises. It is the bills of hundreds of soon-to-be ducklings, pecking at their eggshells in impatience to hatch. A Canadian with the Baptist Mission is encouraging Bangladeshis to switch from grain-eating chickens to omnivorous ducks that forage on vegetation and snails.

Every few miles Moti stops to visit another project of another organization:

- A field office of Planned Parenthood International, struggling to rouse rural women to reduce the frequency of pregnancies
- Farmers of the Mennonite Central Committee, urging Bangladeshi counterparts to diversify their crops and plant fallow winter fields in fast-maturing vegetables, particularly vitamin A–rich broccoli
- Engineers with International Voluntary Services, promoting efficient irrigation wells and pumps
- UNICEF teams, offering healthful lunches for children
- CARE and Catholic Relief Services, working under AID contracts to improve nutrition

Between stops Moti describes the treadmill existence trapping Bangladesh's millions of day laborers. The man works nonstop through the day, then takes home his pay in rice. His wife cooks most of the rice for the family dinner. The rest they have for breakfast. By dawn the laborer is off to work again, to earn the rice for dinner and the morrow's breakfast. "That's why the family wants more male children—to bring home more rice. That's why the population grows."

Back in Dacca we visit the slums and the starving souls trapped within. Then we head to the airport, to fly away from this melancholy land. I've been beautifully treated in Bangladesh, by a people of singular temperament and politeness. I've stayed healthy, by eating more bananas than a tribe of red monkeys. But I yearn to leave; too much humanity, too much sadness. Inside the terminal seemingly a billion people press hotly together and consume the air, and I fear they all will try to board our plane. At last we are aloft, and the chartreuse mosaic of rice fields tilts away from the banking jet. My relief is shameful. Steve has different feelings. In a few months he will return and photograph a haunting picture story, "The Nightmare of Famine," that will accompany our joint article.

Our destination is New Delhi in neighboring India, and now a new apprehension disturbs Steve. Other *Geographic* photographers have had trouble entering India—not victims of malice, as it seemed in Niger, but simply of India's mildly paranoid bureaucracy. Steve suspects it's his turn. The problem lies with his eleven bags of photographic equipment. Much of it is electronics—high-tech lights, timing devices, and other black-box mechanisms. To an unversed customs official, these devices could look like bomb controls, surveillance equipment, or costly contraband to be sold on the black market. Even the carrying cases, made of shiny molded aluminum with no-nonsense locks for thwarting weather and robbers, look like those carried by CIA officials. And in the early 1970s, India is on hair-trigger alert against both China and Pakistan.

Our 747 lands before sunrise at an airport cool and blissfully uncrowded; at the moment it may be one of the least populous microenvironments of the Indian subcontinent. Only the stale odor of residual tobacco smoke hints of busier hours.

We queue up for the checking of passports, no mere formality in India. The line moves slowly, but at least it moves. We proceed into the baggage room, where Steve's silvery cases still ride the rattling conveyor. One by one we snatch them off. As the pile grows, men sweeping the floor begin eyeing us covertly—they know a sideshow when it's brewing.

We take our places in the baggage inspection line. Far ahead, a brown-uniformed customs official diligently inspects each piece of luggage. Half an hour later I submit my two carry-ons and in due time pass inspection. I turn and join the floor sweepers and remaining passengers in morbid fascination with Steve's impending encounter.

The customs official watches, intent but impassive, as Steve fills the low stand with his cases, aligning the overflow on the floor. One by one he unlocks them and swings back their lids, revealing the electronic gadgetry within. With each revelation the official's impassivity shades into darker suspicion. Simultaneously his body seems to inflate, as if to arm him physically with a size advantage for enforcing his duty. Magisterially he turns and points to a distant office, manned by another clerk. Steve must go there with his offending bags.

To be passed endlessly from clerk to clerk—that seems Steve's likely fate. We slide his cases to the office and step inside. The scene is vintage India, replicated in government and business offices across the subcontinent. A central overhead fan stirs papers on a large wooden desk. These are kept from blowing by platoons of ornate brass paperweights of varied shapes and designs. The clerk, a portly soul in a black suit, sits guardedly, chip on shoulder (we imagine), awaiting our indignation.

"I'm a photographer with National Geographic," says Steve politely if tensely. "These are my cameras and gear. The government knows we are coming. What would you like us to do?" The clerk blinks, then studies Steve's passport and Geographic ID card. He studies another document Steve has slipped before him—a letter addressed "To Whom It Might Concern," explaining in ornate calligraphy the benevolent purposes of our mission, embossed with the seal of the National Geographic Society, and adorned with a blob of sealing wax holding a blue-and-white ribbon. This masterwork of pomposity, contrived by the magazine's art staff and designed to overwhelm the most paranoid official, is known in-house as a "dazzler." It is the ultimate weapon in the stalled staffer's arsenal.

Our clerk digests the powerful missive before him. He shifts two paperweights. Finally he reaches for a stack of labels, tears off receipts for Steve, and methodically marks each bag. A porter moves the marked cases to the back of the room. "Contact your embassy later this morning," suggests the clerk noncommittally. "I will," replies Steve politely. "Thank you."

"Pretty quick, for a confiscation," observes Steve appreciatively as we flag a taxi. "Those guys can keep you in limbo for hours before they seize your stuff." Later in the morning a call to the office of the U.S. cultural attaché will produce a call to the airport customs official, and we will hire another taxi to spring Steve's equipment. A morning is shot, but not our schedule: Steve was canny enough during our planning in D.C. to factor in the delay.

India is a land of rich soils and skilled farmers. It is also a land of widespread malnutrition and starvation. What explains this contradiction?

We find the answer near Lucknow, in the squalid mud-house village of Itaunja.

It is market day in Itaunja, and food lies in small piles on mats on the hard-packed market ground—little pyramids of rice, wheat, red beans, yellow beans, peas, flour, fruit, unrefined sugar. There is fresh meat on demand: If a customer materializes, a goat tethered near us will be led behind a tailor's shop and butchered.

Beside the piles, an emaciated man stands silently, looking. Food three feet away, and he is slowly starving—not because of food shortage but because he lacks money to buy it. Poverty. Multiply this tragic wraith of skin and bones by tens of thousands, and one grasps the primary reason malnutrition and hunger haunt Indians and other peoples around the globe. Headlines highlight famines caused by war and drought because their victims are clustered for the camera and also can be reached by relief. Poverty is unexciting, uncomfortable to see, difficult to remedy, and tempting to overlook.

For the journalist seeking problems and pathos, teeming India is an easy target. But Steve and I have also come to India to see success. It abounds, both here and in neighboring Pakistan. It was Indians and Pakistanis who embraced the wonder wheat and miracle rice of the Green Revolution. The two nations became the theater for an epic struggle between Malthusian overpopulation and the Green Revolution's Norman Borlaug.

When I met Borlaug during my coverage in 1974 he was at his research center near Mexico City, where the revolution began. Three decades earlier the Rockefeller Foundation had sent him to Mexico to improve the nation's then-dismal yields of wheat. In that period the intense Iowan had genetically transformed wheat as a crop, introduced his wonder wheats around the world, and saved tens of millions from starvation. In 1970 he won the Nobel Peace Prize. Yet the remarkable man sitting before me was still tormented. Borlaug was desperately worried about the onrushing avalanche of population. He feared too that misguided environmental concerns would distract from feeding hungry mouths.

From his first days in Mexico, Borlaug was a driven soul; lacking machinery, he at times yoked himself to a plow. By 1963 he had tripled the country's yields. Alert officials in India and Pakistan invited him to introduce the wonder wheats there. Within five years both nations were planting them on millions of acres, storing the unexpected bounty in schools and stadiums, and amassing grain reserves. Simultaneously the International Rice Research Institute in the Philippines, modeling its experiments on Borlaug's, produced the miracle rices that quickly spread around the world.

Before leaving India, Steve and I meet with Dr. M. S. Swaminathan, the top agricultural official in the government of Indira Gandhi. His New Delhi office is uncluttered by stacks of papers or brass paperweights. Speaking with flawless flow and logic while Raymer orbits with camera clicking, Swaminathan emanates a depth and breadth of understanding and of human concern that produce an aura such as one imagines surrounding prophets and saints. He has used this personal force to transform passivity-prone India at a critical moment. Recognizing the promise of the miracle grains, Swaminathan has instituted a voluntary government extension program that prepares Indian farmers mentally and physically to accept and adopt them. The result has been a reshaping of millennia of agricultural tradition and the productive surge of India's Green Revolution. In later years on later assignments I will see this remarkable man again, always with the awe one feels in the presence of the mystery known as greatness.

With Borlaug trouncing Malthus, with the Green Revolution blooming, why has famine struck?

The revolution's reach has not been total. Initially favoring those who irrigated and were progressive, it has come slowly to the illiterate and backward. Further, farmers planting the high-yield varieties have fallen victim to the worldwide fertilizer shortage. With the resulting fall in food production, food prices have soared. It is a bad time to be poor.

THERE ARE MORE Asian countries to visit, each with its own food problems or solutions. In Pakistan I travel up the old Silk Road to the lofty foothills of the Himalaya, where an exploding population has deforested the mountains and erosion is washing the mountainsides down into tributaries of the Indus River, clogging the nation's vast irrigation system.

In beautiful Taiwan, green with rice terraces, I find a heartening success story based on land reform and on rigorous education that includes family planning, farm cooperatives to provide fertilizers and credit, and the Chinese work ethic.

In the vibrant Philippines, scores of scientists at the sprawling International Rice Research Institute continue breeding more miracles into the receptive rice grain: disease and insect resistance, drought and flood tolerance, ever-higher yields. IRRI is one of fourteen agricultural research centers operated by the Consultative Group on International Agricultural Research (CGIAR), conceived of by the Rockefeller and Ford Foundations and now supported by twenty-nine nations and administered by the World Bank. IRRI and Borlaug's Mexico center are the most famous; collectively the CGIAR centers improve agriculture and livestock production in every major world environment, from desert to rain forest. They are a powerful weapon against Malthus.

Homeward bound! En route the plane stops at Anchorage, and passengers file through customs and immigration. "We'll have to burn your boots," announces the immigration official. He's right: While in Taiwan I visited a test plot for controlling an Asian soybean fungus. If introduced into the States via my boots, the pathogen could wipe out the nation's most valuable export crop. Good riddance.

Once in the air again, I dutifully take out my blue expense-account booklet to make a boots notation. I scan the familiar categories: hotel, meals, air travel, taxis, postage, publications purchased, tips, and miscellaneous—the place for my boots. A final category, a quaint vestige of the past, reads "gifts to natives." The words transport my imagination back to earlier *Geographic* times and places: in the jungle in my pith helmet giving trinkets to the pygmies; in the royal palace of the maharajah presenting my credentials and a *Geographic* map of his dominions.

My trip has lasted thirty-one days, the maximum allowable under my one-month rule. Jes has survived admirably, and the boys—can I detect a slight growing up during that short absence? I have several weeks of office work and daytrips before my final major excursion for the article.

During this break I find myself filling a niche in the food chain. Six months ago our older son, Yellott, now twelve, ordered twenty-five Rhode Island Red chicks through the mail, which arrived merrily chirping. Since then they have grown, fledged, and commenced laying eggs in prodigious numbers. The home market is glutted, and I am Yellott's delivery man to the Society. Several days a week I bring in two or three cartons of large brown eggs, hawk them along the corridors of the writers and researchers, and turn in the take to our entrepreneurial offspring.

To complete my coverage, I must go to South America, where malnutrition, the phantom killer, sucks at the vitality of the continent like a leech, inviting disease.

Consultants at both the World Bank and AID suggest that I focus on Colombia. Stretching from Atlantic to Pacific, embracing mountains, rain forest, and savanna, Colombia in its geography, peoples, and problems typifies much of South America.

After landing in Bogotá I head for the town of Leiva, several hours north. Leiva is storybook colonial—wide cobbled plaza surrounded by low white-stucco buildings flanking the Roman Catholic church. Wealthy Colombians on holiday stroll unseeingly among bent *campesinos*, both sexes of whom wear ponchos and felt fedoras.

Thirty Peace Corps volunteers, almost entirely young women, are meeting in a Franciscan convent to discuss the welfare of the *campesinos* they work among. Their stories are grim: abandoned babies, left starving at volunteers' doors because mothers can't support them; families that have never heard of malnutrition or the importance of vegetables; starchy diets of yucca, potato, and plantain so bulky that children's stomachs can't hold enough to sustain them. And the cruel cost of *machismo:* male pride in having mistresses, whom they abandon with illegitimate children; the frequent abandonment of wives and their newly born; the beatings.

Back in Bogotá, Children's Hospital is overflowing with emaciated little bodies like those the volunteers spoke of. I visit many:

- Sixteen-month-old Luz, brought in by her parents because of incurable diarrhea, 40 percent under normal weight, bloated by acute malnutrition known as kwashiorkor, stricken with attendant anemia, pellagra, edema, and urinary infection

- Marina, six and a half months old, brought in from the hot low country by parents mystified by malnutrition, now recovering

- Juan, a two-year-old Indian whose resistance is so lowered by malnutrition that a host of diseases are in advanced stages and will soon claim him

- Year-old Angel, body scarred by pellagra, racked by diarrhea and anemia, abandoned by a widowed mother of eight

- Luis, age three, kept in a box in near starvation until discovered by a hospital worker, nicknamed "the

Buddha" because he could only sit, now rallying nicely
on rice, meat, potatoes, and green veggies

Hungry Colombians have a dream. Like westering North
Americans of a century ago, they will advance onto their great
plains, their *llanos*. The dream is powerful because today their tiny
farms terribly overcrowd the healthy highlands, as in Kenya. But it
remains a dream because the immense llanos are cursed with acid
soil, toxic to most crops.

I fly across the Cordillera Orientale, the eastern range of the
Andes, out into the mightiest llano. An ocean of grassland spreads
to the horizon and far beyond—one of the world's great outbacks,
room for numberless homesteaders. The Meta River, en route to the
Orinoco, coils like a serpent beneath shadows of drifting clouds.
One cloud hugs the ground: the dust of a cattle herd being trailed
to market, reminiscent of the Texas long drives. This *is* the
Old West.

We land at Carimagua, an agricultural research center in the
heart of the llano. Here eighty-five agronomists and soils scientists
grapple with land so acid that Colombians can buy it for the equivalent of forty cents an acre. Massive amounts of lime and potassium
can sweeten the soil—at prohibitive transportation costs. The goal
is acid-tolerant plants, and it appears to be woefully distant. There
will be no immediate land rush onto the llano.

In a 1970 Ford pickup an agronomist and I set forth on the
dirt trail for Bogotá at the crack of dawn. Soon we overtake an Indian family, and they clamber aboard. The man holds a bow and two
long arrows, for shooting fish in a tributary of the Meta.

We pass a rare homestead—a ranch of 12,000 acres supporting
a mere 200 cattle on the llano's nutrient-shy grass. More Indians
clamber aboard. The dirt trace grows slick from the last night's rain.
The agronomist, suddenly in a hurry, cranks the speed up to sixty,
and we fishtail wildly along, the Indians hanging on. Such speed
seems insane, but why worry? In the llano there's almost nothing to
run into.

At the small city of Villavicencio the llano ends abruptly against the sheer wall of the Cordillera. The road climbs steeply, and I look back at the great earthen sea we have left. The annual burning of the grass has started, and puffs of smoke rise like distant shell bursts. We wind sharply upward and at 11,000 feet reach the pass over the Cordillera. Ahead, toward the setting sun, ranges of the Andes march chaotically, as if tossing off the clouds that invade their crags.

The agronomist stops while a bulldozer clears the road of a slide. He tells the story of the unfortunate town in the valley we are approaching.

Several months ago a mighty slide swept away the town's one-lane bridge, severing contact with the llano. With a month's furious toil the government rebuilt the bridge. Four hours after it reopened, a top-heavy truck overturned and collapsed it. Ten days later the bridge reopened. Weeks later another slide swept it away. Again the government rebuilt and opened the bridge to traffic. Soon another truck overturned, collapsing the bridge once more. Fifteen days ago it reopened.

During that trying time, irate motorists who had waited forty-eight hours to cross forced their way onto the bridge and plunged to their deaths in one of the collapses. Now government troops armed with submachine guns are controlling traffic, permitting one vehicle at a time to cross the narrow span. Arrive in the town at the wrong time, and you can wait half a day to cross.

We are lucky; traffic moving from our direction is crossing. But s-l-o-w-l-y. For an hour and a half we inch along. Now only four vehicles are ahead. One creeps across. The next one gets the wave—and stalls at the abutment! Surely the soldiers will wave on the other side, and we will sit for half a day. In an eruption of fumes, the staller starts up, he lurches across, and we follow. It's been another long day.

HOME ONCE MORE. I've logged more than 58,000 miles on this assignment, a lot even by *Geographic* standards. I have twenty-two notebooks filled with food and famine information of every sort. If I don't understand the subject now, I never will. Rebecca Beall somehow transforms herself into a one-person protective cordon around my office. Now it's the typewriter and me.

Fortunately I've already decided on a lead, a vulnerable point that can block a writer even before starting. We writers worry colossally over leads: a poor one will lose readers at the outset, and a good one might pull them into an article they never expected to read. My lead is the Indian at the market in Itaunja, standing beside the little piles of food, too poor to buy, starving. It dramatically makes the point that the most common cause of malnutrition and starvation is plain old poverty.

For one who edits himself a million times over, I crank out text at a pretty good clip; after three weeks the end is in sight. Science editor Ken Weaver is relieved; the publication schedule calls for the article to be completed in another week. Now it's time for my text to answer the Big Question: Can the world feed its people?

Whom to believe? There are the optimists, a.k.a. cornucopians, who exult that the world can feed 15 billion people, nearly four times the population at the time. Many of these optimists are responsible people, solid scientists. I want to agree with them, but can they be right?

There are the pessimists, the doomsayers, who claim we've already had it—that we're running out of water, land, and productivity, that the population bomb is already armed and ticking, that we'd better let the weak drown or we'll swamp the lifeboat. I dislike their alarmism, but they might be right.

And there are those in the middle, those who say that the world can feed itself for the next few decades but by then we'd better have corked the population bottle. These are the solid strugglers in AID, the U.S. Department of Agriculture's Economic Research Service, the Rockefeller and Ford Foundations, the CGIAR centers, and the moguls at the World Bank. They inspire confidence, and I feel they probably are right. I realize that my confidence in this position has probably guided my writing from the start.

I hand in the manuscript to Weaver, a mild doomsayer, who gives it a quick read. "I'm surprised you're so optimistic, Tom. But the story looks balanced. Let's see what Gil Grosvenor says."

The verdict arrives via Edward J. Linehan, the assistant editor who works with in-house manuscripts like mine. Gil is disturbed. The lead—the starving Indian—is too morbid, too unpleasant. He's afraid people will read the first few sentences and then stop, finding the subject distasteful. Start out with something positive. Linehan has seen a passage in midarticle extolling sweet potatoes as a potential salvation of Asian farmers. Let's lead with the sweet potatoes.

I'm not much for infighting, but this won't do. Talk about rose-colored glasses! Fortunately, Ed Linehan is as reasonable as he is competent, and I sense he doesn't entirely agree with Gil. He rejects my urging to return to the starving Indian, but suggests I find something else. We settle on a lead mentioning catchy but undramatic advances in food production. Every editor involved with the article winces. But none wants to argue with Gil.

A knock at my office door brings three researchers from across the hall. I know why they're here. "The team of Feeney, Sweeney, and Wendt, come to check your manuscript," announces the senior member, Ann Wendt. She, Kathy Feeney, and Mickie Sweeney are seasoned veterans, alert to the small error and the big picture. But three researchers—that's unusual. The editors want no mistakes in this article.

In the twenty-five years since that article appeared, much that has happened foodwise has followed the article like a script. As foreseen, the world's population has climbed frighteningly, from 3.9 billion to nearly 6 billion. Yet the world has fed itself and—except in Africa, where the Green Revolution never took hold—eaten better than before. Behind the general improvement lies astonishing growth in crop yields, springing from intensive agricultural research.

Much has also varied from that script. Where those variations have occurred, the cornucopians have outforecast the doomsayers. There has been no "gigantic inevitable famine," although several

African nations have suffered politically caused starvation. Population growth has slowed from 2 percent worldwide—and much higher in developing countries, where food was scarcest—to 1.5 percent and falling, most markedly in developing nations and largely as a result of family planning initiatives and improved economic growth.

What lies ahead? On the basis of past performance, perhaps the cornucopians deserve the last word. One such optimist is Pierre Crosson, food expert with Resources for the Future. He sees the next two decades unfolding much as the past two have—decades of sufficiency and perhaps a little more. Two possible weak points concern him: Will nations continue funding needed agricultural research, such as CGIAR and national programs? Will the world preserve its irreplaccable genetic material, its biodiversity, on which improved yields heavily depend? "The cup is half full, not half empty," he asserts, "but it's not a sure thing by any means."

At the *Geographic*, meanwhile, assignments continue rolling in fast: on the Apollo program, on predicting earthquakes, on climate change, on the magic metal aluminum. And then I take on a particularly thorny challenge, in the fascinating field of archaeology. The article that results will be titled "The Search for the First Americans."

Chapter 5

THE MYSTERY OF THE FIRST AMERICANS

O n the surface it is a dream assignment, this plum Ken Weaver hands me in 1978. It offers mystery, romance, travel, and controversy—all the ingredients of the ideal article. But I soon discover that this plum may harbor a worm, or maybe a can of them; I have been asked to cover one of the most complex and contentious subjects in archaeology. It's also the assignment on which I come closest to killing myself.

My task is to answer three seemingly simple questions: Who were the earliest settlers of the Americas? When did they arrive? How did they get here? The quest for the answers has puzzled and divided scholars almost since Columbus first encountered the New World's bronze-skinned inhabitants and misnamed them Indians. Enormous research has gone into uncovering their origins, and exciting discoveries have traced them back in time. But no artifact or archaeological site has clearly established the identity of the

New World's first Paleoindian pioneers: who they were, when they came, and from where.

Indian cultures past and present have intrigued the Society since its birth in 1888. Across the decades more than 150 *Geographic* articles have dealt entirely or in part with Indian topics—far more than on any other subject. The Society's best-selling book was *Indians of the Americas*. This enormous interest probably reflects the fascination we all feel for our fellow man, for what makes us human.

Conversely, much that is known about Indian origins and cultures is the result of research sponsored by the Society. Its Committee for Research and Exploration, which dispenses several million dollars a year for basic research in geography-related fields, has funded more than 200 grants to prominent and promising scientists investigating Indian sites and cultures in North, Central, and South America. The academic payoff has been profound. Society-backed scholar/adventurers excavated the lost Inca city of Machu Picchu, solved riddles about Southwest pueblos and Midwest mound builders, illumined the civilizations of the Mesoamerican Olmec and Maya, unearthed the incomparable artifacts of the pre-Incan Moche. Less splashily and more often, these researchers endured the tedium of sifting ancient hearths and middens to add a few more brush strokes to the picture of early Indian environments and lifeways.

Yet the picture still has large holes in it concerning the first Americans. Surprisingly little is known about how and when human beings first entered the New World. Pursue the earliest known Americans deep into the past and eventually their trail vanishes into mystery.

Tantalizing hints first came to light through dazzling discoveries decades ago in New Mexico and Colorado.

In 1908 a former slave named George McJunkin, foreman of the Crowfoot Ranch near Folsom, New Mexico, spied enormous bones protruding from an eroded bank. He told others of the discovery, but two decades passed and McJunkin died before scientists responded. Tardily visiting the site in 1927, they found the bones still there—fossilized skeletons of extinct giant bison. Embedded in their ribs were distinctive stone points, indented along their lengths in a style known as fluting. Suddenly a continent assumed to have been settled for only a few thousand years revealed a human population dating back to the Ice Age, perhaps 10,000 years ago.

Soon larger fossil bones were found in a gully near Dent, Colorado, and in an arroyo in eastern New Mexico near Clovis. At both kill sites the prey was mammoths. Among the carcasses and cookfires lay fluted points even larger than those found near Folsom. By the early 1960s similar kill sites had been found across the West, each featuring Ice Age animals and fluted points that acquired the name Clovis. All were carbon-dated at 11,000 to 11,500 years before present (B.P.).

Similar fluted points, many with similar dates, cropped up by the thousands throughout North America and in Central and South America. Two possible explanations emerged: Either a single people, fashioning a point often called the first American patent, spread rapidly across the hemisphere soon after 12,000 B.P., or a point-making technology spread rapidly among a preexisting people.

At the time of my article, many respected scientists held that the Clovis hunters were the first Americans south of the ice sheets; no archaeological site or carbon date proved incontrovertibly that human beings had occupied the hemisphere any earlier.

Other highly respected scientists disputed this tidy claim. They scoffed at the notion that within a few hundred years a hunter-gatherer people could possibly disperse across a hemispheric frontier stretching south for more than 10,000 miles. They also pointed to archaeological sites in both Americas that strongly indicated human presence hundreds and even tens of thousands of years before Clovis hunters had wielded fluted points.

Strongly, but not *indisputably.* None of the alleged pre-Clovis sites could be dated beyond all doubt. A lively schism divided those who believed the presence of pre-Clovis Americans was proved and those who did not. This schism defined much of my article. It also meant ticklish going. As a journalist I would not have to take a stand; but I would have to be very, very fair, for the sake of the academic protagonists and the *Geographic*.

The academic rock on whom these waves of opposing opinion dashed was C. Vance Haynes, geosciences professor at the University of Arizona in Tucson. Preeminent among Clovis authorities, unflamboyant and steadfast, Haynes was exacting in his criteria for site validity. Over time his unaggressive credibility cast him as judge and jury in the matter of Paleoindian site antiquity—a role he convincingly claimed to find "wearisome."

Early in his archaeological career, Haynes had shared the view that another people had preceded the Clovis hunters. Conviction weakened as he examined, often with the Society's support, the sites on which the claims were based. Each claim, he discovered, harbored a weakness, usually disturbance of the soil by erosion or diggings by man or beast, contamination of the carbon used for dating, or uncertainty that objects claimed as tools had actually been made by humans—were artifacts, not "geofacts." One site after another failed to qualify as unarguably older than Clovis. Thorough in his analyses, persuasive in presentation, Haynes did much to shape contemporary thinking about the peopling of the Americas.

Yet many felt that Haynes' exacting criteria imposed an unreasonable burden of proof on credible sites, and that the cumulative evidence of early occupation was persuasive. A leading spokesman for this populous camp was Alan L. Bryan, a prolific writer and fertile thinker at Canada's University of Alberta.

Like Haynes, Bryan had wide field experience on both continents. In Venezuela he had excavated a mastodon kill in which the lethal, non-Clovis points might predate Clovis; in his Edmonton office he showed me twigs exhumed from the great beast's gut and carbon-dated to 13,000 B.P. Bryan did not exclude the possibility that the first arrivals in the New World might even have been *Homo erectus*, *H. sapiens'* beetle-browed predecessor, whose trek out of Africa brought him as far as northern China half a million years ago.

The potential solution to these conflicting claims lay in archaeological sites and professorial dens scattered from Siberia and Arctic America to windy Patagonia. While pursuing answers in that vast arena I would travel at times with Kerby Smith, a talented freelance photographer, and more often with David L. Arnold, the project's picture editor. Quite often the more energetic picture editors broke out of the office to shoot part or all of an article. Dave Arnold, competent, civilized, quietly humorous, was the right companion for demanding coverage in which we routinely worked by day and traveled nights as we leapfrogged down the hemisphere.

To do our subject properly, we three should have begun our field work in eastern Siberia, whence came the earliest Americans. But in the Cold War climate of 1978 the struggle to obtain clearances from the Soviet Union and likely restraints on our movements made the effort seem futile. Instead Dave and I headed toward the Alaskan shores of the Bering Strait, where the first arrivals had crossed into the New World.

A BUSH PLANE drops us at Alaska's westernmost edge, in the Inuit village of Wales. Here the Seward Peninsula separates the Pacific and Arctic Oceans and rubs noses with Siberia, fifty-six miles across the Bering Strait. We are incredibly lucky. For the past month, overcast skies and storms have suffocated Wales. Today the sun's rays ricochet off both oceans. Across the strait we see the snow-capped highlands of Siberia, through which those migrants passed millennia ago.

On our map, the International Date Line cleaves the strait, projecting Siberia into tomorrow. But in my mind's eye I see it in a distant yesterday, during the Ice Age, as the lost world known as Beringia. Looking westward, I see not two great oceans, but their floors, now drained of seas and undulating as vast vegetated plains hundreds of miles to south and north. The exposed ocean shelves fuse the continents of Asia and North America with a geologic weld a thousand miles wide.

This is the celebrated Beringian Land Bridge.

Looking again I see the strange beasts that roam this largely treeless realm. They share a gigantism peculiar to the Ice Age and are known as the Pleistocene megafauna. Many are vegetarian grazers and browsers: high-shouldered mammoths standing twelve feet tall and with tusks even longer, lumbering mastodons, jumbo bison, sloths twice as tall as a man, camels, yaks, horses, musk-ox, stag-moose. Among them prowl formidable predators: short-faced bears dwarfing today's grizzly, lion-size panthers and saber-toothed tigers, massive dire-wolves.

Out there too are those adaptable omnivores, *H. sapiens sapiens*, slowly advancing across the Beringian steppe, destined to forsake their Asian citizenship and become Paleoindians. But they remain well beyond our gaze, hidden in the haze of prehistory.

Asian Beringia offers surprisingly little evidence of their advance. A site on Siberia's Kamchatka Peninsula contains the dwellings and tools of a people who hunted mammoths, bison, and reindeer perhaps 14,000 years ago. A hunting site near the Arctic Ocean brings them slightly closer in time and space. But no known remains show them within a thousand miles of where we stand in western Alaska. Asian Beringia is largely a blank space still awaiting archaeology's trowel.

Dave and I climb the huge boulders of Cape Wales, aligned along the ramp like petrified vertebrae. Far below, immense swells roll in from the Pacific's Bering Sea; northward, the chill Arctic Ocean gnaws at the Cape. Out in the strait, black ramparts of the Diomede Islands stand silhouetted against Siberia's ermine heights. It is a scene of vast geography.

Next morning we walk the Pacific beach and feel it shudder underfoot to the rhythm of the crashing combers. We pass an Inuit grave: A skull and lower leg bones thrust from the sand beside a funeral offering of rifle and knife. In the strait, clouds the Diomedes have snagged clouds and resemble whales surfaced and blowing. Dotting the beach are flat bones the size of salad plates; I will take one back to the Society and learn it is the vertebral disk of a whale.

We make our way to the village's tiny airstrip to catch another bush plane. This time we are headed for an archaeological site known as Onion Portage, above the Arctic Circle. Below us a lace-work of trails of introduced reindeer scribes the fragile tundra. Galaxies of lakes spangle the wilderness, fringed with early ice and flecked with swans preparing to fly south. Across the miles, the sur-face wears the strange landforms associated with permafrost: geo-metric polygons, made up of ice wedges linearly connected; pingos, ice mounds formed by the upward expansion of freezing surface water; and solifluction, the downhill slumping of thawed surface soil that often buried and preserved remains of Ice Age animals.

We pick up the Kobuk River and follow its path upstream. Coiling restlessly in tight meanders sheathed with small trees, the river provides welcome relief to the tedium of the tundra.

Our pilot spies the excavations of Onion Portage and prepares to land on a short gravel bar along the riverbank. "We'll touch down first to see if it's firm," he announces. Down we plummet. Wheels smack the gravel with a whiplash jolt, and we bounce back into the air with engine roaring. "Feels good," he opines. We circle, cut throttle, and smash down again, in a series of diminishing bounces that cease just where the bar does.

The commanding bluff at Onion Portage obviously served its Paleoindian hunters well. As it serves hunters this day. An Inuit and his wife have just dressed out a slain caribou, stashed its meat in their outboard, and sent its innards floating downriver.

Onion Portage, with its distinctive stone tools, provides a strong link to the Asian origins of early Americans. But not to the earliest Americans. Once thought to be extremely old, the site is probably not earlier than 10,700 B.P. Yet standing here, Dave and I feel a kinship with those who first passed this way on their journey south.

We reboard the bush plane and strap ourselves into our seats, mentally and physically bracing for our takeoff run down the gravel bar. How short it looks! Engine roars, wheels pound, teeth rattle. At the bar's far end—on surely the last rock—we struggle above the river.

Unwelcome thoughts of small-plane safety intrude again as we near Fairbanks, our destination. Crashed aircraft litter the hillsides, attesting to the area's fierce storms and opaque fogs. I conjure up some gallows humor, in the form of a question to Dave Arnold: "How can a bush-plane pilot find the Fairbanks airport in a fog?"

"Dunno," responds Dave, busily cleaning a camera.

I point down. "The more wrecked planes he sees, the closer he's getting to the runway." Dave is not amused, the pilot less so.

During the Ice Age, when unglaciated Beringia was a refugium of the megafauna, its eastern flank lay in the Canadian Yukon, in the great valley of the Porcupine River. The area became a key arena for early-man research, in part through the keen eye of a Yukon Native American.

In 1966 Peter Lord, a school janitor in the Loucheaux village of Old Crow, joined a field expedition of Canadian paleontologists studying bones of extinct animals along the Old Crow River, a tributary of the Porcupine. Five days out, working a bone-rich bend of the river, Lord straightened with an object in hand: "Is this what you're looking for?" He held a fossilized caribou bone with one end beautifully carved into saw-teeth. The scientists instantly recognized it as a flesher for scraping hides.

The flesher passed into the hands of archaeologist William N. Irving of the University of Toronto, who also was working the Old Crow area. Carbon dating gave it an extraordinary antiquity of 27,000 years. The flesher offered dramatic evidence of early occupation of Beringia. Intriguingly, it suggested that in a riverine environment where rock is scarce, Paleoindians fashioned their tools of bone: a people not of the Stone Age but of the Bone Age.

From Fairbanks Dave heads back to D.C.; as a picture editor he works on several articles at once, and the others demand his attention. I fly by bush plane to Old Crow, named for a past chief and located where the river flows into the Porcupine. There I board a helicopter dispatched by Irving. Copters are costly tools for archaeologists; this one reflects the importance Canadians assign to this exciting early-man site.

Forty miles upstream we dip down at a loop in the river, where Irving is harvesting many of the bones that build his case for the presence of the first known Americans. I greet Kerby Smith, now well into his first *Geographic* assignment. I will appreciate him most a few months hence, in Florida.

Bill Irving joins us, and we head for the river. "You arrived at a good time," he explains. "The water level is dropping, and the bar has surfaced."

"The bar" is Irving's bone mine, the river his conveyor belt. Each spring the melt-swollen Old Crow picks up fossilized bones by the thousands and drops them where the flow slackens at the river bend. When the water recedes, bones pave the top of a sandbar and lace its depths. He and assistants sort them, keeping those that show signs of human alteration. Each year they classify 8,000 to 10,000 specimens. "It might be the world's greatest bone source," observes Irving.

I spend three days here, absorbing Irving's work. To earn my keep I join the bone excavators at the bar. With every few thrusts my shovel clinks against Ice Age fossils of the megafauna. As I work I quickly discover that one dread carnivore—a member of the minifauna—still flourishes. More bloodthirsty than the Asian dhole, more fiercely armed than the saber-toothed cat, seemingly larger than the lumbering mastodon, this nemesis is the arctic mosquito, bane of the tundra. Humans are not the only creatures to writhe in misery under the insects' hellish swarms. The great annual migrations of caribou, of which the Porcupine Valley herd is the largest, are driven in part by the beasts' feverish urge to escape hatching mosquitoes.

We boat upriver, where Irving's group is examining fossils embedded in a near-vertical bluff towering eighty feet above the water. Halting to discuss his work, we are drowned out by a *whoosh!* of rushing air, then a crash like a thunderclap. A hundred feet downstream a cloud of dust marks a thaw-loosened slide that would have crushed and buried anyone working beneath.

It is late afternoon, and the arctic sun is slowly sliding toward brief oblivion in Asian Beringia. Someone informs me that archaeologist Jaques Cinq-Mars is leaving on an aerial reconnaissance of the area and that his float plane has an empty seat. Do I wish to go along? Yes! We cleave a wake in the broad Porcupine River and soar above the green arctic Eden of the Old Crow Flats.

Below us lakes shine everywhere, crowding so densely they resemble multipaned windows, framed by muntins of muskeg. Each bears a flotsam of waterfowl—swans, ducks, geese. They recall paleo-ecologist R. Dale Guthrie's observation that today's nesting grounds reflect migratory patterns established back when the great ice sheets sealed off much of the North.

We head east, into foothills of the Richardson Mountains. We begin to see caribou—hundreds, thousands. The pilot descends between the walls of a long valley, where the densest numbers feed. "Seven, maybe eight thousand," he estimates, eyes fixed on the herd. "Earlier, on the North Slope, we saw ninety-five thous . . . *holy Jesus!*" We are hurtling toward a mountain wall. With admirable self-possession the pilot nurses the stick—climb hard but don't stall. Reflexively we lift in our seats to help our floats clear the rocky rim.

Swinging westward, we fly over the sparse spruce of boreal forest near the Yukon/Alaska boundary. Each spring the 170,000 caribou of the Porcupine herd leave the basin and drift north through the mountains in one of the planet's greatest wildlife migrations. Reaching the North Slope, they calve and feed on the exploding plant life of the summer tundra. They are the unknowing center of a political tempest. Beneath their feet and those of four other herds lie vast oil reserves. These two great resources, caribou and petroleum, create the environmental conflict that in the United States focuses on the Arctic National Wildlife Reserve.

Beneath our float plane, the nubile curves of rolling tundra sprout man-made structures resembling long picket fences. Constructed of vertically placed spruce logs and trending north–south, they are caribou fences, erected centuries ago to turn migrating animals past hidden hunters or into snares or enclosures. Some stretch for a few hundred yards, others for miles. In a land virtually devoid of human imprint, the mute runic shapes relate a vivid saga of hunters and herds.

Back at the river, we again thrust our shovels into the bar, bringing forth profusions of Ice Age fossils. But our treasures are of limited value: Bone, which does not lend itself to carbon dating, must get its geologic time fix from the sediments in which it is buried. These bones, though, have washed downstream, eroded from sediments whose location is unknown.

Archaeologists harbor another doubt about Old Crow. Are those "altered" bones really the result of human activity—of Paleo-indians seeking marrow and flaking tools? Or could they have been fractured by natural forces—the gnawing, trampling, wallowing, and kicking of other wild animals? Conceivably those fractured bones could be either.

Nearly a decade after my visit, scientific scrutiny will discredit the famous flesher. A team of Canadian scientists, testing the artifact by a refined carbon-dating process known as accelerator mass spectrometry, will derive an age of only 1,350 years—a shocking 26,000 years younger than earlier estimates. What could explain an error so enormous? The scientists surmise that the portion of the flesher dated earlier probably suffered from "massive contamination by groundwater carbonates."

WHILE CANADIAN ARCHAEOLOGISTS pursued the earliest Americans in the Yukon, U.S. counterparts led by the National Geographic Society were launching a major manhunt called the North Alaska Range Early Man Project. The ambitious campaign, which took shape in the late 1970s, was joined by the National Park Service, whose Denali National Park encompassed much of the search area. This decisive archaeological assault on the land bridge was orchestrated by the Society's Committee for Research and Exploration, which allocated $300,000—then a princely sum and its largest grant ever. It placed in charge two respected academicians, archaeologist W. Roger Powers and paleoecologist R. Dale Guthrie, both of the University of Alaska in Fairbanks. Both were highly qualified, Powers uniquely so. Realizing as a graduate student the importance of Siberian Beringia, he studied Russian, visited East Asian sites, and wrote his doctoral dissertation on Siberian archaeology. Dale Guthrie ranked as a leading authority on the Ice Age environment and enjoyed a gift for verbally recreating that ancient past. For several seasons the two men had excavated an Alaskan site known as Dry Creek, which had yielded unchallenged remains dating back more than 11,000 years.

As the Early Man Project took shape, I followed its progress at meetings of the Research Committee. These were impressive sessions: distinguished scientists and a sprinkling of staff executives, fostering research that would decisively increase the world's body of knowledge. Their financial support also shaped grantees into international folk heroes—Jacques-Yves Cousteau, Frank and John Craighead, Louis and Mary Leakey, Eugenie Clark, Robert D. Ballard. Rigorous in its academic requirements, the committee nevertheless occasionally supported graduate students and, more rarely, researchers not yet enrolled in graduate work. This category included Jane Goodall and Dian Fossey. Both were launched in primate studies by Louis Leakey and, along with primatologist Birute Galdikas, became known as "Leakey's Angels"; both gained enthusiastic committee support and later obtained graduate degrees at Cambridge University.

The dignified proceedings of the Research Committee seemed undisturbed by a top-level editorial eruption that convulsed the *National Geographic* during my early-man coverage. It flared between the Board of Trustees and editor Gil Grosvenor, and saw Gil achieve the pinnacle of his editorship.

The difficulties began with the January 1977 *Geographic*. It carried an informative article, "Inside Cuba Today," that reported on life under Castro without taking the anti-Communist tack many expected. Some trustees were unhappy. The next month's issue ran "To Live in Harlem," an upbeat article but definitely new turf for a magazine that in the past had given little coverage to black America. More trustees complained, including the chairman, Melvin M. Payne. In March a Geographic television special on the Volga River drew the wrath of the anti-Communist group Accuracy In Media. By now the board's more conservative members were seething. Chairman Payne suggested formation of a committee to examine whether the magazine's editorial policy had changed. Gil, father Melville, and former editor Ted Vosburgh held the threats at bay. Still, the schism leaked to the national press and stimulated front-page articles from coast to coast. And bigger trouble was on the way.

The month after the Volga program, the magazine published Peter T. White's article "One Canada—or Two?" describing the powerful tide of Quebec separatism. Rumblings on the board reached ominous proportions. Then came the June issue with "South Africa's Lonely Ordeal," a moving article about apartheid South Africa written by William S. Ellis and photographed by James P. Blair. An outraged South African government published advertisements in the *New York Times* and *Washington Post* condemning the *Geographic's* "anti-white racism." At this point the board's conservative wing insisted on forming a committee to investigate whether indeed Gil had surreptitiously changed editorial policy.

The committee included a balance of conservative and non-conservative board members, among them the prime protagonists, Payne and Gil Grosvenor. It also included two level-headed associate secretaries of the Society, Leonard J. Grant and Edwin W. Snider. Two negative outcomes were possible: The committee could find that editorial policy had indeed changed, in which case the new policy would have to be approved by the board, or, more dire, the committee could recommend that the board create an oversight group to control the magazine's content.

Gil deflected the second threat first. "The editor should be able to control the magazine," he contended. "Either you like the way we have been running it, or . . . if you don't, get a new editor." The committee concurred and moved on.

The question of policy change was more difficult. Policy *had* changed; the magazine was more relevant, more attuned to current topics. Gil argued that the change had been evolutionary, not revolutionary; that the magazine was merely changing with the times. The committee responded by asking for a written statement of the magazine's editorial policy. Working closely with Associate Editor Joseph R. Judge, Gil brought forth the following statement: "Geography" includes "the historical, cultural, scientific, governmental and social background of people. The magazine strives to present timely, accurate, factual, objective material . . . Advocacy journalism is rejected. As times and tastes change, the magazine slowly evolves . . ."

The committee accepted his statement, and so, ultimately, did the Board of Trustees. The reality of a changing magazine had been accepted, an oversight group avoided. Gil Grosvenor had triumphed.

UNFAZED BY EDITORIAL TUMULT, the Early Man Project has moved ahead, its mission set. After finishing their excavation at Dry Creek, Powers and Guthrie will assemble a team of geologists, biologists, paleontologists, and other specialists to scour Alaskan Beringia for sites likely to yield evidence about those who first passed this way, and when. Then they will excavate, down through successive layers of soil and artifacts, until they find the answers in tools, Ice Age animal bones, and cookfires.

Meanwhile Powers and Guthrie have returned to Dry Creek, and in early summer I fly to Alaska. I arrive at their camp at dinnertime. Dale Guthrie is serving, and the special of the day is pork, in Stone Age cuts.

"I've never tried this before," the ecologist confesses, holding a sharp, freshly broken rock and standing over a former pig. "But it's coming along pretty well." He stoops, holds the rock against the pig's back, and slashes along the spine. The jagged flake easily parts the thick hide and cuts into the flesh. More strokes extract the ten-

On assignment to cover rats around the world, photographer James L. Stanfield (*left*) and author Thomas Y. Canby hold rodents killed during rice harvest in the Philippines. Some rats were cooked in the field for the workers' lunch, some were saved for dinner for all. (James L. Stanfield/National Geographic Image Collection)

At the Hafkine Institute in Bombay, the previous night's kill of rats is checked for signs of bubonic plague, which claimed 12.5 million Indians at the turn of the century. (James L. Stanfield/National Geographic Image Collection)

Catholic missionary Father Guy Mary-Rousseliere devoted much of his life to the Eskimos (now Inuit) of eastern arctic Canada. An excellent photographer, he recorded Eskimo traditions through the lens of his camera. Here Father Mary captures an Eskimo family sprawling across a sleeping platform inside their igloo. (Guy Mary-Rousseliere, Courtesy National Geographic Society)

The view from a dog sled on the sea ice of arctic Canada. Unlike the sled dogs of Alaska, the dog teams of eastern Canada run in a fan hitch side by side, each pulling a separate line. (Thomas Y. Canby)

Paleoecologist Dale Guthrie butchers a pig with stone flakes at a
Paleo-indian archaeological site in central Alaska. (Kerby
Smith) *Inset:* Hands hold a pair of fluted stone tools known as
Clovis points, used for killing or butchering Ice Age animals.
(Warren Morgan)

While reporting on world hunger, photographer Steven L. Raymer and the author travel by rickshaw near Chittagong in famine-stricken Bangladesh. (Steven L. Raymer/National Geographic Image Collection)

Honoring *National Geographic* policy of submitting illustrations for review in advance of publication, in Moscow Canby has the delicate task of asking Soviet cosmonaut Vladimir Dzanibekov to examine drawings of secret rockets, spacecraft, and cosmodromes. (Steven L. Raymer/National Geographic Image Collection)

The 750-mile-long San Andreas Fault, contact point of restless continental plates, runs nearly the length of California. (James P. Blair/National Geographic Image Collection)

Melville Bell Grosvenor (*right*), editor-in-chief and president of *National Geographic* from 1957 to 1967, and famed *Geographic* photographer/writer Luis Marden attend the 1967 coronation of the King of Tonga. (Edwin S. Grosvenor/National Geographic Image Collection)

Society president Gilbert M. Grosvenor (*center*), the third generation of his family to head the *Geographic*, and editor Wilbur E. Garrett (*right*) present a globe and atlas to President George Bush in 1989. Shortly afterward, Grosvenor abruptly fired Garrett. (James L. Stanfield/National Geographic Image Collection)

Occupying half a city block, National Geographic Society offices embrace a landscaped plaza north of the White House in Washington, D.C. The Headquarters building at right houses the editorial and executive offices and Explorers Hall, while the tiered "Maya temple" holds the photographers' offices, cartographic department, library, and cafeteria. (Joseph H. Bailey © National Geographic Society)

Barry C. Bishop, chairman of the Society's Committee for Research and Exploration 1989–94, was a member of the first American team to climb Mt. Everest, in 1963. Frostbite claimed the tips of both little fingers and all his toes. He died in an auto accident in 1994. (Sam Abell/National Geographic Image Collection)

The author and wife Susan vacation in Portugal. Susan is director of the Society's library and indexing departments.

derloin, which a student slices with another stone flake and places on the campfire. "The idea," Guthrie explains, "is to show our student archaeologists how Paleoindians might have carved an Ice Age bison at a kill site such as this."

His progress slows. He examines the dulled flake and tosses it aside. "Theirs was a throwaway society like ours," he observes. *Wham!* Behind us, assistant Tim Smith smashes one rock against another, selects the sharpest fragment, and hands it to Guthrie. "This is really good for us," comments another student, "to see how they used the stone tools we find."

They find them in profusion. Not dramatic trophies such as Clovis points. Dry Creek's artisans mass-produced less showy lithics: stone microblades, blade cores, flakes, tools called burins, scrapers, and small projectile points, along with knives up to five inches long. In all the site has given up more than 30,000 lithic objects, each accurately recorded as to location.

Many are bifaces—tools worked on both sides. These are the Stone Age's high tech, far more sophisticated than the simple flakes of our pig-butchering. Bifaces characterize the Russian site in Kamchatka and could be precursors of Clovis.

"The large number of stone flakes makes us believe this was a kill site," explains Roger Powers. "They dragged their bison and sheep here, made their tools here, and butchered here. We're seeing the end of the Ice Age, when the glaciers were retreating. Many of the animals belonged to the megafauna, but their niche was fading."

Our camp looks out over the valley of the Nenanna River, flowing north from the distant Alaska Range, crowned by snow-clad Mount McKinley. Strong winds from the mountains sweep up the valley. At the time of the Dry Creek Paleoindians, a glacier hung at the valley's south end, spawning powerful winds that lifted soil, or loess, from the valley floor and covered the hunters' remains. But those same winds could have swept away the soil covering even earlier artifacts, limiting Dry Creek's age as an archaeological site. The archaeologists need deeper, older loess deposits, permitting a longer record of human activity. Promise of this lies in the Teklanika valley, paralleling the Nenanna to the west. Topographical maps show the Teklanika holding deep loess deposits, accumulated during several glacial epochs.

That is where the survey party of Powers and Guthrie will seek out the decisive site of the Early Man Project and attempt to pin down the entry of Paleoindians into New World Beringia. I will meet the team in the field in mid-August to learn what their test trenches have yielded.

I RETURN TO MY OFFICE DESK in July and find the usual Mount McKinley of mail, mostly publicity releases from business and professional associations. I glance at each, alert for interesting science ideas and materials helpful to colleagues. Although most articles in the magazine originate as ideas of us staff members, some of those ideas are sparked or reinforced by the press releases that pour in from every source; my rats article, I recall, originated with a release from the pest-control association. More commonly these flyers contain information useful to fellow magazine writers; each of us routinely keeps track of subjects being covered by colleagues and funnels appropriate materials. The pile before me reflects this policy. In it are several articles and clippings about early Americans, sent by the National Geographic Library and that informal network of staff members. It is a stupendous support system.

The pile also contains a thick packet wearing the red-stamped label "Comments: Criticisms." Inside are photocopies of letters from readers about recent issues of the *Geographic*. Reader complaints make juicy and informative reading, and I whip through them.

An article discussing evolution invites letters of pained outrage; a significant hard core of *Geographic* readers adheres to creationism. They feel betrayed when one of America's most trusted institutions accepts a biological process they reject. An article making use of the metric system's meters instead of standard feet touches an equally raw nerve. Here too reader objections run deep and vocal. Over time the *Geographic* has attempted to convert to metric measurements, but massive and vehement reader objection will eventually force a retreat.

A substantial number of criticisms deplore a natural history article that showed animals preying on others. A significant segment of readers objects to violence and gore and to pictures of animals mating, whether shown in the magazine's pages or on Geographic TV programs.

A final batch of letters reacts to an article on Malaysia. The specific problem is an old one: the *Geographic* and bare bosoms.

I recall the offending photograph. It showed two village women in a longhouse, one holding a child. The picture's lofty point, made in the legend, is that traditionally in rural Malaysia two or more families may live under one roof. Slightly less lofty, the women wear flowered sarong skirts but no blouses, and their shapely breasts salute the world. The indignant readers object that this is gratuitous pornography huckstered under the guise of geography and no way to run a family magazine. A shrill few contend that it's sexism, exploiting the female body in a magazine that does not give equal space to penises.

There's no question that bare bosoms vie with the yellow border as the trademark of the *National Geographic*. The bosoms even preceded the border; the November 1896 issue, wearing a terracotta-colored cover, carried a picture titled "Zulu Bride and Bride Groom" and showing a man and woman holding hands and both topless. In 1899, fresh on the job, young Gilbert H. Grosvenor published a photo of robust young Filipino women harvesting rice and bare from the waist up. Against later criticism he defended the picture as "a true reflection of the customs . . . in those islands," a policy encouraged by his boss and future father-in-law, Alexander Graham Bell. These "true reflections" crescendoed in a 1928 article on Bali, enhanced with early Autochrome color; one inspired print assembled seventeen bare-breasted Balinese maidens, all staring innocently at the camera, with the legend "Bali Has No Blondes."

Defying the global spread of Western fashion in attire, toplessness continued strong in the 1970s and 1980s under the editorships of GHG's grandson Gilbert and successor Bill Garrett.

For us staffers this editorial fixation has been a mixed blessing. Easily a thousand times I have listened to male acquaintances confide, when learning I was with *National Geographic*, their childhood fondness for thumbing through old magazines in the attic looking for topless tribeswomen. In fact I did it myself.

It is the ides of August, and Alaska's fickle weather is at its shining best over Mount McKinley National Park, since renamed Denali. Towering over sister peaks of the Alaska Range, the snow-crowned lord of the continent supports a Wedgwood sky of blue and white.

I board a helicopter and hop out to Powers' and Guthrie's final survey camp. During their weeks along the Teklanika, the multidisciplinary team has traveled on horseback, carried its gear by packhorse, and lived in tents. As the pilot sets down, my view of the encampment recalls movie sets of cavalry patrols in the days of the Wild West.

The mood is apathetic, downcast. Misunderstanding, I think they are unfriendly, perhaps resentful of an office jockey chartering in when they have roughed it for weeks in the wilderness.

I seek out Roger Powers. Polite but grim, he quickly explains: The survey has been a failure. The topographical maps erred; there was no deep loess in the Teklanika valley. There, as in the Nenanna valley, glacier-spawned winds removed the soils that might have held remains predating 12,000 B.P.—blew those soils clear to Fairbanks. The Early Man Project is back to square one.

Meanwhile those early Americans, whatever their timing, are in Beringia, poised to begin their long advance down the Americas. Dauntingly, massive ice sheets smother most of Canada and much of the United States. What route southward did they take?

Some authorities believe they followed the Pacific shore, probing southward as coastal glaciers briefly receded to open a way.

Most believe they "lived their way" southward along a narrow gap between the two great continental ice sheets along the eastern side of the Rockies. Thirty miles wide at the narrowest, shifting position with the waxing and waning of the ice, this ice-free corridor offered a pathway for animals and human beings throughout much of the Ice Age.

I team up with Dave Arnold again. It is time to explore the world of the Clovis Paleoindians, the earliest identified inhabitants of the New World south of the ice. We head for the University of Wyoming in Laramie, to the office lair of an archaeologist spiritually close to those formidable hunters.

Big, rawboned, and rustic, George C. Frison seems more rancher than academic. And that he was, until, in early middle age, he yielded to a fascination with ancient hunters, earned college degrees, and won his colleagues' respect for his understanding of the lifeways of ancient hunter-gatherers. Frison himself is a hunter of elk, moose, and buffalo. "I butcher them with stone tools," he explains. "I've trained my muscles to register the effects of different blades. They have to be *sharp*; that's why we find so many flakes of tool resharpening."

Frison came face to face with the mammoth hunters while excavating a kill site known as Colby, in Wyoming's Bighorn Basin. His insightful interpretation of the Colby archaeological record vividly brings to life these remarkable hunters of 11,200 B.P., at the end of the Ice Age.

Frison's Bighorn Clovis band is small—perhaps two or three families—taking their living from an area about seventy miles square. They share their turf with a herd of mammoths, which they systematically harvest. The upcoming hunt is a crucial one. Winter has arrived, with cold so deep that meat can be stored in the natural deepfreeze of the outdoors. If they down a mammoth, they'll survive until spring. If they fail . . .

The hunters know that the herd's feeding pattern, which repeats about monthly, will bring it near a steep-walled arroyo. Their best spearmen hide on the rim of the arroyo where it narrows to a choke point.

The mammoths appear, near the foot of the arroyo. The fleetest hunters isolate a juvenile animal that has wandered from the herd. They drive it up the arroyo. The narrowing ravine forces the animal against the wall at the choke point. The spearmen plunge their sharp stone points deep into the beast, then patiently wait for the crippled mammoth to slow, lie down, and die.

Where the animal falls, there the Paleoindians butcher. Their stone blades slash quickly so the meat will not freeze before they finish. Stacking the massive cuts, they assemble a protective fence of bones from earlier kills—a shield against scavenging Ice Age lions and cheetahs. In the process the Clovis hunters leave behind several stone projectile points, along with tools of camel and sheep bone. These bones and stones, meticulously excavated, are the hieroglyphs that Frison deciphers to recreate the ancient hunt.

Did the Clovis Paleoindians possess spiritual beliefs? If so, could fading strains of that faith still linger when Clovis physical remains are so ephemeral? Dave Arnold and I find the answer in southern Montana, on a snowy slope that has recently surrendered the bones of two Paleoindian children.

Here, at a site known as Anzick, Clovis people performed an elaborate burial. With the children's bodies they entombed more than a hundred handsomely crafted tools: fluted stone projectile points, spear foreshafts made of bone and ceremonially broken, and scores of large bifaces, one a mighty cleaver twenty inches long. Over the human bones and artifacts, the ancients scattered a dusting of red ocher, made of burnt iron oxide and perhaps intended as a magical substitute for fire or blood. Obviously intended for the afterlife of those buried, the Anzick offering is held up as the New World's oldest evidence of religion.

Ignoring Montana's winter chill, Dave Arnold spreads out a collage of Anzick artifacts on the snow and photographs them close-up, a scene simple but strong. Months later, when our travels are over and the editor performs the monthly ritual of selecting a cover picture for the September 1979 issue, Dave's photograph will win out over competing scenes from other articles. It is a coup. Photographers and writers alike take vast satisfaction from seeing their artistry, their article, highlighted in the yellow border.

The heyday of the Clovis hunters and explosion of fluted-point makers coincided with the final passing of the Ice Age megafauna. Did human hunters play a role in this extinction? The question is almost as troublesome as that of the earliest Americans themselves.

The scythe of extinction swept wide in North America as the Ice Age waned. Thirty-five genera vanished—80 percent of the continent's large-animal species. Most were gone before 12,000 B.P. But many, including mammoths, mastodons, camels, and horses, died out at the time of the Clovis hunters.

Did these hunters cause it? Yes, according to the appealing "overkill" theory propounded by Paul S. Martin of the University of Arizona. He sees the hunters emerging from the ice-free corridor with their deadly weaponry, advancing some ten miles a year in an ever-broadening front, and doubling their own numbers about every thirty years. In three centuries they number 300,000, have felled perhaps 100 million large animals, and camp at the Rio Grande. In a thousand years they have reached the Strait of Magellan, and the megafauna is no more.

Many archaeologists delight in reviling Martin's theory. Most reject it at least in part: Far too few kill sites have been found; certainly changing climate played a role; rational humans would not have stormed around slaughtering giant animals. Nevertheless, many believe that human hunters contributed to the extinctions. At the close of the Ice Age, spreading aridity and drying lakes would have shrunk animal niches and increased vulnerability to the fearsome new predator. There may indeed have been overkill, but perhaps of species already doomed.

Martin's theory could weaken fatally if the site known as Meadowcroft Rock Shelter achieves its potential. This beautifully excavated Paleoindian camp in western Pennsylvania has the best chance in North America of proving beyond doubt that humans lived south of the ice sheets before Clovis.

Strange rock shelter, this. Double doors guard it, not from the elements but from vandals. Electric lights illumine it. Electronics regulate temperature and humidity. Computers trace its millions of itemized contents. In every way, Meadowcroft Rock Shelter is state-of-the-art archaeology or beyond. If it doesn't shatter the Clovis barrier, the fault won't lie in the negligence of its excavator, James M. Adovasio.

Of average height, bearded and burly, Adovasio projects physical strength but has a light touch; where soil strata were too fine for a trowel, he and his high-tech team excavated with razor blades.

A million animal bones, a million and a half plant remains have come out of Meadowcroft, left by Indians and Paleoindians who used it as a transient hunting camp for . . . how many millennia? The meticulous control maintained by the excavators has yielded a prodigious fifty-two carbon dates. Most interesting are six strong dates from the lowest stratum, all associated with artifacts. They range from 12,800 to 16,175 B.P.—all healthily pre-Clovis.

Can anyone doubt Meadowcroft? Some do, among them Vance Haynes. A lobe of the last ice sheet hung only fifty miles north of the site, yet none of the excavated bones are of Ice Age animals, only deer, squirrels, and passenger pigeons. Was Meadowcroft really Ice Age? The carbon dates, too, permit faint doubt. Western Pennsylvania is coal country, and deposits lie near; Haynes believes that coal solubles borne by groundwater may have tainted the readings.

From Pennsylvania I head south to Florida, where a bizarre archaeological discovery is clamoring for attention. A Paleoindian site has been discovered deep in a now-flooded sinkhole. I need scuba lessons because the site lies nearly ninety feet underwater.

Scuba diving brings out the wimp in me. Long dives revive a claustrophobia originating in childhood nightmares of suffocating in a sack of sugar, dreams that tortured my nights for years. Sparing my diving instructor qualms better suited for a psychoanalyst, I go through the motions and get certified. Still, I can't help but worry that I'm not really qualified. I repress such thoughts by telling myself I'll be making only one simple dive.

I fly to Sarasota, Florida, dragging a bulbous bag of diving gear—fins, wet suit, mask, weight belt. A short drive southeast brings me to Little Salt Spring. The "spring" is actually a giant sinkhole nearly 300 feet across and 190 feet deep. The archaeological site is on a ledge 87 feet underwater. In itself it isn't much, only the remains of a single cookfire, but its implications are enormous.

What were Stone Age people doing down there?

Underwater archaeologist Carl Clausen has pieced together the unlikely answer. Some 12,000 years ago, Ice Age Florida was dry and the water table much lower—down to ledge level. A Paleoindian fell into the sinkhole and scrambled onto the ledge. With a wooden skewer he killed a now-extinct giant tortoise that also had fallen in. Then he lit a fire and cooked it.

Excavating on the submerged ledge, Clausen has uncovered the fire-baked clay and the tortoise atop it, still impaled by the wooden skewer. He has also found bones of an extinct ground sloth, remains of other species of tortoises and turtles, and a section of a wooden boomerang, probably used as a weapon by hunters at the surface. Carbon dating of the skewer has yielded a reading of 12,000 B.P.

As for the tortoise-eating Paleoindian, Clausen has not yet found his bones but hopes to. Unfortunate as he doubtless was, the Paleo escaped a worse fate. Had he not reached the ledge and instead sunk to the bottom, he would gradually have been swallowed by an ooze of bottom muck. The sinkhole is a doorway to oblivion, a geologic black hole.

Clausen and I suit up, along with photographer Kerby Smith, whom I last saw in the Yukon and who is an experienced diver. We don inflatable vests, strap on weight belts and air bottles, and swim to the center of the sinkhole. There a float moors a line that descends to the ledge. With Clausen in the lead, we descend the rope, into the gathering gloom. It is a splendid experience—a trip into a realm I never expected to enter.

We reach the smooth limestone ledge, slick with algae. Clausen trains his light. In a yard-wide trench he points out the tortoise bones and sections of the carapace. Nearby protrude bones of the extinct sloth. Only the softening presence of water differentiates this from a terrestrial dig.

We explore beyond the trench, surveying rubbled areas awaiting excavation. Feeling a slight tendency to sink, I keep a supporting hand on the slippery ledge; I forget that my density has increased with the water pressure and fail to inflate my vest for greater buoyancy.

Clausen and Kerby Smith move ahead. My hand slips from the ledge, and I slide slowly down the slick sinkhole wall. I awaken to the problem and push the button to inflate the vest—push it futilely again and again. With each moment of descent my density increases and I fall faster, bumping down the wall, pushing the inflate button, kicking with my flippers, forgetting such remedies as removing my weight belt. I think of that bottom I am speeding toward—an oblivion of ooze, my nightmare sack of sugar. Bumping down the slimy wall . . .

Pain rips through my body, starting at the crotch. But it is delicious pain—I have smashed onto a limestone outcrop and straddle it as if riding a horse. Before I can react, the hand of Kerby Smith starts me upward.

Because Kerby and I have descended perhaps 150 feet, we take time to decompress while ascending the rope. Searching for the problem, I discover that my inflate button is jammed—too great a challenge for the unprepared mind. Mentally I cross diving articles off my wish list of future assignments.

The skewer's date of 12,000 B.P. places its Paleoindian owner earlier than Clovis, possibly even earlier than Meadowcroft. How do archaeologists explain this could-be oldest site in North America? Many simply call it a fascinating anomaly and move on to other locales.

And so do Dave Arnold and I. South America awaits, beckoning our cameras, notebooks, and expense accounts. There are people and places down there claiming to be older than Clovis, some much older.

We land in Caracas, Venezuela, and drive northward with Professor José Cruxent, one of the continent's most productive archaeologists. Fame came to Cruxent for his work at Taima-Taima, the site of an early mastodon kill. Digging in an ancient spring in cactus-spiked desert only a few hundred yards from the Caribbean, Cruxent unearthed the bones of four large mastodons. In its pelvic cavity, one carried a cigar-shaped point of a kind known as El Jobo, first identified by Cruxent years ago. From organic matter in the spring soil he derived the imposing date of 13,000 B.P. Fellow archaeologists responded with skepticism, but independent investigators from North America corroborated Cruxent's findings.

Caribbean breezes soften the noon heat as Cruxent leads us over Taima-Taima. A small herd of goats tiptoes daintily to the spring and drinks. Cruxent's pride in his site is tainted by resentment that a South American archaeologist's claims have required verification from the North.

Dave and I fly south to Peru, to picturesque Ayacucho in the highlands. There, set into a rocky hillside, the great rock shelter known as Pikimachay yawns each day at the morning sun. In its depths archaeologist Richard MacNeish has found dramatic evidence of an encounter some 14,000 years ago between Paleoindians and giant ground sloths, with the humans victorious. Other evidence links human artifacts with the bones of extinct horses, camels, and giant cats as far back as 25,000 B.P. As with so many other sites I have visited, authorities question the carbon dates and authenticity of the artifacts.

Into the air again, to two Paleo sites in Chile, both excavated with Society support. One, known as Tagua Tagua, gives evidence of the use of fire drives in hunting Ice Age horses. On our first day,

Dave is trembling with fever but works on, kept afloat by the myriad remedies in his Geographic medicine bag. I silently congratulate myself on the blessing of an iron constitution. Next day I am the one who turns to the medicine bag, though I manage to continue taking notes. It will be my only bad day in a career of travels.

Illness and injury are familiar risks on assignments that take writers and photographers into war zones, malarial swamps and jungles, dubious aircraft, dives into the unknown (and among sharks), and vehicles driven by madmen over treacherous terrains. We staffers have been "amazingly lucky," in the words of former editor Bill Garrett; the only fatality has been assistant editor George W. Long, whose Portuguese aircraft vanished en route from Lisbon to Madeira in 1958. Injuries have struck harder. A helicopter crash into Great Salt Lake shattered the leg of photographer James L. Amos and killed the pilot. Photographer Emory Kristof took shrapnel in the eye while flying over Vietnam. A Society freelance photographer, Reid Blackburn, died when Mount St. Helens erupted in 1980.

Virtually every Geographic field worker has suffered illness on assignment: malaria, debilitating intestinal afflictions, hepatitis, frostbite, bends while diving, irksome jungle parasites that lodge in the belly or beneath the skin and defy medical remedies. Kurt Wentzel's half-century of photography and writing embraced the spectrum: broken ribs and clavicle in Ethiopia, more broken ribs in Nepal, amoebic dysentery in India, two bouts with malaria, and multiple hernias. My good health often tempted me to overlook purifying the water or taking prescribed pills. Sanity invariably returned at the sight of one of the forlorn health clinics encountered so often in remote places, its stucco walls mildewed, the outdoor light smashed, the sign peeling paint, the sagging door open to a dark interior I wished never to enter.

In Chile Dave and I suffer a self-inflicted misfortune, far worse than our bouts with a bug. While there we fly over but do not visit the site known as Monte Verde. When we planned our itinerary, Monte Verde had not yet achieved its present recognition as one of the most important archaeological sites in the Americas.

Some 12,500 years ago, according to Monte Verde's numerous carbon dates, a band of twenty to thirty people lived beside a stream in southern Chile. After perhaps a year they abandoned it, and soon afterward a peat bog encroached, preserving the village remains in its muck. Excavations led by Tom D. Dillehay of the University of Kentucky in the 1970s and 1980s illumined unique details of a hunter-gatherer society that apparently existed a millennium before Clovis.

Monte Verde's inhabitants left traces of wooden structures covered with hides that rank as the hemisphere's earliest architecture. They made tools of stone, bone, and most particularly wood; they utilized a rich variety of native plants—seeds, stalks, leaves, fruits, nuts, berries, roots—and they may have begun domestication of the wild potato. They slew mastodons with stone points possibly linked to those at Taima-Taima. The intimate remains included leaves they had chewed, perhaps for stimulation, two dozen hearths, and even a child's footprint.

Nine carbon readings give Monte Verde a range of dates extending to 13,565 B.P. At the time of our trip, critics still doubted that Monte Verdeans predated Clovis. Better than any other site except perhaps Meadowcroft, Monte Verde illustrated that the mere act of lodging a pre-Clovis claim invited the doubt of colleagues.

Flying directly over Monte Verde, Dave Arnold and I land at Punta Arenas, southernmost of cities, hard by the Strait of Magellan. In a nearby rock shelter known as Fell's Cave, Paleoindians left undeniable evidence of their arrival by at least 11,000 years ago. In so doing, they closed the immense frontier they had opened at Alaska's Bering Strait, at a time still unknown.

A tourist's urge diverts Dave and me before we head for the cave. We go to Punta Arenas' sea wall, dip our hands in the strait's icy brine, and stare beyond Ferdinand Magellan's wake to the somber heights of Tierra del Fuego. Here, as at the Bering Strait, unfolds a scene of vast geography.

We slide into a dusty black pickup truck sent by Mrs. Peggy Fell and set forth across the stupefying flatness of Chilean

Patagonia. A hundred twenty miles to the northeast lies Mrs. Fell's sheep station, Estancia Brazo Norte.

Patagonia: abode of sheep. They graze in seemingly motionless clouds across sparse grasslands that stretch to the horizon. Periodically to our right the land drops off to the strait. Occasionally we pass a town-size *estancia*—stately main house, bunkhouses, church, wharf at the strait, elaborate shearing sheds, dipping sheds, blacksmith shop, cookhouse, clubhouse. Trees sheltering the cluster bend to Patagonia's incessant wind, now at our backs. This *estancia*, says our shepherd/driver, grazes 160,000 sheep.

We pass animals other than sheep—a few. A small flock of ostrichlike rheas, nearly as tall as a man, return our stares. Two fox pups frisk about a reddish-gray vixen. A male rhea strides ahead of three chicks he has hatched and now will raise. Off toward the horizon, a lone guanaco warily walks where Paleoindians hunted its ancestors, maybe with dogs, 11,000 years earlier.

I glance at Dave and see he is wrapped in thought, and I sense that those thoughts are much like mine: that we are incredibly lucky people. Thanks to the *Geographic*, not only are we in unique Patagonia; we are being paid a good living to be here, we are being welcomed at the private home of someone we have never met, we will see famous archaeological sites visited by only a few handfuls of people before us. Back home I have met extremely wealthy people who, learning of my job as *Geographic* writer, have only half in jest offered to carry my bags or a photographer's cameras if they could share the access we enjoy. We are lucky indeed.

We reach Estancia Brazo Norte and the Fell frame house, set in its sheltering grove. Mrs. Fell is vivacious, perhaps glad to see us. She feeds us lunch of mutton soup and shows us replicas of cave artifacts—distinctive fluted fishtail points, varied scrapers, and unusual discoidal stones, all found at Fell's Cave and a sister shelter, Palli Aike. From the porch, she points our way along the Rio Chico toward the cave, a fifteen-minute walk.

The stream, cutting through a volcanic surface crust, is an artery of life in biologically lean Patagonia. Ibises, ducks, geese, golden plovers, and birds we cannot identify swirl up at our coming and wheel, squawking, overhead. A series of small caves stares from a low volcanic cliff; in one a sheep peers out possessively.

Halfway up the steepening bluff we suddenly see the cave, opening like an empty eye socket. Dave and I ascend over rubble eroded from the cliff and carried from the cave during excavation.

The dark interior is as large as a volleyball court. Boulders obviously spalled from the ceiling litter much of the surface. Contrastingly, part of the floor—the archaeological part—is crisply carved in rectangular trenches that resemble graves awaiting vaults.

The archaeologist who dug those trenches was Junius Bouton Bird. In 1936, at age twenty-nine, he came with his wife to Patagonia and excavated Fell's Cave and nearby Palli Aike. Working with a single assistant, he moved tens of tons of rock that had fallen from the cave ceiling through the millennia. Finally reaching the cave's clay floor, he found stone points and fire hearths in association with the cooked bones of sloths and horses.

Initially Bird was confused by the horse bones. Could these have been animals brought by the Spaniards and cooked here, perhaps only decades after Magellan sailed the strait? Slowly he accepted that they were the remains of extinct Ice Age horses, contemporary with the sloths. Bird's discovery, comparable to those at Folsom and Clovis in the North, indicated that Ice Age Americans swept south through the hemisphere with astonishing quickness.

Bird's academic integrity and boundless energy produced the stuff of legend. To ensure the security of his trenches, he camped out beside them, even though comfort lay as close as the Fells'. When darkness hampered work in the cave's recesses, he fashioned a lamp consisting of an old plate, melted fat, and a rag wick. When his Model T Ford faltered on the windswept pampa, Bird unpacked a blanket, rigged it as a sail, and harnessed the wind to his needs.

Bird's meticulous work set standards for all of archaeology. He was first to submit South American materials for carbon dating, first to submit human coprolites—fossilized feces—for evidence about diet. His discovery of human teeth at Fell's and Palli Aike would prove invaluable to anthropologist Christy Turner, whose studies of dentition helped trace the Asian origins of early Americans.

The Patagonian wind has relented with evening as Dave and I walk back along the creek toward the *estancia*. Hares play on a streambank, and guanacos flow silently through the underbrush. Two horsemen trail in; all day they have drifted with the sheep, watching for fleece-heavy animals that have fallen and require a helping hand to regain their feet. Over dinner of mutton chops, Mrs. Fell recalls Bird's last return to the caves, in 1969, to gather additional materials for carbon dating. Tests yielding an age of 11,000 B.P. have confirmed the site's antiquity.

After breakfast of more mutton—sausage this time—Dave and I are back in the dusty pickup, plying the Patagonian sea of grass with its whitecaps of grazing sheep. Time to return home, to become reacquainted with my wife and sons, to sort out the vexing, contradictory archaeological sites scattered from strait to icy strait.

EIGHTEEN YEARS after I traversed two continents in that pell-mell pursuit of the earliest Americans, many of the sites I visited hold firm as then interpreted—durable brush strokes in the picture of the earliest Americans.

But new strokes have been added, some more deftly than others, many with the helping hand of the Society's Committee for Research and Exploration.

The Alaska Early Man Project, defeated in its 1977 site survey efforts, quickly regrouped. This time the field work fell to Roger Powers and environmental archaeologist John F. Hoffecker. During the 1980s they excavated several sites, recording in minute detail ancient patterns of occupation and environment. Their findings paralleled those from Dry Creek, with the earliest human presence dating to 11,800 B.P.

Secure in their carbon dates and stratigraphic control, in 1993 the investigators presented a sweeping scenario for the peopling of the Americas and Beringia:

Settlement of Beringia, they asserted, came surprisingly late, even on the Siberian side, with no persuasive evidence of occupation earlier than 13,000–12,000 B.P. The scientists suggested that an absence of trees for fuel may have delayed occupation of this game-rich mammoth steppe; not until about 12,000 B.P. did aspens and balsam poplars fringe Beringian streams.

This late arrival in Beringia, the authors ventured, explained the lack of firm dates for human presence earlier than 12,000 years ago south of the ice sheets. Once established, Powers and Hoffecker theorized, these pioneers developed the fluted-point technology of Clovis and other cultures that spread quickly across North America and beyond, including northward back to Alaska.

A tight and tidy scenario. But not one warmly embraced. What about those hunters camping at Meadowcroft? Those leaf-chewers at Monte Verde? That tortoise-eater down in my sinkhole?

In 1997 Chile's Monte Verde site finally shattered the "Clovis barrier," transforming with a brush stroke the picture of the earliest Americans.

The barrier, always strained, began giving way with publication of a comprehensive report on two decades of exhaustive Monte Verde excavation and analysis. The Dallas Museum of Natural History, aided by the Society's Research Committee, organized a team of nine eminent archaeologists to visit the site with excavators Tom Dillehay and Mario Piño. The team included Vance Haynes and fellow skeptic Dena Dincauze of the University of Massachusetts, along with my colleague George E. Stuart of the Geographic and friend Dennis Stanford of the Smithsonian. After surveying the site and debating the report, all nine agreed that Monte Verde met the simple but demanding criteria for authenticity: authentic human artifacts, verified provenience, valid carbon dates.

With the Clovis barrier broken, are all those disputed earlier sites suddenly authenticated? Not at all. "Monte Verde doesn't make them better," observes Dennis Stanford, "only more plausible."

That's enough to send archaeologists trekking back to questioned sites, to see if more digging and analysis can erase old doubts.

My article appears in the September 1979 issue, and in a few months it wins the magazine science-writing award presented annually by Westinghouse and the American Association for the Advancement of Science. Gratifying as that is, it will take second place to my receiving, two years later, perhaps the least-known award in journalism. It is reverentially spoken of as "the Ethel," and its origins are deeply entwined in *Geographic* ritual.

It's a raw, cold Friday in January, with threat of snow hanging heavy over Washington. Downtown at headquarters, the magazine's annual Editorial Seminar is in full swing. This is a time when the whole editorial gang—writers, researchers, administrative assistants, and assorted editors—forsakes all but the most pressing deadline chores and gathers to celebrate the written word.

In the morning we hear addresses from our own top brass—President Gil Grosvenor, always ill at ease before the magazine editorial staff, Editor Bill Garrett, greatly admired and generally liked, and Associate Editor Joe Judge, the spiritual leader of these largely pleasant and informative events. At a fancy luncheon we enjoy the witticisms of humorist Art Buchwald. In the afternoon we attend a series of panel discussions, two featuring critiques and commentaries by outside journalists.

Ignoring the certainty of snow, we drive in early darkness north into Maryland, to the Society's elegant Membership Center Building, known as the MCB. The noted architect Edward Durrell Stone designed this palatial office building and its mirroring artificial lake shortly after conceiving our white marble headquarters just north of the White House. By day its offices hum with some 1,300 technical personnel performing the countless clerical chores generated by 10 million dues-paying, book- and map-buying members.

Tonight this building is rocking. A large room holds several busy bars, a (temporarily) restrained band, and tables of hors d'oeuvres proudly overseen by the Society's Swiss-born maître d', Charles Reichmuth. We will return later to dance to that fine band. We move on to dinner, with filet mignon and filled wineglasses. As plates are cleared and waiters bring on dessert, fellow writer Elizabeth A. Moize rises and advances to a microphone to present the home-grown Ethel.

Four years ago friends of staff writer Ethel A. Starbird, a much-loved and humorously cantankerous Vermonter, celebrated her sixtieth birthday by establishing an annual editorial award, to be presented to the editorial staffer best exemplifying the qualities of "integrity, good humor, and guts." Traditionally, the recipient from the year before presents the cherished trophy—a woman with arms upraised—to the next winner on the night of the Editorial Seminar banquet.

Betsy Moize was last year's winner. Tonight, with a speech warm and flattering, she will pass the Ethel on to me. Over the years I will win half a dozen or so science-writing awards, including the big one from AAAS-Westinghouse. But the Ethel is the one I most treasure. I am proud to see my name engraved at its base beneath those of Bill Ellis, Howard LaFay, and Betsy Moize.

Ellis is probably the best writer the magazine ever had. Exquisite metaphors and similes form seemingly effortlessly in his mind, infusing his articles with warmth and color. Yet he is editorially tough. When he and photographer Jim Blair produced an article fairly depicting apartheid South Africa, its wrathful government futilely attempted to browbeat him into softening his stance, then took out full-page advertisements in leading newspapers berating writer, photographer, and *Geographic*. Ellis is witty as well. When he was on assignment during an anti-U.S. protest in Beirut, Lebanon, a mob turned on his photographer colleague, George Mobley, screaming "Get the American! Get the American!" Recalled Ellis:

"Mobley had jumped up on a rooftop to escape and he looked down at me and yelled, 'Do something! *Do something!*' I did. I yelled, 'Get the American!'"

Howard LaFay is another *Geographic* giant, Ellis' rival for finest writer, large of heart, witty, greatly beloved. Cancer claims him at an unfair age, but he will be fondly talked about for decades. Like Ellis he eschews clawing up the corporate ladder to win editorial titles; these two are writers, masters and slaves of the beauty of language.

Betsy Moize is a versatile Texan, a strong writer, a strong editor and manager, a fishing fanatic with an explosive laugh. She and I served side by side as legends writers, and after I moved on to the articles staff, Betsy succeeded Carolyn Patterson as legends editor. When Bill Graves assumed the editorship in 1990, he tapped Betsy Moize as associate editor, the highest editorial rung a woman has occupied. Yes, the Ethel folks are good company.

The period of covering the early Americans also witnessed the final unraveling of my marriage to Jes, a process that had been under way for several years. With relief I saw our sons, then sixteen and fourteen, endure a difficult period with poise and evenhanded affection.

Two years later I found myself frequenting the National Geographic Library, specifically the office of assistant librarian Susan Fifer, with whom I was falling in love. In 1982 we were married, an event that has brightened my life ever since. Today Susan serves the Society as director of the Library and Indexing. And one more intra-Geographic marriage flourishes.

Meanwhile new article assignments come rapid-fire (by *Geographic* standards). Free-lance photographer Ted Spiegel and I report on the U.S. water situation in August 1980. The oil crises of the 1970s prompt Editor Gil Grosvenor to publish a special energy issue in February 1981, in which I cover the prospects for synfuels with photographer Jonathan Blair. Then to the U.S. Southwest, to write of the amazing Anasazi Indians of a millennium ago, for a November 1982 article photographed by Dewitt Jones and David

Brill. And in September 1983 an article on how we are using satellites . . . by which time I already have circled the globe again, on
the trail of a rampaging El Niño.

Chapter 6

EL NIÑO'S TANTRUM

Until the El Niño of 1982–83 wrought its awesome destruction, most of the world had thought little of this distant phenomenon. It was a localized weather problem best left to South Americans, who had picturesquely named it after the Christ Child because of its traditional arrival at Christmastime. But after this El Niño departed a year later, the world would never again take lightly the power of the Child.

The Niño of 1982–83 stands as the most devastating natural event in modern history. It slowed the rotation of the planet, changed the chemistry of the global atmosphere, threatened Earth's richest ecosystem, took 1,500 lives, destroyed billions of dollars in property, and inflicted immeasurable human suffering. Yet so quietly did it gather strength, so stealthily did it envelop the globe, that scientists were unaware of its presence until five of the six inhabited continents felt the Child's wrath:

Niño-spawned deluges drenched the U.S. South until the gorged Mississippi River nearly leaped its levees above New Orleans and changed its course westward forever. On the West Coast mountainous surf and floods destroyed or damaged 10,000 California homes.

In Ecuador and Peru, ten feet of rain falling on onetime desert brought mountainsides crashing down on villages, buried highways under mudslides, and swept away bridges.

Vicious Pacific cyclones left 25,000 homeless on battered Tahiti and tossed seas that virtually erased other French Polynesian islands. Failed monsoons brought famine and fires to India, Indonesia, and the Philippines.

In Australia, prolonged drought exacerbated by dust storms and raging fires caused nearly 3 billion dollars in damage and claimed scores of human lives.

In southern Africa, drought visited hunger on thousands of villages and death on millions of cattle and wild animals. Europe alone escaped the Niño's tantrum.

Until the Niño caught them by surprise, scientists had been bullish about their growing understanding of Earth's most disruptive climatic force. They had studied the lair from which Niños emerge, the ocean and atmosphere of the tropical Pacific. They had dissected past Niños, placed sensors in the seas, and positioned satellite eyes in space. Should the monster stir again, they felt confident they could detect its cumbrous early moves and warn the world of its imminent onslaught.

When their failure became apparent late in 1982, the chagrined scientists confessed their errors with candor. This Child had been a maverick. Its birth had not exhibited the same symptoms as those of earlier Niños. When symptoms did appear, poor analyses and bad luck had combined to thwart the forecasters.

This much the scientists knew:

In normal times the Pacific trade winds blow steadily from east to west along the equatorial belt. As they flow they caress the waves beneath, pulling sun-warmed surface water with them and piling it up in the western Pacific. There an immense low-pressure system roils over Indonesia, generating powerful convective cells and turbulent rainstorms and releasing prodigious heat—a maelstrom likened to the Great Red Spot of Jupiter. Paired with this "low," a huge high-pressure cell 5,000 miles eastward brings the steady sunshine of paradise to Tahiti and other South Sea isles.

At the start of a Niño, the trades falter and even reverse direction. The relaxing winds release the pile of warm water, which sloshes eastward back across the Pacific. Ponderously the low-pressure system over Indonesia and the high over Tahiti change places, in a colossal seesaw effect known as the Southern Oscillation. Because the warming waters of El Niño and the seesaw effect of the Southern Oscillation are opposite ends of a single phenomenon, scientists identify the combined event with the acronym ENSO.

Such billboard-size signals seem hard to miss. How could forecasters have let the 1982 Niño slip past?

They had seen the trade winds falter but paid little heed because warm water had not yet piled up in the western Pacific. The great pressure cells over Indonesia and Tahiti had begun seesawing—but then rallied long enough to throw off suspicion. Even nature had conspired to blind the scientists. In the spring of the Niño's stirrings, in 1982, the Mexican volcano El Chichón had spewed mighty plumes of dust into the atmosphere, confusing the satellite sensors on which the forecasters relied.

The Niño was finally unmasked on September 23, 1982, with a simple observation in its traditional cradle. At a pier on the Peruvian coast, meteorologist Cesar del Carmen de la Torre immersed a thermometer in the eastern Pacific. The instrument read *hot*. It confirmed that Earth's most powerful rogue force had eluded the scientists' vigilance and already launched a global surprise attack.

Even with discovery of the Niño's arrival, recognition of its scope dawned slowly. Its effects were too varied, too far-flung, to be readily attributed to a single climatic culprit. Over the next months awareness grew of something wrong in the world—of South American deserts awash, of freak hurricanes pounding bewildered Tahiti, of Australia parched and burning, of parts of Asia and Africa starving. At last scientists gained the ear of the press and strove to explain the complex interactions of oceans and atmosphere that had brought the misery. Slowly the world awakened to a realization of what was happening.

The editor in the spring of 1983 was Wilbur E. Garrett. He had succeeded Gil Grosvenor, who had moved up to become the Society's president. A native of Kansas City and graduate of the University of Missouri School of Journalism, Bill Garrett had a genius for the use of photographs and was an able writer. Aggressive as a journalist, considered by many to be the best editor in the magazine history, Garrett also respected the Geographic's educational role, particularly in the areas of geopolitics and science. At the same time, he acted to improve the literary quality of the magazine by hiring novelist Charles McCarry to recruit and develop prominent and promising outside writers.

By April Garrett was persuaded of the immensity of the Niño's impact. He instructed Science Editor Ken Weaver to send forth a writer. Weaver had two troops in his diminutive command, and the other one was far afield, on the ash-strewn slopes of Italy's Mount Vesuvius. I would do El Niño.

The global impact of the Niño called for coverage in kind—a round-the-world survey of its depredations. I would track it from east to west: First to Ecuador and Peru, which were devastated by floods and the spread of disease. Then to Hawaii, where climate experts held forth at the state university and airlines could take me to battered Pacific islands. From there to worst-hit Australia, perhaps to Indonesia, and thence across the Indian Ocean to southern Africa. There was no time to waste. At some point the Niño would abate and disappear; my story would be strongest if I could see the beast at full strength.

Many visas to get! I called Dick Pearson, the Society's able emissary for pressing visa requests to the embassies. Scanning my itinerary, Dick saw one possible problem: South Africa was still smarting from a Geographic article about apartheid. The nonpolitical nature of El Niño would probably ease the government's apprehensions. Meanwhile, the Niño was causing havoc in the United States. I would drop down to northern Louisiana to see the Army Corps of Engineers grapple with a swollen Mississippi River, then hop over to Salt Lake City, where Niño-spawned snowmelt had turned State Street into one of Utah's swiftest rivers.

To my regret, there'll be no photographer keeping company on this trip. Much of the devastation has already occurred and, we hope, been photographed by free-lancers on the spot. Fresh events—fires, flash floods, dust storms, hurricanes—are scattered and often of brief duration. It will be the task of the picture editor, Rob Hernandez, and me to locate and assemble the best of this localized photo coverage.

IN JULY I head for the soggy port of Guayaquil, Ecuador, a moldering, suffering city hemmed by a moat of flooded countryside. Since autumn the Niño, the most savage in local history, has brought almost unremitting rainfall.

The source of the city's ills is a slab of warm Pacific water 450 feet thick, lodged like a massive lava flow against the coasts of Ecuador and northern Peru. Its warmth has heated the atmosphere above and saturated it with moisture, which has condensed as torrential rains pelting the South American littoral. Some areas have received more than ten feet of rain within two weeks. In displacing the cold Peru Current, the invading hot water has also turned off the natural air conditioning that normally blesses the coast. Ecuadorians and Peruvians are sealed in a mammoth Turkish bath.

The slab of heated coastal water has distorted weather patterns far from South America. The towering convection cells spawned by it have pumped latent heat into the upper atmosphere. Pushing against the tracks of the jet streams that steer the world's weather systems, these heat cells have triggered the floods that almost changed the course of the Mississippi, brought the snows whose melt flooded Salt Lake City, and unleashed the waves and slides that crumbled California homes.

Floods and slides plunging down Andean slopes have shattered Ecuador's infrastructure. Large chunks of roadbeds and railroads have vanished, along with scores of bridges. The staggering nation has repaired a few essential bridges, only to see floods sweep them away again. Thousands of homes have vanished. As displaced occupants fled up the slopes near Chunchi, rains loosened those slopes, and slides buried more than a hundred in cars and buses.

Many have gravitated to the Guasmo, a sprawling slum festering on Guayaquil's outskirts. Years of disaster coverage for the Geographic will take me to my share of slums, but few will harbor worse misery than the Guasmo.

In shacks and shanties and lean-tos cobbled from wood scraps, cinder blocks, bamboo, tin, and plastic, 300,000 Ecuadorians are battling hunger and sickness. Many of the flimsy dwellings stand in lagoons of sewage and green slime swollen by the relentless rains. Still the people are gamely seeking jobs; some have even set up little shops in the Guasmo.

"I sell a chicken or so a day, maybe ten on Sunday," says Enriquepa Castillo, a handsome woman ensconced in a gore-spattered, cubbyhole stall. She shows me a rash that covers her arms like a sleeve. Her small son appears, his arms and legs erupting with rash. Other residents, seeing my interest, crowd in to display their afflictions on chests, necks, and limbs, many entreatingly, as if I, a stranger, can heal them. Mosquitoes and other insects, thriving in the slime pools, are spreading infection to all. Guiltily I bless the bulging medicine bag in my luggage, knowing there's no way to share it with so many.

I visit a tiny clinic. "Typhoid is reaching epidemic proportions," says the overwhelmed doctor. "We're also fighting typhus and salmonella infection." Flooding has contaminated the region's drinking water supplies, and sickness is rampant. Around the world El Niño has given impetus to diseases of all kinds: Hepatitis, dysentery, typhoid, cholera, malaria, dengue, yellow fever, encephalitis, schistosomiasis, plague, and hantavirus are all on the rise.

A black sky dumps its deluge as I emplane at Guayaquil and head south to Peru. From Lima I'll travel north along the Pan-American Highway toward Chimbote, yesterday the fishing capital of the world, today brought to its knees by the Niño.

My Lima hotel arranges for a taxi driver who speaks passable English. José Gloque's eyes light perceptibly as he mentally calculates the driving miles to our distant destination; this will not be his typical crosstown fare. Silently I hope that his aged vehicle is primed for the trip. More fervently I hope that his limited English and my poor Spanish will suffice. We'll be traveling a region that's suffered some of the worst of the Niño's devastation—a strategic area for my article.

Language is a problem for every journalist who travels beyond the bounds of his linquistic fluency. For me those bounds were tight: a little high-school Spanish, a little college French, enough to find a destination or order a meal but totally inadequate for conducting a meaningful interview. This meant hiring interpreters, which we writers customarily did. But even this posed pitfalls, especially for a science writer. Often, during interviews with foreign scientists, the interpreter's fuzzy translation and rattled look told me he or she was lost, hoping to bluff it through. The only solution was to repeat a question several times coming from slightly different directions until I felt I understood—and be grateful that the *Geographic* research staff would later clear my quotes with the scientist.

Early on, four lanes speed José and me through miles of wrenching slums and spotty irrigated agriculture. We see few vehicles; coastal Peru is prostrate. Above hangs a gray Niño sky, while to our left spreads a sullen Niño sea.

To our right, rounded hills, seemingly as sterile as the moon, roll upward toward the Andes, lost in a murky haze. An hour north of Lima the Pan-Am narrows to two lanes; still the sterile ridges of stark desert march inland and upward, barren even of goats. We are in the arid zone of a rain shadow. The wall of the Andes halts moisture-laden clouds flowing westward from the Atlantic and channels their rainfall down eastern slopes into Amazonia. Except when El Niños turn the weather upside-down, virtually no rains fall here.

Two trucks approach—the first we've seen on the deserted road. They carry sacks of guano, the valuable fertilizer of bird droppings mined on Peru's celebrated bird islands. For more than a century guano hewn from offshore islands has provided one of Peru's primary exports. Now man and Child seem bent on destroying this resource.

For millennia, birds by the millions have fed on abundant anchovetas and other fishes that flourished in the nutrient-rich Peru Current. They formed the top of the richest food chain on the planet. Roosting and nesting on the islands, the birds deposited guano in prodigious amounts. With no rains to wash it away, the guano accumulated, in places 150 feet deep. When guano fleets began hauling away the fertilizer in the mid-1800s, the roosting and nesting birds generated more. Peru enjoyed a resource both profitable and renewable: Fish fed the birds, birds converted the fish into guano, people mined and sold it.

Late in the 1950s Peruvians began to short-circuit this food chain. Backed by Norwegians who had overfished their herring and Americans who had exhausted the California sardine fishery of Cannery Row fame, Peru elected to go directly for the fish. Ever-larger fishing fleets seined the ubiquitous anchoveta, main fare of the guano birds. Busy plants ashore ground the fish into meal and exported it as a protein supplement for livestock feed. By 1970 Peru's 1,500 modern seiners pulled in 14 million tons a year and flew the pennant of the world's largest fishery. As catches soared, the guano birds sharply declined. The food chain was severed.

Then nature struck another blow. In 1972 a bad Niño struck the Peru coast. The hot slab of seawater corralled the anchovetas into shrinking pockets of cold water. The fishing fleet, now at its largest, closed in on the confined fish—fish in a barrel. Seines hauled in the greatest quantity of living matter ever wrested from the Earth—as much as 180,000 tons a day. The fish and the birds that fed on them took a staggering blow.

Now the wounded ecosystem is being bludgeoned by an even worse Niño.

A hundred fifty miles north of Lima, José and I observe the first clawmarks of the Niño on the land. Gullies carved by recent flooding cleave the desert, rocks strew the highway, and water hides the valley floor. Dodging the worst rocks, José grips the shuddering wheel and moves his lips silently. His decrepit cab faces nature's equivalent of a demolition derby. And if we break down . . . ?

At the former town of Casma, foundations without houses stand beside a broad wash once paved by the Pan-Am. A tractor rests upside-down in muck. Two floods have swept through Casma, killing forty-five. Many of the victims have seldom seen rain in their lives. Nor did they see this one. The deluge fell not on them but on the sterile slopes above, then crashed down on them like an avalanche.

We reach the outskirts of Chimbote. Houses have been swept away, along with our bridge. We detour east, along a small road covered with water.

A pall of quiet hangs over the fish-meal plant, over the long conveyor belt that once carried anchovetas unloaded from the seiners. Down at the wharf, beached seiners rest hull to hull, slowly rusting. But not the entire fleet. The warm ocean water, fortified with nutrients flooding seaward, has generated an explosive proliferation of shrimp. Shipowners alert to opportunity have detoured their craft to the shrimp beds.

As idle as Chimbote's beached boats, fisherman Adolfo Arratia loafs on a pier. "In all my twenty-five years on the water, '82 was the best," he says wistfully. "Maybe it was a 'good-bye' from the fish."

Fisheries authorities and conservationists fear Adolfo Arratia is right. Incredibly, the planet's richest ecosystem faces collapse. This is the doomsday scenario: Desperate fishermen exterminate the sardines that replaced the anchovetas. When the Niño departs, plankton proliferate once again. But there are few fish to eat them. Their dead bodies rain down on the sea floor and decompose, robbing the water of dissolved oxygen. The bottom no longer supports fish and is taken over by anaerobic worms—and the ecosystem becomes a marine desert.

I HOPSCOTCH ACROSS the tropical Pacific, nursery of Niños, home of the tradewinds, the Indonesian low, the Tahiti high—colossal caldron of atmospheric and oceanic perturbations.

Christmas Island, the world's largest atoll and one of thirty-four far-flung islands making up the nation of Kiribati, fries like an egg under an equatorial sun. In normal times the island hosted 17 million nesting seabirds—frigates, boobies, tropics, terns, shearwaters. Their nests crowded under every bush and atop the searing coral. When not nesting the birds soared and dove for fish without need of land—as at home in the air as are fish in the sea.

With the invasion of warm Niño water, the fish on which they fed have vanished, and so have the birds—no one knows where. Prowling the island, I see the feathers and slender bones of countless fledglings abandoned by their parents. But the birds are resilient. They've survived Niños for thousands of years and will survive this terrible one. Tentative new colonies are forming on old nesting grounds, numbering in the thousands instead of millions, but a start. This means that fish have returned to surrounding equatorial waters—a sign that here, at least, the Niño is subsiding.

Tahiti, once an island queen, is now a battered hellhole. A paradise that felt its last hurricane seventy-five years ago has cowered before six in five months. Fifteen hundred houses destroyed, roofs blown off another 6,000. Dislodged roofs are everywhere—hanging from houses and trees, strewing the ground. To the east, the storms have engulfed the atolls of the Tuamotu archipelago; islanders have lashed their boats to coconut palms and ridden out waves clinging to the gunwales.

Even Tahiti's woes pale before those of Australia, hardest hit of all by the Child. Because that continent will be a major focus of my coverage, I had persuaded attachés at the Australian embassy in Washington to contact counterparts in Canberra, the capital, and set up interviews. And so, scarcely pausing in Sydney, I ply Canberra's orderly boulevards. In one trim government building after another, sober agriculturists, economists, meteorologists, soil scientists, and fire analysts reel off statistics detailing the Niño's impact.

Before heading into the field to flesh out those statistics with the human experiences behind them, I fulfill a promise to picture editor Rob Hernandez: to call local newspapers about Niño photographs. The inquiries will pay off; several pages of illustrations in our article will come from leads relayed to him.

At this point I'm halfway through my globe-girdling trip, and I pause to take stock. So far my interviews and experiences have paid handsomely; notebooks are filling steadily. I miss the companionship of a photographer, though less perhaps than if I were traveling in more difficult conditions. But definitely I'm coming down with a tinge of occupational malaise. For two weeks nonstop I've been bombarded by tragedies of every description. Two more weeks of the same lie ahead. Carrying their cumulative weight is demanding a little more effort each day in the field. I've often wondered, when covering disasters, how physicians can practice for decades seemingly unaffected by the endless procession of sickness, injury, and inevitable death. On the positive side, the reactions of disaster victims to their misfortunes are almost invariably heroic. Never do I encounter a victim who has simply surrendered to despair.

For nearly a year drought has withered eastern Australia, pulling moisture from the soil, from livestock dung, from vegetation. Howling out of the outback, winds have picked up the surface soil and dung and the ash from forest fires. The dust has blinded farmers and motorists, clogged equipment, and brought agony to housewives. In early February, the height of the torrid austral summer, the winds lifted an unprecedented cloud of dust and debris and aimed it straight at stately, sweltering Melbourne.

The immense cloud towered like a moving escarpment—a wall of airborne earth and ash thousands of feet high, 300 miles long. An unnatural darkness fell over Melbourne, then ominous stillness, then the suffocating enveloping cloud. For forty minutes Melbourne was a buried and terrified city. My chambermaid, a young woman from the country, is among those who felt the terror. "It was the end of the world," she recalls, eyes rolling. The storm dumped 11,000 tons of topsoil on the city and would bear some as far eastward as New Zealand.

At the same time, bushfires, whipped by the winds and fed by dry vegetation, swirled across Victoria and New South Wales. In the Niño's worldwide frenzy these were the prime killers, claiming seventy-five lives, destroying 8,000 homes. From a holocaust in Victoria emerged a national hero.

A fire was rampaging around agricultural Colac. Astride his motorbike, Senior Constable Steve Williams was doing his duty, urging farm families to evacuate, herding campers and motorists out of the fire's path. A motorist intent on remaining balked; Constable Williams finally turned him around. But by then a wall of fire had moved in, cutting off their escape route. "We were well and truly in it," the genial constable recalled.

Unknown to Williams, a television-network helicopter was hovering overhead, camera trained for the coming contest between men and fire.

The constable urged the motorist into the flames; better to make a run for it than await certain death. But again the motorist balked, out of stubbornness or fear. Ordering the man to follow, Williams took the lead. "I ducked behind the bike windshield and just opened her up—shot into the fire at a hundred miles an hour."

Sitting before tellies across Australia, hypnotized countrymen watched the tiny figure as seen from the copter: Williams disappears into a sheet of fire; moments later he breaks clear. He careens around a bend, but ahead roars more fire. He vanishes into it, then rockets out the far side. Flames are feeding on his face, his unprotected arms. Into more fire—the agonizing wait—and one more escape.

At last pulling ahead of the holocaust, the constable stops and looks back. The motorist is not with him. He turns his motorbike back into the fire. By now fallen trees block the road, and winds are so fierce the flames sweep horizontally. Williams has no choice but to give up; the situation is hopeless. An ensuing copter search finds the motorist burned to death. Yet all of Niño-weary Australia celebrates Constable Williams' escape.

For months the fires gnawed at Melbourne's outskirts, consuming entire suburbs. On the night of Ash Wednesday, half a dozen blazes ringed the city. One swept Macedon, a fashionable exurb whose wooded hills held the homes of many airline pilots and a beloved population of furry koalas, Victoria's state mascot.

The sharp hills of Macedon lie blackened as a Melbourne taxi takes me slowly through the fire area. Some ridges still exhale wisps of smoke, resembling little volcanoes. Charred tree trunks bristle from the ash-strewn slopes like coarse hairs on a hide. Beside the road stand naked chimneys, headstones for the lost houses and in some cases for their occupants. In many burned areas the koalas scrambled to the tree crowns and survived, but not here. So great was the heat that the oily eucalyptus trees exploded as the fire roared through at forty and fifty miles an hour.

Ken Hook owned a tearoom and gourmet restaurant in Macedon. As the fire approached, he left his business to save his house. With foresight he had equipped it with an electric water pump. A flaming tree fell, knocking out the pump, and the house burned to the ground. He returned to his restaurant. It too had burned.

Some 250 Macedonians sought refuge in the Macedon Hotel, near the train station. In the depot parking lot sat 260 cars. Fire surrounded the frame hotel and swept over the roof. The cars exploded in a chain reaction. On the hotel roof, three men trained hoses on erupting fires and on themselves to fight the deadly heat. Inside the smoke-filled hotel, the refugees pressed their faces against the lobby floor for air and held wet towels over their heads to keep hair from singeing. Miraculously the fire passed.

I ask the driver to stop at a charred chimney rising from the foundations of a onetime house. In a nearby camper, which Australians call a caravan, I find Annette Radford; she and her husband, Gerry, lost everything that Ash Wednesday night. Almost everything: She shows me the melted remains of a bracelet, gold wristwatch, and necklace she found in the ashes.

"Let's head for the airport," I say to my taxi driver as we depart Madedon's desolation. "Where are you going?" he parries. "To Wagga Wagga," I reply, "to see the damage to the wheat country."

The driver, voluble Ken Matthews, is large and in early middle age, as is his Ford, a black sedan equipped like many Australian cars with tanks for dual fuel—gasoline and natural gas. As we've driven through the fire zone he's made helpful observations about the fires, the neighborhood, the suffering of eastern Australia.

Ken pauses. "I'm enjoying myself," he finally says. "Why don't I drive you? It won't be that expensive, you'll see the countryside, and maybe I can help you." Help me he does, in understanding his vast country, and in providing welcome companionship in the cheerless business of chronicling human suffering.

And so we are driving northward through Victoria, over the Dividing Range and into the drainage of the great Murray River. Through quaint Bendigo, goal of miners pouring into southern Australia for the 1851 gold rush that nearly trebled the nation's population, and across the Murray into New South Wales, home of a third of the nation's 15 million people.

We move through wheat country—wheat and sheep, farmed on a vast scale. Farm boundaries run ten and twenty miles to a side. Rains have finally returned, and a patina of green softens the huge holdings. A cold drizzle falls as we drive.

A few months ago this was a dust bowl, with two and three "whirly-whirlies" a week. Farmers who raised a sweat found themselves covered with mud. Those who planted wheat saw winds lift it from the ground with the powdery soil and sheep dung and aim them for Melbourne. Where the seeds germinated, emaciated kangaroos came out of woodlands and ate the sprouts, then wallowed

on what they had not eaten. The sheep dung, light and easily
blown, drifted into depleted livestock ponds; a burning sun and
bacterial decay heated the foul soup to nearly boiling. Meanwhile
shire officials bulldozed burial pits, and farmers brought their
starving sheep to be shot, sparing them a slower death. Most had
been through lesser droughts before, for the threat always haunts
Australian farmers. Many of those earlier "drys" would have been
caused by El Niños, recognized only now as global culprits.

I examine the scattered homes as we drive, seeking signs of
suffering, the staple of disaster journalism. Most garages hold two
shiny cars, at least one of them usually a Mercedes. "In the long
pull, these farmers do all right," comments Ken. "Savings in the
good years carry them through the bad."

We stop to talk to a farmer repairing his paddock fence. About
sixty, Hugh Robertson wears a fresh slash across his face where the
barbed wire has raked him. The wound is the least of his worries.

"I don't know what I'll do," says Robertson, gratefully getting
into the car to escape the raw cold. "I'm keeping a thousand sheep,
but only by feeding them seed barley I'd saved for next year's
planting. I planted 1,250 acres of wheat, but it got knocked back by
frost. Now it's blowing out of the ground. The 'roos are stripping my
best paddock.—there's more of them than you'd believe.

"I don't know what to do about my cattle. Too many decisions
to make. I don't know what I'll do." His eyes water. He grows quiet,
but he can't leave the warm car and sympathetic ears. The Niño has
nearly broken Hugh Robertson. He might belie my observation of
the uncanny resilience of disaster victims.

His discouragement dredges up my earliest memory of
drought, on our Maryland farm. Every few years in late spring or
summer the rain gods would overlook our 130 acres: The corn
would wither; the hay would cower, stunted; the pasture would fail
our milk cow and team of draft horses. In those times my father too
would shrivel, physically and spiritually. There he is of an evening
when I am three, bathed clean of the day's sweat and still smelling
faintly of soap, walking after dinner to the edge of the cornfield

with me scampering at his side, then looking long at the sere stand and speaking a single word: "*Ruined*." Unlike Australia's wind-plagued droughts, in Maryland even the air would die, stilling the rhythmic throb of our windmill. Then my mother would have to drive for water for cooking for washing, for flushing. Yet in those trying years the farm, marginal at best and bled by a mortgage, still offered relative advantages: We were better off than the millions who had nothing at all in that time of the Great Depression.

As Ken and I travel, we hear Australian farmers speak as one against kangaroos. As the drought has worsened and the natural vegetation shriveled, the animals have moved in mobs onto the cultivated areas, with devastating effect. "They've denuded my paddock, my wheat," I hear repeatedly from farmers who've been forced to shoot hundreds, often thousands, of sheep. Says one: "They are responsible for our plight; if it weren't for the 'roos, our sheep could make it, even in this drought." The farmers looked at me, an American, with dark suspicion. An American environmentalist has recently published a book anguishing over the shooting of kangaroos and lamenting the animals' imminent extinction. The Australian media, well aware of the millions of 'roos bounding around the nation, have played up the book. The farmers hate the author with a passion.

Ken takes me to Wagga's airport, and I fly to somnolent Charleville, in the Queensland outback.

This is huge country. On their station between Charleville and Wyandra, Neville and Diana Palmer graze 106,000 acres and drive eight miles to see their nearest neighbor. Hundreds of their sheep have died in the drought; the 5,200 survivors and 250 cattle subsist on mulga leaves, browsed from bull-dozed trees. "Even the 'roos are starving," says Neville. "I often find two or three dead ones under a shade tree. We have thousands, and they eat much more than a sheep." A neighbor has hired a shooter who culled 5,000, with little dent in their depredations. No, I assure Neville, I don't share the views of the despised American author.

I fly south to rendezvous with Matthews. "Got your story?" he asks that evening as we down our daily ration of beers from the large cans Australians call tubes. "More than I'll ever need," I concede. "But I think something better is still out there." Tomorrow afternoon my self-set schedule will see me airborne, headed for the Niño's depredations in southern Africa. But I'm uneasy. Despite the notebooks I've filled, I feel in my journalist bones that I haven't yet found the individual(s) whose experiences quintessentially express the Australian ordeal.

"I heard of a small farmer near Charlton in Victoria who went through it all," suggests Ken. "His name is Peter O'Brien."

Clad in padded jacket and rubber boots, Peter O'Brien is finishing his chores when Ken and I accost him on a frigid morning beside the white frame farmhouse. Beneath the gray sky, gentle hills wear the green of recent rains. O'Brien follows my eyes. "The Aborigines called the area *Buckrabanyule*. It means 'last of the hills,' before you reach the flat of the Mallee."

I pull out my small spiral-bound notebook, and Peter O'Brien, wiry, fortyish, black hair beginning to gray, tells his story while standing in the cold.

He and his wife, June, bought their farm in 1979, three years before the Niño, and at once began drought-proofing it. He deepened the ponds that Australians call dams, and asked the shire's help in drawing up a ten-year soil conservation plan. By the autumn of 1982 he was building a fine flock of sheep and could plant heavily in wheat.

Simultaneously the Niño struck Buckrabanyule. Dry winds ripped O'Brien's wheat seed from the ground. The little that sprouted fed the kangaroos. His 750 merino ewes lambed the best ever—but food dried up, the lambs could not nurse, and he sold them at one-tenth their normal value. "Then the dust storms came, the soil blew into the air. I knew we were ruined."

June joins us. "A windstorm would fill the house with dust. I'd wait a few days, until I thought things had calmed, and then clean up. Another storm would fill the house. I had to keep the windows

closed, and the heat was stifling. I told myself, 'There's always someone worse off than we are.'"

O'Brien realized he would have to put down his ewes. He
could dump them in an unused dam. Shire officials came, herded
600 animals into a chute one by one, and shot them; Peter threw
the bodies into the dam. Other farmers brought their beasts. By the
end of that gory day a bulldozer had covered 1,800 bodies.

"I kept 130 ewes, hoping to start over again. Some died. I'd
go out to hand-feed them hay, and they would fall down in front
of me. If the rains hadn't come when they did, we'd have lost
them all."

He has bred the survivors. We walk to an outbuilding, he
opens a door, and I see the first new lamb. Peter and June O'Brien
will rebuild. And I have the story I've come for. The O'Briens'
hardships encapsulate much of what many Australians have suffered at the hands of El Niño. And like their countrymen, they'll
work their way back to prosperity, and perhaps to better prepared-
ness for the onslaught of the next Niño. In the process the O'Briens
have given me what every journalist treasures: a sense of certainty
that this is the lead for my article. For a moment I worry about my
exultation at having found the perfect victim, about profiting, in a
sense, by another's misfortune. But my profession is not unique in
this regard. Doctors and dentists and certainly lawyers profit in this
way, and perhaps it's the way of the world.

I bid good-bye to Ken Matthews, unable to thank him enough
for his help. I've sent a long Telex to Hernandez in Washington,
telling him about photographs of the dust storm that enveloped
Melbourne, of the fires, and luckily of the O'Briens: A professional
photographer covered the shooting of the sheep and published her
pictures in the London *Sunday Times* magazine supplement. The
same Telex has requested more money on my arrival in South
Africa. The Australian beer has been cheap, but not the charter
aircraft.

My passport permits me to stop in Indonesia, but not my
schedule. I bypass it reluctantly. Indonesia's rain forests, baking
beneath the huge high-pressure cell of the Southern Oscillation,

have dried to tinder, and immense fires are ravaging the archipelago. Fifteen years later another El Niño will again desiccate those
forests, and the smoke of their fires will pose a health hazard to
much of Southeast Asia.

I cross the Indian Ocean in endless night that travels with the
plane. In Johannesburg, the metropolis on South Africa's high
veldt, a taxi drops my travel-weary carcass at the Carlton Hotel at
1:30 A.M. On the eleventh floor the elevator doors open onto a
dimly lit corridor. Halfway along it stands an apparition to rouse the
dead—a beguiling woman in a soft negligee smiling a welcome.
What does a starved man do? I embrace my wife, Susan, and tug her
into our room. She has flown over the North and South Atlantic
Oceans, I have crossed the Pacific and Indian Oceans, and we are
at last reunited here.

We arranged this rendezvous a month ago, when I was planning my Niño coverage. Susan has never seen southern Africa, and
while here we will visit my sister, Vertrees, who three decades ago
married Paul N. Malherbe, a South African then studying at the
Massachusetts Institute of Technology. They now live in a suburb of
beautiful Cape Town. Fortunately for us, the *Geographic* has a
spouse travel program, aimed at reducing the marital stresses arising
from the extensive absences of writers and photographers: Business
mileage accumulated by one spouse translates into free travel points
for the other.

Like Australia, southern Africa is withering under the blast of
El Niño. But here many already live at the fringes of survival. With
the Niño, hunger and malnutrition have silently taken up lodging
in the shanties and huts, or rondavels, of South Africa, Botswana,
and Zimbabwe. This is the second time that drought-caused famine
has brought me to the continent. A decade earlier the hunger zone
lay northward, in the Sahel.

With South African physician Michael Lewis, Susan and I
drive through the nation's parched northeast toward the borders of
Zimbabwe and Mozambique. Here in the low veldt, vegetation is
shriveled, rivers a chain of stagnant pools. We cross into Lebowa,
one of the national states established for black Africans by South

Africa's apartheid government. Suddenly there is no vegetation at all. The land lies naked, as if sprayed with herbicide.

"Too many cattle," says Dr. Lewis. "Cattle mean wealth and status. Tribesmen sacrifice to build herds that overgraze even with normal rains." Perhaps 90 percent will die in the drought. Officials privately welcome the loss as a means of removing pressure from the land.

We enter Gazankulu, another tribal homeland, and approach the village of Thoma, an assortment of rondavels and empty cattle *kraals* (corrals) at the foot of a steep hill. Three of Mphephu Shibambu's five small children cling to her, and she is pregnant. "My husband works in town," she says. "He bought seven cows just before the drought, and we drank the milk. Six have starved, and the seventh is dying—gives no milk. We eat once a day." That single meal is cornmeal porridge and, perhaps, a tomato.

To the east sprawls Kruger National Park, oldest of Africa's ninety national parks, larger than my home state of Maryland. Kruger's animals are dying by the thousands—kudus, bushbucks, 10,000 impalas—but warden Dannie Pienaar is taking it in stride. "It's a natural culling process—takes out the old, the diseased, the animals infested with parasites. Survival of the fittest. The elephants do relatively well because they aren't choosy about their browse, but they hammer the habitat. Hippos and warthogs are suffering the worst, but they should bounce back. Some of the private parks outside Kruger let their animals overstock. They're getting the big die-offs." True. In immense Klaserie Private Reserve, adjoining Kruger, 33,000 carcasses have been counted.

Kruger research scientist Anthony Hall-Martin is about to board a helicopter and dart an elephant for a medical study. Would I like to go? The activity has no discernible relevance to the Niño. But who could say no?

The pilot lifts to 300 feet, and we rattle over the bush. To port I watch a hawk intently soaring at our altitude. Below, antelopes crowd a slime-covered waterhole.

Hall-Martin spots our elephant strolling through the scrub, waving his huge ears. Earlier the scientist has inoculated the animal with tritium for studying how his body processes water. The results will be compared with those of an inoculated desert elephant in Southwest Africa (today Namibia). Tentative findings indicate that desert elephants require only a quarter of the water used by their savanna kin.

The pilot dips the copter and expertly herds the elephant toward a park road, to enable a ground crew to reach us quickly when the beast falls.

The animal stops and defiantly waves his trunk. We descend to a few feet above the low-growing acacia trees. Hall-Martin aims the gun, and suddenly a dart quivers in the elephant's rump. "He should go down in a few minutes. If we're unlucky, he could fall forward on his chest. Unless we can roll him, he can live only seven or eight minutes before suffocating. If it's a brisket-fall we have to move quickly."

The elephant trundles into the bush, ignoring the drug and the pilot's nudgings toward the road. A quarter-hour passes. "The drug may have been sold at half strength," Hall-Martin observes.

The pilot dips among the acacias again, and soon a second dart quivers beside the first. Simultaneously the animal grows unresponsive to the chopper. "He's feeling the first dart," says Hall-Martin.

The elephant wobbles and his switching tail sags. He staggers, steps on his trunk, and slumps forward—squarely on his brisket.

The pilot lands, and we race to the five-ton hulk. Shoulders to the elephant! Hopeless. We tug at a front leg propping him on his chest. Hopeless. We push at his head; I lever myself against a tusk. Hopeless. Every ten seconds or so breath gurgles from the beast's trunk with a resonant plumbing sound, as if from a pipe in a cave.

Hall-Martin seizes a fallen acacia log, and he and the pilot pry it against the living mountain. I push at the shoulder. It's rolling!

Thwock!—the elephant's left front leg flies upward into my crotch and sends me soaring. Aarrgghh!

The ground crew arrives, with Susan. One crew member stands guard with a rifle—always a precaution when on foot in Kruger. Another douses the overheated animal with cooling water, and seven others swarm like Lilliputians over him. They take blood from behind an ear, place a plastic bag over the end of the trunk for breath analysis, reach inside for fecal samples, even measure the wind speed to help with water-loss analysis.

Hall-Martin injects the elephant with an antidote to the knockout drug, and we race to the copter. As we rise, the elephant lurches to his feet—awake from a very bad dream.

Along its curved northern border South Africa cradles the France-size nation of Botswana, normally home to 1.3 million people and 3 million cattle. This year a million cattle are dying as the Niño sears a region already midway through seven years of drought.

Southern Botswana embraces the famed Kalahari Desert of the Bushmen. The northern third is a watery wilderness, formed by the seasonal flooding of the Okavango River, flowing from Angolan highlands. In the Okavango Delta and related waterways survives the Africa of yesteryear—the last free-roaming herds of elephants, Cape buffalo, zebras, antelopes. The Niño had shrunk the delta and dried up ancillary marshes, rivers, and pans. The Okavango is reeling.

Here again I have benefited from the influence and good name of the *Geographic*. I visit the Okavango with South African conservationist Clive Walker, a leading figure in the often-uphill struggle to protect African wildlife and habitat. Trained as an artist and successful as a painter, Walker has established the Endangered Wildlife Trust, concerned with creatures ranging from a threatened vulture to the desert elephant and sponsor of trail programs to foster a wildlife ethic among the young. Elephants are his particular fascination—their complex psyches and physiology, their devastating effect on habitat, the difficulties of protecting beasts competing so directly with Africa's desperate agriculturists. His book, *Twilight of the Giants*, eloquently presents these problems. A hands-on practitioner, Walker operates his own game park north of Johannesburg.

Our small plane out of Johannesburg crosses Kipling's Limpopo River, still lined with fever trees but now a ribbon of sand instead of gray-green and greasy. Ahead, Botswana and the Kalahari spread flat and brown to the horizon, like a forgotten slab of Earth's crust still awaiting the gift of life. Walker points out scattered red sores pimpling the surface, as if the land itself has contracted measles. At the center of each sore cluster a few rondavels, their *kraals* bounded by fences of thorn branches. Overgrazing and restless hooves have churned the circular pattern, known to sociologists as a "grazing gradient" and most intense at the core.

Straight as an arrow beneath us, one of Botswana's "fences of death" streaks to the distant horizon. Erected to protect cattle from foot-and-mouth disease carried by wild grazers, the fences have severed hoof-packed trails worn over the centuries by tides of wildebeest migrating from the Kalahari to the watery north. Punished by drought and the fences, 50,000 will die this year.

Even in unfenced Okavango, animals of every species are falling to the drought. Hippos are suffering agonies. As waterholes shrink, the great beasts cluster immobile in congealing muck like sausages in a pot. Unprotected backs burn in the blazing sun—burn badly enough to kill. Singly or in small groups, some have pulled free of the sucking mud and are lumbering toward water still flowing in the Linyanti-Chobe river system forty miles to the north. This is the goal of many animals forced to trek out of the Okavango area. Freedom from fences—freedom to migrate, to trek out if instinct urges—is the salvation of northern Botswana wildlife.

The departing animals have left behind a ravaged landscape. The region's 60,000 elephants in particular have wrought havoc on trees and scrub. "Thank God the drought moved the animals on, to give the land a rest," says Walker.

EVEN THE WORST of El Niños must end. As this one dissipated, the seasons reasserted control. The ordeal left lasting scars, in villages swept by floods, soils removed by winds, families diminished by a death or wiped out entirely. Around the world in uncountable venues, people began rebuilding, taking up life as before. Nature too proved resilient. In the seemingly shattered ecosystem of the Peru Current, anchovies and guano birds returned in strength.

The Niño galvanized the world's climatologists. Its surprise onset and devastating impact had blared out a need to understand and predict Niños—to decipher once and forever the continuous interaction between oceans and atmosphere that shapes most climate and weather.

The international scientific community responded. In 1985 sixteen nations launched TOGA, the decade-long Tropical Ocean and Global Atmosphere program. Research vessels and satellites channeled data into high-speed computers to model the ocean/air interaction across the Pacific basin and predict its effects. A special task force probed Indonesia's great red spot, crucible of global climate. East to west across the equatorial Pacific, TOGA strung an array of sixty-nine buoys into the world's longest antenna to continuously transmit sea-surface temperatures and currents.

Studies also focused on La Niñas—Niños in reverse, when normally cool ocean currents grow cooler, warm pools warmer, and atmospheric pressure cells more intense. Additional studies probed whether global warming could affect Niño intensity and frequency, which some scientists believe to be increasing.

From this research have come predictive and monitoring capabilities that forecast Niños as much as a year before their first stirrings, and shadow their stealthiest moves. Paralleling this, an international agency issues warnings to countries likely to be affected and offers suggestions for mitigating damage.

As I write, scientists are tracking the formation of a monster El Niño, comparable in severity and weather pattern to that of 1982–83. Warned well in advance, vulnerable peoples around the world are responding: Californians and South Americans to the threat of floods, Australians and southern Africans to the scourge of drought. Too big and boisterous to be disciplined, perhaps the Niño can be outmaneuvered through advance preparation.

More assignments await me, and the one first in line marks new territory. The Society wishes to publish a North American atlas; it will make heavy use of satellite images to reveal the continent's cultures and landforms. I will be the text editor, and my friend Jon Schneeberger, the Society's space specialist, will handle the imagery. At the end of a year's strenuous toil, in 1985 we will attend the birth of our handsome offspring, *Atlas of North America: Space Age Portrait of a Continent.*

Meanwhile Schneeberger and I face a still more challenging project. For several years in this Cold War era we have struggled to overcome the Soviets' obsession with secrecy and report on their sophisticated space program. At long last, we may be making headway.

Chapter 7

DUEL IN SPACE

Make the Soviets show you Baikonur, Tom," directed Editor Bill Garrett somewhat snappishly in 1982. "That's the Geographic story—'first Western journalists into secret Soviet launch site.' Don't let them jerk you around."

That was Garrett: Get *the* story. Don't let a mere Superpower slow you up. More important, don't just come up with an interesting article about the Soviet space program. Find something *new*, *different*—the news peg on which to hang the article. I had to admit that being the first Western journalist into secret Baikonur would be a coup—and balm for Garrett's fevered brow. The Soviets scarcely admitted the huge cosmodrome *existed*.

I knew just as well that I'd never get to Baikonur. No one "made" the Soviets do anything, of course. Their bureaucrats were the most trying, opaque people on this planet except the Albanians. In fact at this point they weren't even letting me into the

Soviet Union, much less to their remote launch site in Kazakhstan. That's really why Garrett was so irritated.

Garrett understood all this, of course. But being the consummate professional editor, he had to try.

Bill Garrett had come to the Geographic in 1954, the same year as Gil Grosvenor. The two became fast friends, working together, socializing with their two families—a closeness that would exacerbate the pain of their eventual and cataclysmic falling out. Garrett formed a special bond with Gil's father, Melville, capturing the senior Grosvenor's interest with his constant flow of ideas, sharing Melville's intuitive insight into reader preferences in pictures and text. Energetic and virtually tireless, Garrett was intensely competitive: unrelenting as a journalist, aggressive on the tennis or squash court, an infighter in office power struggles.

Not surprisingly, Gil rose through the ranks faster than Bill, but not by much. Usually they were promoted in tandem. Office gossip had it that the top brass (usually dominated by a Grosvenor) included Bill in Gil's promotions to soften the appearance of favoritism to the Grosvenor dynasty. Those who recognized Garrett's talent did not doubt he earned his way.

Space exploration had won the Geographic's enthusiastic support from the outset. It was a subject custom-made for the magazine: positive in its goals, dependent upon scientific and technological advances, and often productive of breathtaking pictures, taken either robotically or by the astronauts. Further, space flight was by nature an unfolding adventure rich in dramas dear to journalists— peril and suspense, failure and triumph, heroism.

Readers responded warmly. Geographic articles about space achievements, many written by astronauts and space scientists, struck a popular chord. Reader polls showed that even somewhat routine space articles enjoyed the avid appreciation of a large, hardcore constituency of enthusiasts.

Soon after the beep-beeps of Sputnik 1 radioed the dawn of the space age in 1957, the magazine eagerly reported America's climb toward the moon: the seven lunar probes known as Pioneers, six of

which failed; the Ranger moon rockets, which after six failures produced the first useful images of the cratered lunar surface; the five
unmanned Surveyor spacecraft—ungainly space spiders that soft-
landed amid the craters and televised breathtaking panoramas of
lunar soil and rocks, proving that the surface would support vehicles and human feet.

Then daring Americans in space: Alan Shepard in Mercury's
maiden flight and John Glenn thrice around the planet; the
dizzying maneuvers of Gemini astronauts as they perfected space
rendezvous; the ever-bolder Project Apollo flights, until *Apollo 8*
first freed human beings from the silken snare of Earth's gravity and
Apollo 11 fulfilled a president's pledge to put a man on the moon
before the end of the 1960s.

With equal zeal the magazine covered the nation's unmanned
probes in their reach for the planets: the Mariners and Vikings to
our red neighbor Mars; Mariners to scorching Venus and Mercury;
and—most rewarding—the two Voyagers, whose twelve-year grand
tour trained America's robotic eyes on the giant outer planets—
Jupiter, Saturn, Uranus, and Neptune—and on their swarms of
intriguing moons and rings.

I would write five of those articles and edit many more. Naturally I found it heady stuff, working with the astronauts, observing
the shapers of the American space drive—the Wernher von Brauns
and Chris Krafts. And the great space installations—von Braun's
rocket works at Huntsville, Alabama; NASA's vast campus south of
Houston, with Mission Control and the space science offices and
astronauts training in sweltering bayou country abubble with beer
and crayfish. Cape Canaveral, with its cavernous Vehicle Assembly
Building, so huge that rain formed in it, with the tracked crawler
that like a drifting continent gently bore the assembled rockets vertically to their launch pads, with the incredible Saturn V moon
rockets. Nothing was more awesome—*nothing*—than von Braun's
mighty Saturn V rocket poised at the pad, belching steam, tipped
with an Apollo capsule or *Skylab*, erupting flame that would
surely consume it, lifting so s-l-o-w-l-y it had to topple, hurling a

terrifying thunder that literally rippled the cheeks of us stunned journalists perched in the closest viewing stands, three miles away. *How on Earth* did humans control this stupefying release of energy?

But a little cloud dimmed my euphoria. Always a believer in space exploration, unabashed admirer of astronauts and the technical and organizational miracles behind them, I could not resolve a troubling question: What portion of a finite budget should go to manned space, what portion to unmanned? Manned missions were gobbling up funds. But a large part of the scientific community— the community I ultimately believed in—hugely resented the volume of money poured into "space spectaculars," believing it could be better spent. I feared they had a point.

Good arguments supported each side. The manned Apollo and shuttle programs unquestionably advanced science, driving rapid development in computers, materials, and communications— to a degree. And these developments spun off into society—to a degree. More important, perhaps, the space spectaculars possessed enormous intangible value, lifting the nation, giving it pride. We humans had a destiny in space—that I believed.

On the other hand, many of the experiments conducted by astronauts could be done much more cheaply robotically. Further, many of the astronauts' goals—improved industrial processes in space, for example—would be goals for two decades, with little apparent progress. And if Apollo had been an inspirational success, so had the grand tours of the two Voyagers that began in 1977— arguably the greatest journeys of exploration ever. Seizing upon an every-176-years alignment of the outer planets, low-budget NASA scientists had assembled two spacecraft and launched them through that narrow window. As planned, the gravitational pull of each planet flung them toward the next, accomplishing in twelve years a voyage that otherwise would have taken thirty, and yielding data that reshaped scientists' understanding of the planets' turbulent atmospheres, their zoos of weird moons, their jewelry stores of planetary rings.

Comprehensively and proudly, the *Geographic* related America's continuing space achievements. But this conscientious coverage of the U.S. program told only half the story. Similar and often bolder space exploits were unfolding with unnerving frequency in the Soviet Union. The magazine virtually ignored them.

It could do little else.

Soviet space secrecy was as absolute as the Soviets could make it. In part this reflected a tradition of state obscurantism long predating the Communists. Secrecy served the national policy of concealing—from Soviet citizens and foreigners alike—the disasters that punctuated the long climb spaceward. It also reflected the program's dominance by the generals of the Strategic Rocket Forces. The rockets that hurled *Sputnik* and jubilant cosmonauts into space were the same as those used in the intercontinental ballistic missiles whose nuclear warheads pointed by the thousands over the Pole toward American cities. So zealously were the three Soviet spaceports concealed that American astronauts participating in the 1975 joint Apollo-Soyuz Test Project were flown into Baikonur during darkness. Space was a militarized zone— tomorrow's battlefield.

Far from copying American ways, the Soviets were blazing their own pathway to the stars, with obvious success. While post-Apollo America funneled its resources into a program built around the costly reusable shuttle, the Soviets focused on space stations, and reaching them with mass-produced throwaway space capsules. Their rockets, unlike America's, were both practical and economical. Most telling, the Soviet program exhibited a consistency of goals, dominated by its evolving space stations, that appeared lacking in post-Apollo America.

Like the American space program, the Soviets suffered disasters, grisly ones: the crash landing of the capsule that carried Vladimir Komarov to his death; a capsule soft-landing at Baikonur with its crew of three cosmonauts—staring out, dead of suffocation; and of course the nation-numbing plane crash of Yuri Gagarin, the beloved idol who in 1961 led humankind's way into space. Credible rumors told of other catastrophes. The worst happened in 1960 when a launch-pad explosion of a huge experimental rocket killed at least forty officials and scientists, including the commander of the Strategic Rocket Forces. Costly in terms of rubles if not lives, tens of unmanned probes failed in their missions to the moon, Venus, and Mars.

With space as their showcase, at their pleasure the Soviets broke silence, often to announce their triumphs—*Sputnik 1* as the first man-made object in Earth orbit; the female husky Laika, the first spaceborne living creature; Yuri Gagarin, the first human to fly in space; Valentina Tereshkova, the first orbiting woman; Alexei Leonov, the first spacewalker . . . first after first after first, up the staircase to the stars.

Then in 1982 the door of secrecy opened, a crack—the crack I was squeezing through. The occasion was the twenty-fifth anniversary of the flight of Yuri Gagarin, a dazzling national triumph whose luster was undimmed by time and Gagarin's fiery plane crash in 1968. As part of the celebration, the space-confident Soviets would launch a three-man crew that included a glamorous French cosmonaut. In the geopolitics of the time, this successful wooing of a U.S. ally gave the Soviet space program another savory coup to celebrate.

For a closed society, the celebrating Soviets opened wide. Members of the Western press (properly screened) were invited to visit space facilities in the Moscow area. These included a look at their manned-flight Control Center and a live telecast of the Frenchman's launch, offering outsiders their first filtered glimpse of Baikonur. There would be tours of the prestigious Space Research Institute and of Star City, the campuslike training center for cosmonauts. Not Baikonur, of course, but good stuff.

MEANWHILE, I am not unaware that Soviet intransigence finds a faint echo here at the *Geographic*. My story has faced trouble from the time it was proposed. Part of the problem has been Garrett's understandable distaste for Soviet secrecy and censorship. Part has been the low survival rate of all story suggestions for the magazine. Many times I have marveled that enough proposals survive the selection process to fill each issue.

The main cause of this attrition is competition—too many story ideas competing for few publication slots. Each month scores of written story proposals bombard the editor, often with the proposer attached and demanding the editor's ear. More proposals pepper him from friends and friends of friends who have an idea or seek to publicize a cause. Yet each month's magazine carries only five or six titles. Theoretically, the paring process follows established, civilized procedures. In reality, success rewards a variable mix of merit and cunning.

Like the Soviet space program, the formal selection of topics for *Geographic* articles takes place behind closed doors, a practice all the editors approve of. This is not because the *Geographic* likes secrecy; far from it. Rather, it stems from a vulnerability to being scooped during the long lead time required to produce a *Geographic*-quality article. The magazine's insistence on thoroughness, accuracy, and quality control, together with the long press run, burden most articles with a full year's gestation period. A competing magazine such as *Smithsonian* can learn of an article in preparation and easily beat us to publication—a thunder-stealing experience we loathe.

Being scooped this way is especially vexing because so much thought and effort go into selecting articles in the first place. The process begins with the Planning Council, an elite editorial group that convenes monthly. The Planning Council meeting is a ritualized *Geographic* tradition.

At approximately 10:30 A.M., council members converge on the ninth floor, the domain of the editor, president, and top assistants, and proceed along a carpeted corridor to a large, windowless chamber known as the Control Center. During a normal workday the center's staff and customized electronics, presided over by senior assistant editor Lou Mazzatenta, dedicate themselves to what the *Geographic* calls scheduling—the important and complex task of keeping track of the hundred and sixty or so articles already approved and now in various stages of planning and preparation, many with writers and photographers working in the field.

This morning the center becomes the arena of the Planning Council. In attendance are about twenty associate and senior assistant editors and editor Bill Garrett. They form their chairs in a circle. The circle includes the editor, but he is not in charge and indeed is uncharacteristically quiet.

Eyes focus on Joseph R. Judge, the senior associate editor and Planning Council chairman. In 1980 Judge was Garrett's chief rival for editor, but he is now his righthand man. Like Garrett, Judge is smart, quick, and decisive. A gifted writer and true Irish poet, he is the idol of most of the writing staff. He also runs a good meeting—not difficult in an organization whose hallmark is civility.

Before each editor reposes a stack of photocopies half an inch high. These are the story suggestions, twenty-two of them this time. Some have been submitted by council members, others by junior staffers and outsiders. Scores of other proposals have been eliminated by prescreening. Now the council must narrow the twenty-two before them to a number approximating the half-dozen published each month. Even fewer may be approved if quality does not measure up. A majority vote in favor will send a proposal on to the editor, who usually accepts the council's advice.

"I trust you all did your homework," says Judge, glancing at the pile of Xeroxes, then scanning the circle for guilty faces; each editor is expected to read each proposal carefully, for informed selection is a serious responsibility. Judge turns to a list of the suggested topics. They fall into three main categories—geography, science, and culture—all of which are further subdivided by region or subject.

"Africa," he says, citing the leadoff area of the geography agenda. "A nice suggestion on Lesotho. Any interest?" This is my suggestion, inspired by my sister, who lives in South Africa and has talked often of this tiny black kingdom surrounded by the Republic.

Silence from the editors. They are aware that a number of other Africa subjects are in the mill. No need to push this low-interest article.

"Asia/Indian Ocean," recites Judge. He sifts through his stack and extracts a proposal. "We want to snap up this one," he opines, confident that others will agree. It is a suggestion that Paul Theroux write about his experiences and observations during a train trip across India. The editors approve by acclamation. Theroux's presence on the agenda reflects Garrett's goal of strengthening the magazine by aggressively enlisting free-lance writing talent.

No suggestions relate to the next two categories, Australia/Pacific and Canada/Arctic. "We need a Canada story," says Judge in a familiar lament. "I'll prod the area specialists," he says, referring to the staff members responsible for generating suggestions on Canada and the Arctic.

"Europe." Five proposals treat this topic-rich realm, and two win the editors' approval, on Italy and Catalonian Spain. Both were persuasively presented by their proposers, and both met four broad criteria for approval: rich photographic possibilities, high reader interest, importance as a subject, and correct timing. As a rule, an eligible subject should not have been covered by the magazine during the past decade.

Quiet greets the next four categories: Soviet Union, Mexico/Central America/Caribbean, Middle East, and South America/Atlantic. Reader interest in these regions is low, and the area specialists win few approvals.

Judge moves on. "Let's look at the U.S. proposals. I'd say they're pretty anemic." A buzz of agreement emanates from the circle; good American subjects are difficult to come by, and this batch doesn't cut it. One reason for the short supply is the high consumption rate. The magazine insists on publishing at least one U.S. subject in every issue; most Society members are Americans, and they like to read about their country. The chronic shortage also reflects the fact that not every American locale offers story

ingredients; the magazine is unlikely to base an article on the covered bridges of a Madison County. Judge good-naturedly jots a note
to schedule another meeting with area specialists.

The agenda advances to the science category. A proposal on
air pollution wins approval, as does one on ants; natural history
articles enjoy high reader appeal.

Now, a long three-pager. It proposes a comprehensive article
on the Soviet drive into space. The subject stirs interest, but there
is uncertainty and much debate: What about the secrecy?
Will there be photo possibilities? Who will write it? Judge asks
science editor Ken Weaver to answer these questions in a memo for
the next month's meeting. A good sign: Weaver is a master memo
writer. And at the next session he will carry the day, including his
proviso that the author be one of his science writers—Canby.

A final proposal completes the agenda. It flows out of the
Society's prestigious Committee for Research and Exploration,
which grants several million dollars a year to peer-reviewed appli-
cants in a wide variety of disciplines. These grants carry no obliga-
tion to produce a *Geographic* article. But many such projects generate article material, particularly those in which the researcher uses
photography in documenting findings. Identifying and shepherding
these researchers through the editorial process is the task of council member Mary G. Smith. Her subject this time is a tad frothy—
the world's largest flower, a rare parasitic colossus found only in
Indonesia. But Mary has lobbied beforehand among her colleagues,
and *Rafflesia arnoldii* will become a short article.

By 12:15 the council has done its work. Of the twenty-two
proposals considered, six have survived the editorial gauntlet and
await the editor's final and decisive vote.

Time for another monthly ritual. The editors troop across the
courtyard to Hubbard Memorial Hall, the first Society-built headquarters. Erected in 1903, it is named for the Society's first president, and decorated with dramatic paintings by N. C. Wyeth.
Round tables seating eight offer appetizers and wine, with waiters
poised to bring on the next courses. The editors relax, recounting

clever stories of experiences in strange lands, and work's petty frictions gradually melt away. The Planning Council luncheons are one of the perks I'll treasure when I succeed Weaver as science editor.

Garrett's approval of the Soviet space article automatically triggers photography director Robert E. Gilka to assign a cameraman. The nod goes to Otis Imboden, a veteran staff photographer possessing valuable experience with the American space program, but who with age seems to have slowed. Without powerful pictures, we will not produce a usable article. I worry.

For weeks I've plodded regularly to the Novosti Press Agency office at 1706 18th Street N.W. There, squirming in the small reception room, I've handed in visa application forms and added relevant information as requested by Messrs. Skripko, Isachenko, Tagashov, and Kamenev. Without comment the information disappears into what seems to be a bottomless bureaucratic maw, eliciting no reaction. I fester.

My office phone rings. Our visas are ready. Our Aeroflot and Moscow hotel reservations are booked. Now we're off for the Soviet Union, bolstered by Garrett's farewell suggestion: "Get your asses to Baikonur."

Often, on trips to sensitive lands during the Cold War, I wondered if I'd be approached by someone from the Central Intelligence Agency, asking if I would cooperate on some chore vital to the nation. And I thought of an answer: "No, regretfully no." This is not because I don't wish to help my country—far from it. It is because my saying yes could bring down catastrophe on the Geographic and possibly myself and my colleagues. To my relief, no CIA agent ever approached me. Nor did I hear from colleagues of any such approach to them. During coffee breaks one occasionally heard rumors of CIA contacts after World War II, of agents seeking Geographic photographs of sensitive areas. Espionage is exciting stuff, but best left to the pros.

Otis and I alight in Moscow, where melted snows have nurtured colorful window-box flowers and emerald lawns in public parks. The Cosmos Hotel is far from the Kremlin and Gum Department Store and older, fancier downtown hotels, but my room looks out on a towering titanium obelisk that supports a Vostok rocket such as lifted Yuri Gagarin into orbit. Sculpted at its base stand Konstantin E. Tsiolkovsky, Russia's pioneering genius of rocket science, and a smiling, dimpled Gagarin. His titanium foot is raised in a first step to the stars, and his upthrust thumb shines from the grasp of countless hands of worshipful Soviet citizens standing next to him to be photographed. It seems I am off to an auspicious start.

In the lobby of the Cosmos I meet Alexei Perezostchikov, the youthful and fluent interpreter who will accompany us during most of our visit. He is serious, sincere, and eager to excel.

In a chill drizzle, we board a bus with a knot of other journalists and their interpreters and head toward the cosmonaut training center known as Star City.

I take stock of my journalist colleagues: three from Japan, a Spaniard, a Swedish television crew, a Dane, an Indian, a Finn, a Pole, an Austrian, a Czech, a Yugoslav, an East German, and numerous Americans representing magazines, newspapers, television. The Soviets have a fine turnout for their space party.

Our bus leaves the highway and eases past military guards into a complex of low brick buildings set amid well-tended gardens and lawns. Star City is a privileged haven of material abundance and physical comfort. But for those who would be cosmonauts, it also can be a living hell, demanding total, relentless dedication and imposing grueling demands on mind and body.

We enter a small auditorium and take seats. Before us are three rather distracted-looking generals. They wear the dark green uniforms of the Air Force, and their tunics are resplendent with campaign ribbons and the gold stars awarded a Hero of the Soviet Union, the nation's highest honor. The harassed men confer with aides and whisper among themselves, their faces florid with concern; perhaps they are unaccustomed to giving press conferences before unpredictable Western journalists.

One general in particular arrests the eye. Balding and power-ful, slightly bent in his walk, he suddenly straightens, turns toward us, and fractures his face with a mighty grin. "We'll be ready in a minute," announces Alexei Leonov, obviously pleased with the English he learned while commanding the Soviet crew in the joint Apollo-Soyuz mission of 1975. Avid amateur painter, fun-loving extrovert, agile before a camera, Leonov is a consummate cosmo-naut who has brought glory to his country and thrice defied death, twice on a single mission.

The near-fatal flight, known as *Voskhod 2*, carried him and Pavel Belyayev aloft in 1965. Their secret assignment was breath-taking: Leonov would be the first human being to leave his orbiting spacecraft and become a human satellite—to walk in space.

Once in orbit, Leonov moves confidently. Carefully he pres-surizes his space suit, opens the *Voskhod*'s rear hatch, and thrusts himself into space with tether and television camera. His brief pic-ture footage records images of the spacecraft and the Earth below. All has gone as planned.

Victorious, he moves to reenter the spacecraft but cannot. His inflated spacesuit has become so cumbersome that he can't bend his body; he can't put his feet back inside. Heartbeat and breathing rates, telemetered to Mission Control, leap to near-panic levels, telling ground crews of his plight. Seizing his only option, Leonov boldly reduces his suit pressure to gain flexibility, virtually guaran-teeing that his blood will bubble with the bends. Now the tops of his toes catch the hatch opening. Slowly he eases inside. Death cheated—temporarily.

The cosmonauts prepare to land, near the Baikonur cosmo-drome from which they blasted off. Now their autopilot fails. They make another orbit, then maneuver manually. *Voskhod 2* lands in deep snow, and the men scramble from the hatch door—2,000 miles off course, in the deadly cold of the forested Ural Mountains. They hear growls and see dark shapes moving—a pack of wolves. The freezing cosmonauts scramble back aboard until dawn, when they venture out to start a fire. A full, frigid day will pass before search parties locate and extricate the shaken pair.

The two other generals also are celebrated cosmonauts. In 1969 Vladimir Shatalov commanded a flotilla of three spaceships flying in formation—an armada as has never again assembled in space. Georgi Beregovoy, Star City's commanding officer, won his nation's adulation by successfully piloting the new Soyuz space cap-sule after an earlier test crashed into the Urals during touchdown, killing colleague Vladimir Komarov.

Proudly the generals lead their rapt audience through Star City's training facilities, to see the simulators, to watch cosmonaut candidates training in the weightlessness of a huge water tank, to enter a Soyuz spacecraft and Salyut space station replica, to ogle a fearsome centrifuge that spins cosmonaut candidates at cruel veloc-ities to hone their fitness for the stresses of launch and landing.

One of the generals approaches and seizes my hand—beaming Leonov, bursting with good spirits, itching to speak more English. He likes the *Geographic*, the short piece I did on his joint mission with Americans, the Apollo-Soyuz project. Yes, he still paints; a big showing will take place next week on the twentieth anniversary of his historic spacewalk. No, he probably won't fly in space again; his terrestrial responsibilities are grounding him. But I suspect he wish-es to; never will I meet a cosmonaut or astronaut who doesn't yearn for another flight.

Outside the auditorium, a walkway leads past a parking lot toward a small space museum. I look at the parked cars. Many are Mercedes-Benzes, one of them Leonov's. The privations of Soviet life lap harmlessly at the insulated shores of Star City, where cos-monaut families shop in a well-stocked grocery store offering ample fresh fruits and meats, where no lines form for shoes.

Inside the museum, I see the memorabilia of Yuri Gagarin, more than 1,000 items: clothes, medals, tools, toiletries, photos as youth and celebrity. Yet these represent only a tenth of the relics of the hero's short life: His Volga auto, for example, slumbers in a glass sarcophagus in his hometown, now named Gagarin. In this officially atheist nation, some of people's spiritual needs seem to have transferred to their Soviet space heroes. Busts of cosmonauts stand everywhere; only Lenin's likeness appears more ubiquitously than Yuri Gagarin's.

Back in Moscow our hosts are ready with their main show, the televised launch of the three-man crew including the handsome French cosmonaut. We gather in the Novosti auditorium, before a large TV screen. The scene flickering before us is the Baikonur cosmodrome—the closest I will get to it. A great white-and-red rocket exhales wisps of steam like a chained dragon panting with suppressed power.

Another camera takes over, filming inside the Soyuz capsule atop the smoldering rocket. Jean-Loup Chrêtienne sits contentedly between his crewmates, wearing an armband labeled "France." Now we see the rocket again in the final seconds of countdown. Steadying gantries fall away like toppling trees. A mighty explosion envelops the rocket in flame, and it lifts on its pillar of fire. Throughout the tumult, calm comments flow incongruously from crew members inside the inferno. The launch takes place on time to the second. We journalists burst into applause.

Later, a press conference features the exuberant Leonov. Beside him, petite by comparison, sits Patrick Baudry, backup for Chrêtienne and like him a noble specimen of *Homo gallois*. Leonov and Baudry report that the Soyuz capsule has linked up with the space station *Salyut 7*, and all are on board and in good health.

Leonov genially asks for questions, and the journalists revert to type. "Why," asks one accusingly, "have no more women flown after Valentina Tereshkova's historic 'first'?" Rumors abound within the press corps about cosmonaut and Soviet chauvinism, about Tereshkova's alleged panic in space, about fellow cosmonauts' resentment of favoritism won by her charms. When we journalists first arrived, our Soviet hosts told us we could interview Tereshkova but not ask about her life as a former cosmonaut—only about her present role as national chairperson for women's rights.

Leonov is unruffled. Laughing contagiously, he explains: "Women in space want vacuum cleaners . . ." The journalists respond with a nervous laugh, worrying about political correctness, and Leonov grows more serious. Cosmonaut training is physically punishing and involves high risk. One cosmonaut in ten will die. It is not right to subject women to such rigors. But some are in training, and they will fly. I will recall Leonov's reservations four years later when the shuttle *Challenger* explodes, killing all seven crew members, and the nation's mourning focuses on teacher/astronaut Christa McAuliffe.

We disperse. As I leave the building I pause to observe a reporter from the authoritative weekly magazine *Aviation Week and Space Technology*. He is struggling mightily to persuade two Soviet officials to admit him to Baikonur. They are politely not budging, and he is taking defeat poorly. Admiring his gumption, I heed the futility of the request.

A last valuable visit caps the celebration agenda. A bus scoops up our dwindling ranks and takes us to the Space Research Institute. The institute's respected scientists have mounted the unmanned missions to the moon and to the inner planets: probes to Mars that largely failed, capsules to Venus that miraculously survived the searing acids of its toxic atmosphere and soft-landed to photograph the cratered landscape and analyze the soil. Otis Imbodin draws my attention to the institute's aged American computers, testifying to the Soviet lag in electronics.

I am struck by the institute's English-speaking director. Serious, intensely polite, possessing a sense of mission, academician Roald Z. Sagdeev has insisted that his scientists collaborate as closely as possible with foreign counterparts, especially Americans. His passion for world peace warms the cordiality with which he greets us journalists and responds to our queries. A decade later he will marry Susan Eisenhower, granddaughter of the former president and herself a crusader for world understanding, and they will pursue their mutual concern from the Washington, D.C., area.

Most of the invited journalists have now left Moscow, but Otis and I stay. Our hosts are opening doors especially for *National Geographic*, permitting glimpses of important, little-known space agencies scattered about Moscow. We retire to the Cosmos Hotel and await our interpreter's summons.

The calls come, in a trickle—one visit today, none tomorrow, two the next day, but all friendly and informative. We discover a quaint custom: If an interview ends at the close of a workday, our host may reach in his desk for a bottle of vodka and order a plate of sliced cucumbers, and we set about thawing the Cold War.

A Sunday arrives, sunny and warm, and we hire a car with a driver named Viktor and an Intourist interpreter, Marina. Our goal is the small town of Vladimir, near Moscow, where in the spring of 1968 a plume of smoke curling above the forest told numbed Soviets that Yuri Gagarin had crashed and died. "When people learned of it," recalls Marina, "they quietly began filling Red Square, each carrying a flower."

During the drive, Marina dwells on Gagarin: "He had a great spirit." Then, mindful of her American companions, she tells a story. On a Moscow street a decade earlier she had recognized the American astronaut Vance Brand, who had rendezvoused in space with Leonov in the joint Apollo-Soyuz mission and was visiting after the flight. He had politely stopped to talk with her and her friends. In the car she opened her bag and brought out a card with Brand's autograph.

We pass tiny, rustic towns with complicated names and approach the crash site. It's a tranquil place. A long avenue of spruce and birch hides whistling birds. Ferns and profusions of blue lupine line the macadam road. A small monument quotes Tsiolkovsky: "Don't stop. Always go ahead. The universe belongs to mankind." Marina asks Viktor to stop the car; we get out and pick lupine.

Marina translates a sign at the shrine's gate: "The world bowed to the human being." We join others at the monument. A low marble wall describes a circle sixty feet in diameter. Within it at one side, a great marble slab rises spaceward. Marina places her flowers at the foot of the wall, and we follow suit. Only birdsong and the shuffling of feet break the silence.

Since arriving we've heard of an intriguing space temple, housed in a crypt beneath the titanium obelisk across from our hotel. On the final day of our visit, the *Geographic*'s good name

gains us entry. In company with the curator, we enter a dimly
lighted foyer and slip sanitized booties over our shoes. A heavy door
swings open, and we cross into the temple's first room, dominated
by a large stained-glass window; the hush is reverential. A metallic
frieze pictures Yuri Gagarin returning from space to greet the joyous
earthlings he left behind—a depiction, the curator murmurs,
symbolizing all mankind. Other chambers open beyond, awash in
moving light and relics of space triumphs. Gagarin's many medals
gleam like jewels on tufted cushions. Spotlights play on venerated
items of space hardware: moon capsules, Venus probes, Leonov's
space suit. We have penetrated the cathedral of the cult of cosmo-
nautics. A far cry from India's Rat Temple, yet similar in the devo-
tion it represents.

Our hosts have shown us much of the Soviet space program.
Otis has taken pictures—precious few, I fear, but we will see. We
pay the substantial departure fees levied by the dollars-shy Soviets
and board another Aeroflot plane.

A SIDE TRIP interrupts my journey home. I want to meet a master of space espionage, a Brit whose hobby is spying on Soviets
in space.

In spontaneous response to Soviet secrecy, around the world a
cadre of clever observers has independently embraced the challenge
of baring every Soviet move in space—each launch, each satellite
maneuver, each radio communication with space-station occupants. One of the leading figures is Geoffrey Perry, who lives an
hour north of London by fast train.

I join Perry in Kettering at the boys' school where he teaches
physics. He shows me the radios and shrublike rooftop antennas
with which he tunes in to the beeps of newly launched Soviet satellites. Each type of satellite, he explains, communicates via a distinctive language of beeps, and on meaningful frequencies. By
interpreting those beeps and frequencies, he can deduce a satellite's
mission: weather observation, communications, earth resources
mapping, or spying on the West, the satellites' primary task.

He has also deduced more. By intercepting the beeps of one suspicious Soviet satellite and calculating its orbital track from routine reports by the U.S. Space Command, he has discovered it was launched from a secret cosmodrome hidden in forest north of Moscow. Sixteen more years will pass before the Soviets acknowledge the existence of Plesetsk, the world's busiest spaceport.

Aware that other space sleuths share his interest, Geoffrey Perry has formed the worldwide Kettering Group of amateur Soviet space analysts. Some, like Perry, seek out satellite radio signals; others comb the most obscure Soviet publications for clues carelessly published. The fruits of the tenacious surveillance of these amateurs, freely shared with the world press, will provide valuable information for my final article.

Back in my office, I set about writing an article. I develop a lead about the three cosmonaut generals at Star City. For an inherently slow writer, I feel I'm making fair headway.

Then the Soviets do the unforgivable. Over the eastern Soviet Union their fighter planes shoot down a South Korean airliner, Flight 007, that strayed off course. All 269 on board perish. President Ronald Reagan denounces the downing as a "horrifying act of violence." People around the world are outraged. I cannot write—the *Geographic* cannot publish—a dispassionate article about a rogue Superpower. I shelve my manuscript and reams of research material.

For two years the subject sits, abandoned but not forgotten.

IT IS A TUESDAY MORNING at headquarters when a knock comes at my office door. In steps Society vice president Leonard J. Grant, a friend of long standing and a versatile administrator, whose steadying hand and diplomatic skills have helped guide the Society through its decades of tremendous growth. Grant served as aide-de-camp to Melville Grosvenor during that heady era of innovation and expansion. On occasion Grosvenor's exuberance led to misunderstandings among others—jobs seemingly offered, magazine assignments seemingly approved, projects seemingly backed. Grosvenor often needed extricating. Grant's tact and superior writing skills had helped in these difficulties.

Grant had been a special friend to me. A year and a half after I'd started work at the Society, escalating differences with the chief of the Book Division had led the latter to discharge me, giving me six weeks' notice to relocate. Learning of this, Len arranged for me to continue on as a book writer but outside the Book Division. From there I'd followed the path to the present.

Now Len has come with another glittering offer: Would I like to become a member of the Cosmos Club? As a former president, he, Len, would be glad to sponsor me. I snap up the offer. Not only is the Cosmos Club one of Washington's premier social/scientific institutions, offering a stimulating blend of camaraderie and academically oriented entertainment; it also was the birthplace of the National Geographic Society, and the two organizations still enjoy a close relationship.

On January 10, 1888, club member Gardiner Greene Hubbard and five other gentlemen, all eminent scientists and explorers, issued an invitation to colleagues and friends to gather "for the purpose of considering the advisability of organizing a society for the increase and diffusion of geographical knowledge." They would meet three days hence at the Cosmos Club, then located just north of the White House. Then as now, the club was a gracious social focus for the elite of American science.·

By eight o'clock on that cold, raw Friday night, thirty-three men had arrived, warmed themselves before the fire, and taken their places at a large round mahogany table for coffee, brandy, and discussion. Their callings were varied—a banker, educators, lawyer/businessman Hubbard—but the majority were scientists or explorers attached to government agencies or the military. Several wore the wounds of battle or their professions: geologist John Wesley Powell had lost his right arm in the battle of Shiloh and risked his life exploring 900 miles of the Colorado River; meteorologist Edward E. Hayden had lost his leg in a landslide; Brigadier

General Adolphus Greely had been stranded in the Arctic for three years, lost eighteen of his twenty-seven-man party, and himself was near death when rescued.

The time was propitious for their plan. Belief in science—in a beneficent science—was sweeping America. Further, much of the world remained unexplored in its details; neither pole had been reached. In this meeting and another soon afterward, again at the Cosmos Club, the thirty-three founders adopted a resolution that the National Geographic Society be organized, "on as broad and liberal a basis . . . as is consistent with its own well-being and the dignity of the science it represents."

In another week a committee had drafted a constitution and elected Gardiner Greene Hubbard president. His introductory address, enunciating the Society's goals, set a tone for the future: "that we may all know more of the world upon which we live."

His election set the Society upon another, enduring path. Hubbard had financed experiments of inventor Alexander Graham Bell, who had married Hubbard's daughter. Bell succeeded Hubbard as Society president and, equally important, hired as editor young Gilbert H. Grosvenor, who soon married the Bells' daughter, Elsie. The Society's tradition of dynastic succession was firmly established. Gil Grosvenor, my contemporary, is the great-great-grandson of Gardiner Greene Hubbard.

AT THE MAGAZINE, two years roll by after the collapse of our Soviet space story, and I crank out two more articles, on satellites and El Niño, and edit several more. But I haven't forgotten our project. How could I, with C. P. Vick materializing periodically at my office door?

Charles Patrick Vick, a nuclear engineer by trade, has straight, black hair, wears a white shirt and black suit, and walks with a glide. C. P. has a driving passion: to crack the secrets of the Soviet space program by a relentless sifting of small clues. And he has a second passion: to inform the world of his discoveries. *National Geographic,* he reasons, is the proper vehicle for informing the world. Thus his gentle nagging.

Red flags fly all over editorial offices when such zealots appear. Ninety-nine times out of a hundred, they are not to be taken seriously; most proselytizers are quirky, flaky, and time-consuming. The *Geographic*, with its enormous influence and downtown D.C. location, naturally attracts more than its share. Caution reigned when C. P. first laid siege to the editorial offices.

Implacably persistent, C. P. also is warm and mannerly and thus difficult to rebuff. And his huge artist's briefcase holds hypnotizing revelations: detailed diagrams of Soviet rockets, of hidden cosmodromes, of fascinating space vehicles known only by their Russian names.

Meanwhile we've checked out C. P.'s credibility with other members of the Kettering Group and, in an oblique manner, with an intelligence arm of the Pentagon. Not all responses are favorable; some complain that his drawings are too creative, showing more detail than he could have gleaned from available sources. On the other hand, he has been a valued protégé of Charles Sheldon, respected Soviet space authority of the Library of Congress. Even the sharpest critics concede that C. P. Vick is a walking database, uniquely equipped to interpret the unlikeliest clue. His discoveries are legend. Unearthing a sketch of an unusual launchpad in an obscure Soviet text, he accurately derived from it the configuration of a new secret rocket. A glance at a Soviet photo of a lunar capsule told him it was designed to carry cosmonauts—refuting Soviet denials that they were in a moon race. C. P. is for real.

Before long, associate art director Jan Adkins has transmuted C. P.'s sterile line drawings into a stunning double-page lineup of ten secret Soviet rockets—a panorama guaranteed to knock the socks off the entire Politburo.

With time, horror at the downing of Flight 007 has slowly faded. Periodically C. P. glides in and out of my office and that of picture editor Jon Schneeberger, lobbying us in his low-key way (the artist, less patient, has by this time closed his door to C. P.). Simultaneously Schneeberger is assembling potent pictures of

Soviet space activities: shuttle and satellite images of their cosmodromes; TASS photos of nonsensitive rocket launches, capsule
landings, Venus probes, and crew activities in the Salyut space stations; and assorted shots from the Kettering Group. Schneeberger
and I take pleasure in rebuilding a launchpad for our article—a pre-
rogative of all writers, editors, and photographers who believe in
their subject.

It's time to repersuade Garrett about the merit of our cause.

Happily for us, the cosmonauts themselves do the persuading.
The Soviet space station named *Salyut 7,* temporarily abandoned
during a crew change, loses electrical power and becomes an orbiting iceberg, its interior coated with rime like a leaky refrigerator.
Worse, it is tumbling in a decaying orbit, making it an almost
impossible docking target. Then in the summer of 1985 two daring
cosmonauts miraculously board the wallowing hulk and nurse it
back to life. The space community is agog with the feat. The Soviet program deserves reporting.

Garrett agrees. This time I'll return to Moscow with an eager
and dynamic camera bearer, Steve Raymer, my fellow traveler on
the food/famine article. We'll attempt to interview the now-
legendary commander of the *Salyut 7* salvage job, Colonel Vladimir
Dzanibekov. And yes, we assure Garrett, we'll do our best to get to
Baikonur.

The Soviets will have none of it. We get the silent treatment.
Week after week Raymer and I trek the six blocks to the Novosti
office near DuPont Circle to present our case. Our requests vanish
into thin air. Soviet foot-dragging on our earlier visit now seems
like Open House. We are unwelcome and don't know why.

At Garrett's suggestion, I write a letter for his signature to the
head of Novosti in Moscow. In it Garrett suggests that during my
proposed visit to Moscow I not only pursue our space interest but
also negotiate a number of other editorial matters the magazine has
pending with the Soviets: articles on the Bering Sea, on wool, and
on Ukraine. By this time Ken Weaver has retired as science editor
and Garrett has named me to succeed him, giving me reasonable
credentials for such a mission. This is a heady time. Earlier this year

Susan has been appointed director of the National Geographic Library. We are a fortunate family within the larger family of the *Geographic*.

The logjam begins to loosen. In due time come cool but encouraging indications that Raymer and I may soon be granted Moscow visas.

Editorial preparations are in order. It is *Geographic* policy that the words and pictures we intend to publish be shown in advance to the involved party, in this case the Soviet space establishment via Novosti. This courtesy contributes greatly to the trust and cooperation accorded the magazine, as well as to its accuracy. As our plans jell I begin gathering these materials: the article layout, copies of photos likely to run, and, with mounting nervousness, the provocative artwork for the article. Along with the lineup of secret rockets are detailed drawings of other highly secretive projects: the soon-to-be Soviet shuttle and the heavy booster that will launch it; a futuristic configuration of the newly launched *Mir* space station, a map locating the three Soviet launch sites; and satellite images of the major ones, Baikonur and Plesetsk, with maps identifying secret launchpads and other forbidden features. To my way of thinking, the Soviets can only regard the bearer of such sensitive materials (me) as a deranged CIA operative, come to the USSR to check his homework.

Arriving travel-weary and wary at the Moscow airport, Raymer and I both are worried. Raymer shepherds his eight bags of cameras, which always inspire suspicions of high espionage. I watch with dread as the clearance official finishes poking through my packed clothes and turns to my thick sheaf of documents. The airport is chilly, but I am sweating. All five of this guy's senses, I know, are honed to detect the most minor no-no, such as smuggled papers and pornography. What will he do when . . .

He flips through my notebooks, their blank pages yearning to be filled. He checks out my three novels. He reaches the artwork. He stares at the future shuttle and the fearsome launch booster. A redness suffuses his face and neck. He digests the *Mir* space station, with its futuristic modules, and ponders the satellite images of the secret cosmodromes. Now most of his blood supply resides in the head area, as red as a bowl of borscht. He turns a final page—and ten secret rockets leap out. With superb self-control and crimson head he stares at nothing while reflecting, I fancy, on the gulag. Without a word he waves me through. I muse on whether he will sleep that night, wondering if he has admitted an enemy of the state.

The Cosmos Hotel again, with the titanium Yuri Gagarin outside my window. A message awaits: Tomorrow Raymer and I will appear before Aleksandr Makarov, chief of Novosti's North America Section. I met Makarov on my last visit, and he is a good man. Earlier he spent five years in Washington, came to know the Geographic, and duck-hunted with Bob Gilka, the photography director. Makarov will decide our success or failure.

We are punctual, and so is he. Beside him sit two impassive assistants. Makarov clearly has something on his mind. His eyes fix on mine. He says, in effect: The Geographic obviously doesn't understand the realities within which he and Novosti work. The Geographic asks for, and apparently expects, enormous cooperation from the Soviets: Four articles are in train at once, on space, wool, the Bering Sea, Ukraine. Novosti doesn't have the staff to work with all these projects at once, to make the appropriate contacts and so on. Worse, sometimes our writers and photographers slip into the country behind Novosti's back, on tourist visas, and then expect his help. Time, Life, and other magazines do this also. Novosti can only refuse to cooperate with such miscreants.

His eyes drill into mine: The Geographic space story has caused particular problems. Three years earlier Novosti made unprecedented arrangements for me to visit the space agencies. Busy officials blocked out valuable time. Yet not one word about the Soviet space program appeared in the magazine. The officials were disappointed, sorely disappointed, and the blame fell on Novosti. That is why we were ignored when we first asked to return. The fact that we are now here rests on Novosti's trust that after this visit, a space article will appear. With his case presented, Makarov's eyes relax.

I reflect on the fact that Novosti's workload results largely from the encumbrances imposed by Soviet secrecy and the lack of freedom granted journalists. I reflect that they might have opted not to shoot down Flight 007. I reflect too that these transgressions are not the fault of this forthright individual, and that Steve and I must either work within the system or not work at all. I also know a truth I cannot explain to this decent man: I cannot promise that this time we *will* produce a Soviet space story. Only Bill Garrett can promise that, and Garrett can play hardball: no Baikonur, no article. But I must act as though I can promise Makarov, or everything will fall through.

I thank him for his explanations and imply that I agree with all he has said and asked. He accepts my inability to be more specific and sits back, satisfied. His assistants will talk with me later about the other *Geographic* articles. Coffee appears.

The discussion moves on. The chairman of the board of Novosti wants to discuss an exchange of cultural and conservation films. The Novosti first vice chairman is willing to meet, as is the deputy administrator. For the millionth time I am appreciative of the *Geographic's* respect and influence.

I have a question. What about interviewing General Dzanibekov, the cosmonaut who saved the space station? Prospects are good, says Makarov with obvious pride in what he can deliver. The general is in the city and hopes to be available.

I am on a roll: "And Baikonur?"

My host calls upon his best American slang: "Not a prayer."

The morrow is Gagarin Day, celebrating the anniversary of the hero's birth in 1934. A main observance is taking place at our obelisk, right outside the hotel. In a cold drizzle, Steve Raymer and I join hundreds of rapt spectators.

Scores of schoolchildren are massed at the base of the obelisk. Boys and girls wear similar outfits: white shirts, red sashes, gray trousers or skirts. Each carries a flowing red banner. Their vibrant colors defy the gray day and give them the look of an animated bed of flowers.

The rain increases, but the crowd stands firm. Eight uniformed cosmonauts appear, scorning raincoats, bearing flowers and two stout linden trees. Among them I identify Vladimir Dzanibekov, his hat agleam with the new gold braid of a recently promoted general. The two tree-bearers lower the lindens into holes and shovel in the soggy earth, then carefully tamp it with shiny black shoes.

A phone call arrives from Makarov. Cosmonaut Dzanibekov will meet us the next day at eleven. Bring any artwork we wish to show. I call a cheered Garrett and tell him of our progress with the space story and the three other articles.

At Novosti Raymer and I convene around a long wooden table with Makarov, three assistants, an Air Force colonel, our interpreter, and General Vladimir Dzanibekov. He is a superb specimen: sensuous face resembling Yul Brynner's, broad shoulders, narrow hips, quiet but commanding manner. Only the American astronaut John Young matches his achievement of five rocket rides into the void. It is Dzanibekov's fifth flight—to salvage the frozen derelict Salyut 7—that has brought me to Moscow.

Speaking in measured Russian interspersed with halting English, Dzanibekov tells his story:

Ascending from Baikonur in the space capsule Soyuz 13, for two days he and crewmate Viktor Savinykh pursue the lifeless space station. Catching up, they slowly circle the station and realize the magnitude of their problem. Salyut 7 is tumbling in all three planes, posing a nightmarish docking challenge. Docking will be like threading a tumbling needle.

Dzanibekov describes taking control from the navigating computer ("after all, a machine is only a machine") and moving in, Savinykh calling out ranges to the station. They find themselves blinded, dazzled by the fierce sun of space. They must wait until the two spacecraft orbit into the nighttime of Earth's shadow.

Carefully Dzanibekov aligns the Soyuz to rotate precisely with the twenty-two-ton Salyut. A misjudgment can be fatal; even in normal times dockings pose risks. Ever so slowly he closes in . . . only feet away . . . inches . . . capsule nose into Salyut's docking assembly . . . snap! Docked, in a brilliant feat of maneuvering.

Now the cosmonauts face more questions crucial to the mission. Has the dead station lost its internal atmospheric pressure? If not, has the air been poisoned by an electrical fire? Either event will end the mission. Dzanibekov opens the valve connecting the two space vehicles. *Salyut* has maintained pressure—and the air is good.

Good, but bitter cold. Following the beams of their flashlights into *Salyut,* the cosmonauts are in a spaceborne Siberia. Ice clings to instruments and control panels, blocks the windows. Frozen mold from past occupations covers the walls. Their thermometers measure only to zero Celsius, and *Salyut* is colder. To find out how much, the men spit on the walls, time the freezing—ten seconds—and radio the finding to Mission Control. Word comes back that their workplace is ten below zero.

The cosmonauts retreat into the *Soyuz* and bundle up in fur-lined clothes "like babies in a Moscow winter." Fingers aching, feet numb, they set about recharging *Salyut*'s batteries by replacing connections to the solar panels. With each brief nighttime in Earth's frigid shadow they huddle in *Soyuz,* now fast losing its own heat because of a need to save fuel for the return. Without ventilation, the carbon dioxide of their exhalations collects in toxic clouds about their heads. Brains and muscles numb like their limbs. But the first battery begins recharging.

Without stopping for sleep the men fight cold and exhaustion as they work on successive batteries. After twenty-four hours, six of eight show recharge. They trip the power switch. Lights flood *Salyut.* Ventilators whir. Although days of punishing toil remain before the station is de-iced and dried out, *Salyut* is saved. Dzanibekov will remain aloft 110 days, Savinykh 167.

The cosmonaut grows quiet. He doesn't mention his return, to a tumultuous hero's welcome. Not since American astronauts repaired the stricken *Skylab* in 1973 have spacefarers performed such a feat—one that transcends national rivalries and rightly earns global acclaim.

Now a cloud of tension forms above our Novosti table. It is show-and-tell time. Raymer and I spread out the article layout, the copies of likely photos, the satellite images of the secret cosmodromes, the damnably detailed artwork of the secret rockets. A hush falls. We have their attention. Will they challenge our drawings of their secret hardware? Deny it exists? If they do, will we still have the confidence to publish?

The official reaction will come from Dzanibekov. In a difficult spot, he represents his country well. If he challenges the details of a spacecraft, rocket, or cosmodrome, he acknowledges it exists. If he denies they exist, he embarrasses himself and his nation by clinging to a secrecy that already is shredded. As he sorts through the piles, he astutely elevates the discussion to one of national policy.

"We have a tradition not to talk about things that have not yet been done," he explains through the interpreter while looking at the shuttle painting. "If we start publishing target dates, it will affect the pace and safety of our development." He moves into the valid question of a shuttle's practicality, which the Soviets doubt. "Today, we do not need a shuttle; we do not need to bring much down from space. We can send men and materials up safely and economically in vehicles that will be used only once. They are made on the production line, and are reliable and cheap. We do not wish to spend all our money on a shuttle." Throughout he is calm, courteous, and obviously fascinated. I suspect he may be impressed with the thoroughness of our exposé.

Our mutual formality has been accomplished. The Geographic has submitted its material; Soviet officialdom has neither approved nor disapproved. Both sides are satisfied. A done deal.

I have one more item of business before we adjourn. I know that Dzanibekov, like Leonov, is a talented amateur artist. Will he prepare a painting for National Geographic, depicting a scene from the salvage operation? We will pay at the going rate. Yes, he likes the idea. But he is so busy—what is our deadline? Next June, months away. A pause . . . agreed!

Raymer and I are out of there. Just as Dzanibekov salvaged a space station, we have—we hope—salvaged an article, thanks to the doors that open for the Geographic. In the cocoon of our departing Aeroflot I write my new lead for the article, based on the personal account of a remarkable cosmonaut.

Vladimir Dzanibekov does not find time to complete a painting. But he does come through with a pleasing pen-and-ink drawing of Savinykh and himself in fur-lined suits repairing rime-coated *Salyut 7,* which graces a page and a half of the October 1986 issue. And I am sure we paid him generously.

W ITH THE SHRINKING of the Soviet Union to Russia-size and the final thawing of the Cold War, U.S.-Russian cooperation has blossomed. As I write this, an American astronaut is orbiting with two cosmonauts in a rickety but functional *Mir* space station, and the two nations are working with others on a long-delayed international space hub.

It is as it should be. Virtually every argument for space exploration cries out for space cooperation. Claims of sovereignty fail in space, much as they fail in uninhabitable Antarctica. Nationalistic space rivalries, one hopes, expired with the Cold War; we do not need a Mars race. Nor of course can we afford it.

As science editor I worked with astronaut Michael Collins on his 1988 *Geographic* article, "Mission to Mars." Mike Collins is big medicine: unflappable pilot of the flagship *Columbia* on the *Apollo 11* moon-landing mission, first curator of the National Air and Space Museum, valued trustee of the National Geographic Society, member of the NASA Advisory Council, author of four thoughtful and exciting books about the space age.

In preparing his article and a closely related book, Collins consulted with cosmonauts and Soviet policymakers, including Roald Sagdeev. All agreed that space logic dictates joint missions, whether the goal is distant Mars or the nearby space suburb of Earth orbit.

Mike Collins did something else as he prepared that article I edited. It pleased Editor Garrett immensely, though it did nothing for me.

He got to Baikonur.

Chapter 8

EARTHQUAKE
COUNTRY

Like many Americans, I switch
on the television each morning while downing breakfast, looking
for any late-breaking news and the relevant sports scores. On this
October morning in 1989, I tune in especially to catch results from
the third game of the World Series, scheduled for last night at Candlestick Park. Maybe the Giants bounced back against the Oakland
Athletics, as they were supposed to in this all-California slugfest.

There's no sports news on the screen. Instead, a mighty fire
leaps above a nighttime cityscape that anchorman Dan Rather
identifies as San Francisco. Broken gas mains are feeding the con-
flagration in a part of the city known as the Marina District. Thank
God there is no wind, such as fanned the flames that devoured the
city after the great seismic tragedy of 1906.

The TV image shifts to a jumble of crumpled concrete and
flashing ambulances. Rather reports that scores of motorists have
been crushed beneath fallen spans of Interstate 880 across the bay in

Oakland. He is bivouacked there with his producers and technical team, gloomily recounting the extrication of each mangled corpse.

Another earthquake has bludgeoned California. Registering 7.1 on the Richter scale, centered south of San Francisco in the Santa Cruz Mountains, beneath a dark peak named Loma Prieta. Strong enough to ring the planet like a gong and set seismometers dancing as far away as Burma. Nature's wrecking ball.

I plod to the bedroom and stuff a carry-on with clothes and toilet kit. As science editor I am also the Geographic's unofficial disasters editor, and I know I must hightail it to California. I have mixed feelings about going, but I'll have time to sort them out on the plane.

Fortunately I've prepared for such an event. The magazine's response to the quake is already in motion. Two years earlier I had sat down with Tom Kennedy, Gilka's successor as director of photography, to draw up a plan for a calamity we knew was inevitable: a major earthquake in California. In the event of a horrendous temblor, I would immediately head west if I was in town; if I was on assignment somewhere, one of my three science writers would take my place. At the same time Kennedy's free-lance and contract photographers living in California would swing into action. Because all communication lines would probably be severed, we would headquarter in a designated photographer's house, in Marin County if the quake struck the Bay Area, and in Santa Monica if it hit Los Angeles. I carried their addresses and phone and fax numbers in my wallet, along with the National Geographic credit card that could buy me a plane ticket in an instant. In addition, photographer James A. Sugar had shot numerous structures considered likely to fail in a quake, giving us a file for "before and after" presentations.

This morning I have time to head into the Geographic, where everyone is talking about the quake. News reports speculate that as many as a hundred people are dead, and billions of dollars of property destroyed. A span of the San Francisco–Oakland Bay Bridge has fallen, severing the only direct surface link between downtown and the East Bay. The San Francisco airport is shut down, its radar consoles hurled through control tower walls. Santa Cruz, Los Gatos, and Watsonville are devastated. Among California quakes of this century, this temblor ranks second only to the 1906 disaster.

Breaking news! Editor Bill Garrett is in his element; here is an outlet for the zesty journalistic aggressiveness he normally represses. "Tom," he observes cheerily, "I guess you know you're on your way."

For most media, breaking news is something you'll publish quickly—instantaneously "live" if you're television, next day if you're a daily newspaper. For the *Geographic*, a "rush" article still gestates for six months or so. This is because the *Geographic* article must encompass not merely the drama and damage of the disaster but its entire meaning: how it happened and why (the science), the physical and psychological effects, and the outlook for the future. Photographers require time to identify and shoot meaningful targets; artists must interview scientists for their graphics (in this case the quake's causes and mechanics); an illustrations editor must orchestrate all this and assemble worthwhile photos from amateurs on the scene. Simultaneously the roving writer records observations and quotes that he can later distill into a comprehensive word picture of the disaster. And then there is the painstaking checking for accuracy and the month on the presses to print 10 million yellow-bordered issues.

But even with a lead time of months, hours make a difference this morning. The reason is that disasters, particularly abrupt ones like earthquakes and flash floods, can quickly lose their immediacy: fires are extinguished, roads cleared, injured evacuated, bodies extricated. For me, time's a-wasting.

Winging west to San Jose, whose airport is miraculously undamaged, I have six hours of air time, sufficient for psyching up for the only unpleasant part of my wonderful job. I know that I'm simply not pushy enough for disaster journalism; I lack the visceral impulse, the journalistic toughness necessary for ambulance-chasing. I know that if some brassy reporter poked a microphone or notepad in my face at a time of anguish, I'd resent the exploitation of my misfortune to sell more newspapers or improve TV ratings. We journalists joke cynically that "bad news is good news," but I want no part of it. Better to dance to a quake aftershock than to see in a victim's eyes that he or she regards you as one of the paparazzi.

At times like this, when I'm reluctantly disaster-bound, I often ask: Why does a positive magazine like the *Geographic* cover natural disasters? There's a good answer, especially if you're a science editor. Disasters, with their compelling human element, provide matchless vehicles for teaching science. Natural disasters are the punctuation marks of geography. A person who understands hurricanes or El Niños understands a lot about meteorology and climate. Similarly, coverage of a biological disaster such as diabetes or cystic fibrosis brings the magical world of cells and DNA into focus. A person who understands quakes or volcanic eruptions understands the elegant geologic concept of plate tectonics—why we have mountains, ocean trenches, and continents.

Until tectonic theory emerged in the 1960s, Californians could not explain the seismic violence that wracks their state, were not aware that beneath their feet the Pacific and North American plates are grinding past each other edge to edge, fracturing the state with the 750-mile-long San Andreas Fault and its countless side faults.

That tortured terrain has been one of my beats. My first magazine article described the fault as brought into focus by the destructive 1971 San Fernando quake. A little-known side fault had ruptured, killing 64, collapsing two hospitals and five overpasses, and nearly breaching an earthen dam whose escaping torrent could have killed 80,000. Traveling the fault's length, I've seen the colossal power that hurls up mountains and grinds others to rubble.

That early assignment posed a professional challenge. The photographer, James P. Blair, was a devout liberal, and I am more conservative; I found his agenda squishy and he found mine barbaric. Frequently thrown together at headquarters during coffee or lunch, we baited each other, intending to joke our way out but often ending up snarling. Suddenly we were locked together on assignment as tightly as the two tectonic plates grinding beneath us, with the same likelihood of sparking destructive tremors.

In the first days of quake coverage, we reacted warily, both knowing a flare-up would be ruinous. Fortunately, both of us were absorbed in the awesome fault zone we walked, drove, and flew over. Slowly we relaxed our guard. Invisibly Jim's natural kindness flowed over me; my approval of conscientious effort embraced him. Out of quake country came an enduring friendship.

As the continent unfurls below me on this trip, I'm still moping over my impending chore. But I admit there's a bright side too. People who've suffered catastrophe are usually grateful for sympathy—grateful that the world cares, or appears to care, about their plight. Of the hundreds of victims I've forced myself to interview—survivors of quakes, floods, droughts, hurricanes, tornadoes, slides, blizzards, fires, famine, war—most have willingly responded to questions, and many, once started, had trouble stopping. This willingness, perhaps helped by the *Geographic*'s wholesome reputation, is my salvation in a task I don't like.

I also remind myself that disasters seem to awaken our unsuspected strengths. Few victims are pathetic or despairing. A quake or El Niño may erase their past and destroy their planned future, yet they stand unbowed beside the ruins, ready to rebuild. I'm never more proud of our species than when I see this resilience and fortitude standing tall before calamity.

Another thought disturbs me on this flight: Am I leaving a potential quake behind? In recent years, top-level tension has been growing at headquarters. In effect, a National Geographic Fault exists, a seismic zone dividing the offices of the Society's two strongest forces: Chairman and President Gil Grosvenor and Editor Bill Garrett. Once the closest of friends, the two have grown increasingly critical of each other, dropping remarks that show a deteriorating ability to cooperate. We junior editors naturally side with Garrett. But Gil, who is the ultimate arbiter, calls the quakes at National Geo . . .

THE NEXT MORNING, mist lifts from the shattered Marina District as I join a long line awaiting breakfast at a relief center at the Marina Middle School. A few blocks away, smoke still rises from the great fire shown on TV. All around, houses are bent, broken, and collapsed. Snatches of overhead conversation dwell on the city's plan to issue a list identifying houses as safe or unsafe. The latter cannot be entered, must be evacuated, could be torn down. All homeowners dread the possibility that they might not be allowed, even at their own risk, to tiptoe inside and snatch up their most cherished papers and photographs. Oddly, with communication lines shattered, Marina residents know less about their future than do people thousands of miles away tuning in to TV and radio. Enlightenment will arrive at noon, when the mayor visits the district to talk about disaster relief efforts.

Standing in the line has enabled me to size up the people here and figure out whom to interview. The attractive couple just ahead look promising. I wait for a lull in their chatter. "Hi. Do you live nearby? I'm from *National Geographic*."

They exude friendliness. Aida works at I. Magnin and does television commercials for Pacific Bell. Craig appears in TV ads for the National Fish and Seafood Board: "Eat fish twice a week." The quake has smashed their stereo, TV, and furnishings and brought down some plaster. "We don't care, because we're glad to be alive. For a couple of spoiled Marina brats, we're doing okay."

I write down their addresses, but this couple's story will never make its way into print: They haven't suffered enough to produce good copy. But their politeness gives me confidence that I'll be similarly welcomed by others.

I leave the line and go out onto Fillmore Street. Throngs of people are carrying armfuls of clothes and suitcases from evacuated homes to stay at shelters or with friends. To the left stands a monstrous pile of debris crowned by a bathtub; thirty-six hours ago it was a frame apartment building. Nearby a Salvation Army van dispenses food to all comers. Purposeful city and utility inspectors remove sidewalk covers to turn off gas mains, and water engineers search for ruptured pipes.

Down on Marina Boulevard, million-dollar mansions stand intact next to others that are now worthless ruins. The mayor's noon appearance will be staged at the flagpole on the green that extends from the boulevard to the bay. At 10:30 hundreds are already gathered, craving information about their houses.

Returning to the ravaged side streets, I detect a pattern in the house failures. The Marina's early builders, working on swampy fill, eschewed basement garages and placed them at street level, with living quarters perched above. With few interior bearing walls, the garages formed what engineers call a "soft story," which buckled easily under seismic duress. Many Marina homes simply sagged or collapsed around the inhabitants.

Some structures remain intact but sit tilted, one end sunk into the soil. Around such buildings the soil has bubbled up in small vol-canolike cones. In these locales the shaking has turned the moist fill into quicksand—a phenomenon known as liquefaction.

A few blocks away, the topography radically changes. Granite hills climb from the Marina and support the community of Pacific Heights. Here the rock withstood the shock waves, and the houses show almost no damage. From this height, I look down on the bay. Baby blue and tranquil in the sunlight, it looks like a giant egg cupped in the nest of surrounding brown hills. Two days earlier it would have churned and frothed.

Back at Marina Green the crowd has swelled to thousands. The day is warming, the sun pounds down on hankie-covered heads, and the restless victims pass around bottles of donated Arrowhead water. A fine-looking group—stylish fall fashions, stud-ied casualness, many women in sweatpants, everyone in Reeboks and Nikes.

At 12:10 a Fire Department spokesman interrupts a mounting growl of impatience, asking people to come forward if they know of anybody still unaccounted for. Some of the fidgeting crowd carry pocket radios. They hear the mayor talking at another site. The Reeboks and Nikes begin stamping the ground in anger. The mayor may be doing his best, but that is not good enough for this stressed crowd.

On a curb at the edge of the green, a woman sits sobbing. A TV crew trains its camera while an interviewer holds the mike in

her face, skillfully inducing more tears with his sympathetic questions. The group gets its footage and moves on, and a crew from
another channel moves in, generating another torrent of tears.
More news crews await their turn. The scene makes this journalist
squirm.

At 12:23 a policeman comes onto the mike, announcing that
the mayor is en route. The nervous chatter around me repeats a
theme: "I've got to get the stuff out of my house." "I've got a hundred thousand dollars worth of stuff in my house." "I've got to feed
my cats!" Yet every evacuee has already heard about the woman
who died reentering her damaged home to retrieve a diamond ring.

Cadenced clapping begins at 12:33 and steadily gains volume.
A cavalcade of police motorcycles putts past, evoking cries of
derision. The police chief takes the mike and futilely pleads
for patience. A water official, chosen because he lives in the
Marina, delivers bad news about water prospects until catcalls
drown him out. Where are the fortitude and resilience that disasters usually tap?

At last the mayor hustles to the mike. "I know how you feel!"
The crowd stills, though the silence smacks of skepticism. "No
houses will be taken down without telling you in advance." Cau-
tious cheers. Information about individual houses will be dispensed
at the middle school. A green tag signals an inhabitable house; a
yellow tag allows homeowners limited access to remove only essential items; a red tag means no access under any circumstances—too
dangerous. "Tell us now!" howl some. "I can't," shouts the mayor.
"Eight houses have not yet been classified. Just a little more time!"
The distraught multitude surges toward the school.

Standing at the school, I can easily ascertain the fate of those
exiting. People with exultant expressions bear green cards, those
with a confused look have yellow ones, and those who look stunned
invariably have red cards. Still, almost all have shed their anger and
petulance. Knowing their fate has made it possible to live with it.

The gymnasium of the middle school has been converted to a
shelter for the homeless. One hundred forty cots stand in orderly

rows, obscuring the floor markings of two basketball courts. In a chair along a wall sits Alice Legare, a trim and gracious retiree of seventy-nine.

Alice Legare's three-story apartment building heaved and bucked that horrible evening, and the power went off. Her battery radio told of the shelter, and she gratefully moved in. Once there, she experienced the emotional aftershocks so often triggered by natural disasters. For hours she brooded, fearful that her home of forty years would be red-tagged. She loves comfortable San Francisco and its considerate people. What if she suddenly found herself homeless? She'd probably return to her family in Massachusetts.

Then word came—a green tag! Joyfully she returned. Then the crusher: There'd been a mix-up; the building had been red-tagged after all. The city granted her fifteen minutes to pack her things and leave: period. Back at the Geographic I'll learn that Alice Legare's ordeal exacerbated a heart condition, that the Red Cross looked after her until her family could take her back east.

Across the bay, along the mile and a half of the collapsed I-880, men, women, and machines are toiling around the clock to remove the 26,000 tons of steel-reinforced roadway entombing the cars and forty-two human beings it has crushed. Words of an early witness ricochet in my brain: "We saw this Camaro, and it was only ten inches high."

The collapsed highway yields its dead grudgingly. On the lower deck, men crawl on their bellies beneath the forty-four slabs of fallen roadway, searching for trapped vehicles. At each find, they transmit the precise location to a volunteer above—nurse Alison Mueller from nearby Oakland Navy Hospital. At her direction, highway equipment drivers chip daintily through the stubborn roadbed until they reach a car roof. Then Oakland firemen gently peel back the roof until they find human remains. Mueller extricates some bodies almost intact; others must be recovered in small pieces. She searches also for possessions, to confirm identity. Advancing from wreck to wreck, sleeping little, Nurse Mueller repeats the grisly process for five days.

These lives should never have been lost. It was already well known that earthquakes destroy not in a wide bomb-burst pattern but like a sniper's fire, fixing their crosshairs on bad soils and bad structures. Yet many jurisdictions have ignored maps pinpointing those bad soils, and have permitted construction of unsafe buildings on unsafe ground.

Soon after the 1906 earthquake and fire devastated San Francisco, studies showed that the intensity of shaking varied remarkably, depending on the soils. Buildings that stood on bedrock or firm ground suffered little; those on unfirm sediments or fill suffered severe damage.

In the late 1960s, Robert Borcherdt of the U.S. Geological Survey confirmed that soil structure governs the intensity of shaking. The shaking is worst where the sediments are softest. He saw also that shaking has different effects on buildings of different heights. In 1975 Borscherdt and two colleagues published a detailed soils/shaking map of the Bay Area.

For both the Marina District and the area around I-880, the map predicts "violent" shaking in a quake. Yet many of the Marina buildings lack proper reinforcement, and the scheduled strengthening of I-880 is not yet complete. Thus the needlessness of the two disasters.

Many experts have said that virtually *no* part of California is so far from active faults as to be beyond the reach of a quake's deadly waves. The tragedies of the Marina and I-880 have made that point. Both lie a long seventy miles from the quake's epicenter. San Jose is three times as close, but has suffered relatively little. Why? Because the sediments on which it sits are old and consolidated, and thus withstood the shocks. Santa Cruz, closer yet, has suffered worst of all—but largely in areas of soft sediments instead of rock and firm soil.

This pattern of selective destruction applies to earthquakes worldwide. The epicenter of the 1985 temblor that killed 10,000 people in Mexico City was 220 miles away, about the distance from Washington to New York; the culprit was the quivering soil of a former lake bed beneath the city. In the 1988 Armenia quake, shock waves raced with little damage through nearby towns, only to kill tens of thousands in more distant cities resting on unstable soils.

The behavior of soils and the buildings that ride them will be a focus of our article. William L. Allen, the on-scene picture editor, has arranged for a meeting with Failure Analysis, Inc., a prominent San Francisco engineering firm, to advise him on illustrations. I join the group to learn more about the behavior of buildings during quakes.

It is rainy and dismal—a good day to be indoors. We meet in FA's comfortable offices at the western abutment of the San Mateo Bridge, whose towering single-column supports easily rode out the quake. FA president Bernard Ross almost unconsciously casts an appreciative eye at his building's walls, unmarred by a single crack. San Francisco, he allows, is the world's intellectual center for earthquake engineering. He has words of praise for Candlestick Park and its capacity crowd on earthquake night: the park holding firm to its bedrock, the quake-wise crowd heroically resisting an impulse to panic.

Bill Allen describes the article we intend to produce, the wide readership it will enjoy, and its various elements: photographs, text, satellite imagery, and other graphics to complete the quake portrait. He's an impressive spokesman—articulate, credible, well mannered, obviously competent. It isn't difficult to envision Allen as someday occupying the editor's office. Nor is there a lack of precedent for someone from the Illustrations Department making the big leap; Bill Garrett was primarily a picture man before being named to the top job.

FA's damage experts reconstruct the quake's progress for us, unfolding its destructive path.

With the initial snapping of the fault crust beneath Loma Prieta, waves surged outward at about two miles a second, racing principally in the north–south direction of the rupture. In a twinkling they rippled the soft ground beneath Santa Cruz, Watsonville, and Los Gatos, cracking buildings like eggs, setting them to swaying.

For eight seconds the rupture unzipped the mountain rock, twelve miles in each direction, sending new waves to abet the old.

These reinforcements intensified the shaking, shattering weakened homes, leveling entire business districts.

Roaring up the peninsula, the waves vibrated stable Palo Alto and Menlo Park. At Stanford University, they shook the soil beneath venerable masonry buildings and left many damaged or ruined. The waves swept on to Candlestick Park, tossed the mammoth bowl with its 62,000 fans, but failed to wrench it from its bedrock.

Speeding farther up the peninsula, shaking cities across the bay, the waves slowly lost force. But in the man-made fill of the Marina and the soft sediments under I-880, the spongy ground responded. Reinforcement waves reached the surface, then doubled back, amplifying in force. Houses and apartments shattered and collapsed. The slabs of I-880 wildly snapped their moorings and fell, crushing life from the motorists below. In ten seconds the macabre dance party was over.

If diminished waves from a great distance can wreak such havoc, what happens when the epicenter is closer to vulnerable soils beneath a densely populated city? The 1994 Northridge earthquake provides some answers. Measuring only 6.4 on the Richter scale, compared with Loma Prieta's 7.1, the Northridge quake takes sixty lives, destroys or badly damages more than 3,000 homes, and fells ten highway bridges. Total damage exceeds 20 billion dollars—second only to that caused by hurricane Andrew (30 billion dollars) among U.S. natural disasters. As with Loma Prieta, most of the damaged structures sit atop soft sediments, in this case of the San Fernando Valley and environs—playgrounds for the waves.

The auguries for sprawling Los Angeles are grim.

L.A. floats on a sea of sediments that in places reach down 25,000 feet. Through them runs a lacework of faults. Six are major, excluding the mighty San Andreas only thirty miles to the east. Geologists have counted more than fifty faults capable of producing quakes measuring 6.5 on the Richter scale, and the count continues. Indeed, many faults will not be found until they rupture: The area is riddled with invisible fractures. And atop this seismic sea live 12 million Californians.

The secretive nature of faults has dampened hope that quakes can be predicted. Instead, geologists focus on *probability*: What is the probability that a quake of X magnitude will occur along Y fault within Z years? If people prepare for such an event, the precise timing is not that important.

The probabilities for southern California, derived from a record of past quakes compiled by paleoseismologist Kerry Sieh of CalTech, offer little cheer. In the Imperial Valley, the southernmost segment of the San Andreas is critically overdue—"twelve months pregnant," in Sieh's words. The next segment to the north, centered near Wrightwood, also appears primed. Either fault could unleash a quake much stronger than Loma Prieta. If both go at once, the resulting temblor will surpass the San Francisco killer of 1906. Nearby sits populous San Bernardino, built on a onetime swamp.

The probabilities also bode ill for the Bay Area, with slippage likely on the segment of the San Andreas just north of the Loma Prieta rupture. Still more worrisome is instability in the northern segment of the Hayward Fault, paralleling the east side of the bay, and in a northern extension known as the Rodgers Creek Fault.

In short, Californians almost everywhere live atop a seismic time bomb they cannot control, but can only prepare for.

With *Geographic* colleagues Donald Smith and Mark Holmes I drive into the Santa Cruz Mountains, to a ridge near the dark peak called Loma Prieta. Slides are everywhere, thousands of them. Shattered houses cling to slopes. Occasionally a house foundation stands naked, the structure lying crumpled downslope.

We stop at the house of Lee and Terry Peterson, who were at Candlestick Park when the mountains exploded that afternoon at 5:04. Their frame house has jumped its foundations; its center rests on a rock, the floors slanting off in different directions. I sense it is about to slide down the hillside. Incredibly, the Petersons are cheerful, glad to be alive, thankful their children were safe with a sitter in San Jose. The children—Brooke, eleven, and Morgan, nine—are cheerful too. Only Brooke's black cat, Fuzzy, seems disturbed.

Lee, Terry, and friends have already moved much of the furniture into a small van parked outside. "Every time we move something, the house creaks," warns Terry. When they hear a creak, they move toward a door, just in case.

Lee accepts my offer to help. We encircle an oversize refrigerator and tip it onto a dolly. From where we stand, the floor leading to the van slants steeply uphill. Our grunts compete with the creaking frame as we work the dead weight up to the open door. With the house almost emptied, the Petersons will live elsewhere until they can rebuild—this time on bedrock just up the hill. Already I sense that their experience will be the lead for my article.

Back at headquarters, it's time to sort notes and start writing. It's November 1989, and Bill Garrett wants this article for the May issue—a tight deadline by *Geographic* standards. But localized disaster is a manageable subject, one with inherent boundaries, unlike a broad survey such as the world food/famine story. I see that Garrett is not cheerful. Obviously tension has increased along the National Geographic Fault, the one that runs between his office and Gil's.

I take a break from writing to attend the monthly meeting of the Committee for Research and Exploration. These sessions take place in elegant Hubbard Hall, in the Society's impressive Board Room, reached by opposing curved marble staircases ascending around a bronze bust of founder Gardiner Greene Hubbard. For decades, this room doubled as the Society's library and informal gathering place for early explorers. Since then both room and hall have been tastefully incorporated into the vastly enlarged complex of Society buildings.

The Board Room exudes dignity, achievement, gentility—and a seductive sense that such conditions will prevail there forever. From the high walls gaze life-size oils of past Society officers: Alexander Graham Bell, the first two Grosvenors (Gilbert H. and Melville B.), Melvin M. Payne, Frederick G. Vosburgh, Robert E. Doyle, John Oliver LaGorce. Their gazes converge on the room's centerpiece, a colossal table thirty-five feet long, made of burl maple and polished to a soft glow. It was donated by Thomas W.

McKnew, who joined the Society as a secretary at age twenty-one and rose to become chairman; his likeness, too, overlooks the proceedings.

As a nonvoting observer I sit at one end across from colleague Mary Smith, the senior assistant editor for research. Along the table the other leather chairs fill. Most members are men well beyond middle age—but among them sits a lone woman, Smithsonian archaeologist Betty J. Meggers.

At exactly ten o'clock Barry C. Bishop, the committee's chairman, walks in. His walk is distinctive, his feet kaplunking flat on the floor, his body vertical, lacking the usual tilt forward onto the toes. That is because Barry Bishop has no toes. He lost them and parts of his little fingers to frostbite in 1963, when he and three other Americans first carried the flags of nation and Society to the summit of Mount Everest. During their descent Barry and Lute Jerstad felt their feet slowly freeze as they waited for two companions who had attained the summit by a different route. United, the four exhausted climbers stumbled downward in darkness, descending only 350 feet in three hours, then narrowly surviving a night spent on bare rock at 28,000 feet without oxygen, tents, or sleeping bags.

There's a lot that's different about Barry Bishop. Short and stocky, he's strong as an ox; colleagues have watched in awe as he nonchalantly lifted objects that porters grunted over. He's determined, willful . . . maybe unstoppable. At nineteen he knocked off Mount McKinley by the then-unclimbed West Buttress approach as part of the famous Bradford Washburn Expedition. In midwinter of 1960–61, burdened with twenty-three pounds of cameras, he scaled unclimbed Ama Dablam in the Himalaya, an achievement that astounded the mountaineering world. Then, in 1963, he conquered Everest. And with skillful use of political pitons he's ascended to the top of this prestigious committee. Possessor of a Ph.D. in geography from the University of Chicago, Barry is reverent before the temple of science—respectful of its mission and obligations, deeply disturbed by those who fail the faith, who practice sloppy science. He laughs and groans in perhaps equal amounts and is prone to feel put-upon by those who are ignorant or plotting against him. The latter unleash a combative bristle. One thing he can't beat is cigarettes. He and I shared an office in the early 1960s, and I often flinched watching him grab puffs while training for Everest.

Barry's gavel taps the glowing burl. Members halt their polite chatter and turn to the chairman, respectful of credentials that extend far beyond mountaineering. Barry's decades of field work produced seminal descriptions of Greenland glacial moraines, contributed high-altitude research vital to early days of space exploration and climate studies, and, in a massive survey in Nepal, established a new standard for the study of mountain peoples and environments. His achievements at the Society have been as important: He's established a Geography Intern Program, taken the lead in the Society's effort to overhaul American geography education in public schools, created the Fresh Water Initiative to study the nation's fresh water supply, and, perhaps nearest to his heart, reshaped the Research Committee itself to sharpen its focus on field-based studies of humankind's relationship to the natural environment.

The members lower their gaze to an imposing stack of grant applications. The meeting will be run Barry's way, fairly and with humor, and definitely without time-wasting niggling, which makes him feel put-upon . . .

Barry Bishop will die in an auto accident in Idaho in 1994, only months after early retirement. But not before seeing his son Brent climb Everest (an American father/son "first"); seeing daughter Tara start work toward a doctorate in psychology; and settling with wife, Lila, in idyllic Bozeman, Montana, cupped in mountains he so loved.

MONDAY, APRIL 16, 1990. It's three in the afternoon. I'm paging through my advance copy of the May issue. The quake article looks good. The total story package—photos, graphics, satellite image, text—seems informative and, I fervently hope, will be exciting to the reader.

I turn to another article, "Growing Up in East Harlem." It presents the fascinating, troubled geography of an American barrio—Puerto Ricans and blacks, drugs and crime, and hopeful signs for the future. Such an article would have been extremely unlikely a decade earlier; it is Bill Garrett's kind of geography. But is it Gil's?

The phone rings. It's Gil's office: "Mr. Grosvenor will hold a special meeting in the Control Center at 3:30." Click.

I climb the two flights to the ninth floor, turn south, and enter the Control Center. I'm in familiar country, editorial country, the inner chamber where weekly scheduling sessions and monthly Planning Council meetings are held.

But the scene before me is not familiar at all. The room is jam packed, and at least half of those present are business types, vice presidents and assistant vice presidents. All are hushed. Something big is going on.

At 3:30 Gil Grosvenor walks in, face drawn, body characteristically tilted forward. He stands before the seated crowd, starts to speak, then notices that the Control Center's double doors are still open. Carefully he closes them.

"I asked you to gather so I can make an important announcement," he says. Then he announces that Bill Garrett is no longer editor, no longer with the Society. Because Gil and Bill have developed irreconcilable philosophical differences, no other outcome is possible. The board, Gil declares, unanimously supports him in this decision.

A pin dropping in the silence would have been a cannon roar. Is this the National Geographic Society? The Geographic I know—that all before me have known—is a "proper" place, one of manners, decorum, civility, respect. If someone fails or for other reasons needs to be replaced, he or she is moved aside to a lesser task, and events flow around that individual. The Society may shrink people, but it does not behead them.

A voice projects from the gathering. It is Howard E. Paine, the magazine's long-time art director, the talented innovator who three decades ago helped persuade Gil's father to modernize the magazine cover and layout. "Does this mean Bill Garrett has been fired?"

Gil abruptly dismisses the question and pushes on. Garrett's successor will be William P. E. Graves, currently senior assistant editor for expeditions. Again the audience is stunned. Few if any have thought of Graves in this role. Graves is at my level, meaning Gil has passed over the three senior associate editors: Joe Judge, Charles McCarry, and Tom Smith.

Graves rises and takes the floor. There will be no radical changes in the direction of the magazine. Although he will do his utmost, he cannot aspire to be an editor of the caliber of Garrett. He suggests we get back to work and put the news of Garrett's departure behind us. Graves handles himself well, considering.

In the brief time that Gil has addressed us, Garrett has been ejected from headquarters, directed never to return. So has Joe Judge.

In the days and weeks that follow, all of us, chattering disbelievingly in offices and corridors, exchange explanations (right or wrong) about what transpired and why. This is what I gleaned:

At three o'clock, Gil had called in Bill, told him their philosophical differences had become irreconcilable, and that the Board of Trustees concurred that Bill must be dismissed. Gil had led Bill to an adjoining room and introduced him to an outside "facilitator," who, Gil said, would explain the terms of the dismissal. These included a proviso that Bill would not return to his office or to the Geographic. Bill could have his desk, a beautiful slab of Ohio walnut.

While the facilitator talked with Bill, Gil and Bill Graves had gone to the office of senior associate editor Joe Judge with the word that he, too, was dismissed as of that moment. Judge was considered too closely allied with Garrett, too much a part of the problem—whatever it was—to remain.

Then Gil and Graves had proceeded to the Control Center, where Gil had closed the doors and addressed us senior staff.

Without exception, we editors were dumbstruck by the brutality. All were aware that Gil and Bill had hardened their feelings toward each other. Apparently neither could any longer communicate with the other or forget perceived slights. We had expected a showdown. But not the editorial equivalent of capital punishment.

The causes of the impasse will long be debated.

On the one hand, Gil supporters (few, on the editorial side) and those who tried to see things through his eyes argued that he could not control Bill, financially or editorially.

They said that Bill had not cooperated with Gil's strenuous efforts to trim costs, and pointed to "the holograms." In the March 1984 issue, Bill made journalism history by placing a hologram of an American eagle on the cover. The cost was high, about a million dollars. The November 1985 issue carried a second, intriguing, and more expensive hologram, allowing readers to peer inside the skull of an early hominid. The December 1988 issue, which celebrated the start of the Society's second century and was devoted to environmental issues, carried an ingenious wrap-around hologram depicting the fragile Earth, but the graphic was difficult to decipher in the way intended.

Gil's supporters also said that Bill had carried Gil's early editorial tilt away from "bare breasts and sunsets" and toward tougher reality to unacceptable extremes, as evidenced by an article focusing on AIDS and genocide in Uganda, a picture story that did not ignore America's scamy or shabby side, and the East Harlem article—all upsetting to the magazine's core constituency.

They also thought that Bill had not heeded Gil's often-expressed desire for more articles on U.S. subjects, and that Bill had gone overboard with single-subject issues of the magazine. The February 1988 issue had focused on Australia, and that of July 1989 had celebrated the bicentennial anniversary of modern France.

On the other hand, Bill supporters argued that Gil was psychologically unable to communicate his wishes to Bill and did not appreciate his editorial genius. They speculated that Gil could not stand up to Bill; he could discipline no one face to face and instead took the "bloodless memorandum" route until this violent firing. They claimed that Gil was deeply jealous of Bill—of his innovative creativity and the praise and awards it won him; the holograms were part of this creativity. Bill, they held, was brilliant in a job where Gil had been mediocre; moreover, his editorial boldness had reached beyond a shrinking core constituency to younger readers.

They also asserted that the magazine under Bill had been a financial success, but burdened with a disproportionate share of costs of the Society's services, scientific research, and philanthropy.

One sentiment shared by all was that the firing of Bill and Joe Judge had been unnecessarily bloody and crude. As editor, Gil had depended heavily on Bill for picture guidance and on Joe Judge for word guidance, and now he had destroyed them.

Like most large temblors, the Great Geographic Quake of 1990 was followed by an aftershock. A few weeks later, associate editor Thomas R. Smith, one of Garrett's closest friends and most valued colleagues, joined him and Joe Judge in banishment.

Unlike California, *National Geographic* is not customarily quake country. No tremors of any magnitude disturbed the editorship of Garrett's successor, Bill Graves, who during his five-year reign was confident and competent, though wildly temperamental. Nor should they during the editorship of Graves' successor, the careful, thoughtful, and reassuringly civilized Bill Allen.

For me, a new and unexpected assignment would soon be brewing: to the flaming oil fields of Kuwait in the aftermath of the Gulf War.

Chapter 9

WAR AGAINST THE
ENVIRONMENT

Given a choice, Kuwaiti oil worker Hammad Butti would have politely declined his ringside view of Saddam Hussein's invasion of Kuwait and the environmental atrocities that followed.

From his job in the Kuwait oil field, and from his home near the oil tank farm, Hammad Butti watched with uncomprehending horror as Saddam's Iraqis systematically poisoned the Persian Gulf by releasing a monstrous oil slick, then blackened the sky by igniting the oil wells. When I arrived in battered Kuwait on the heels of Operation Desert Storm, Hammad Butti, his two wives, and their seventeen children were shivering in darkness beneath the towering smoke plume, and felt the tightening pinch of hunger.

Butti was at work in the control center of the Kuwait Oil Company when Iraqi troops seized the oil field on August 2, 1990. Trained as a technician in Houston, Texas, where he learned usable English, Butti operated the switches that regulated the flow of a

211

million barrels of crude a day to three refineries and an offshore loading terminal in the Persian Gulf. Landward of his control center throbbed the hundreds of wells of the Greater Burgan oil field, second in world production only to Saudi Arabia's massive Ghawar field, and the source of Kuwait's legendary wealth. Saddam Hussein, bankrupt after eight years of futile war with Iran, coveted this wealth.

For three months the Iraqi troops hovered menacingly, while Butti and co-workers nervously continued their jobs at the control center. Then in November, counterpart engineers from Iraqi oil operations moved in as understudies: the Kuwaitis were told to cooperate or be killed. In December the intruders took over completely and threw out the Kuwaitis. Butti expected the worst, but not the two-act nightmare that followed.

On January 19, 1991, two days after allied forces declared war on Iraq and launched the aerial blitz of Desert Storm, Butti's Iraqi replacements pushed a bank of buttons. Valves opened along a massive pipeline to the tanker terminal, and the pipe vomited oil into the Gulf at a rate of 35,000 barrels an hour. They pushed more buttons to open an even larger parallel pipe. At the offshore terminal, Iraqi demolition teams boarded Kuwaiti tankers and spilled their cargoes into the sea. They blew up seven loaded Iraqi tankers brought in for the occasion. By the close of Act One, the western Gulf lay suffocating under an estimated 11 to 12 million barrels of crude—perhaps fifty times that lost by the *Exxon Valdez* when it blundered aground in Alaska.

Act Two opened on Sunday morning, February 17, seven days before the launching of the 100-hour ground war. An explosion rattled Butti's home. Out in the oil field an Iraqi team had placed dynamite in a wellhead, capped it with a sandbag to direct the blast downward, and detonated it. Fifteen minutes later another explosion sounded, then another, another, another, as successive wells were fired. Black smoke billowed three and four miles high, filled the sky, and blocked the sun; a chill fell in the daytime darkness, and the scream of escaping gas rent the air. Soft as mist, a drizzle of soot and unburned oil droplets fell from the smoke cloud and coated every exposed surface, including people, animals, and plants. The explosions continued day after day until the signing of the peace treaty in Moscow on February 27. By then the saboteurs had blown up 732 wells and set 640 afire.

Kuwait has become an inferno. In the span of a month, ecoterrorism on an unprecedented scale has reduced its colossal oil field and biologically rich sea to one of the most hellish places on the planet.

I haven't expected to find myself in a place where the stench of rotting bodies mingles with that of oil, and the roar of cannon rolls like thunder. War is not a comfortable subject for the *Geographic*. The two world wars had been covered with remarkable obliqueness during the long reign of Gilbert H. Grosvenor. Not until the Vietnam era, coinciding with the rising influence of future editor Bill Garrett, did articles appear with some frequency analyzing strife around the world. Even so, war is still a side dish on an increasingly spicy menu of *Geographic* titles.

Thus, the Kuwait assignment comes as a surprise. As science editor, I don't think of war as my turf. Geology, archaeology, space, astronomy, climate, natural disasters—these are my beat. But science at the *Geographic* includes the environment, which in a few years will become an editorial department in its own right. This makes Saddam Hussein's war my war. With unmatched viciousness the Iraqi leader has savaged not only the Persian Gulf region but the Earth itself; astronomer Carl Sagan warns that the enormous smoke cloud, by blocking sunlight around the globe, could bring on a nuclear winter.

Surprised or not, I leap at the chance to visit the war zone. Though I served in the U.S. Navy during the Korean conflict, I've never experienced war's devastation. Nor have I traveled extensively in the Middle East. Moreover, the war's impact on the Gulf ecology exerts an irresistible pull on a journalist deeply interested in the environment.

As the unprecedented magnitude of the oil slick becomes known, and the well fires stain the planet like Jupiter's Red Spot, editor Bill Graves shapes a two-pronged strategy for the magazine's

Gulf War coverage. Veteran photographer Steve McCurry, whose bold images have recorded the brutal war in Afghanistan and enhanced eight other *Geographic* articles, is already on scene to shoot the ground war that in four furious days will drive out the Iraqi invaders. Afterward he'll turn his lenses to the desecrated environment—the point at which I'll join him. The picture editor will be Elie Rogers, my worthy collaborator on the world food article.

For me this means playing catch-up. I must scramble for visas for the countries with exotic names that are downwind from Saddam's smoke cloud and oil slick: Bahrain, Qatar, Oman, the United Arab Emirates. Destination number one, of course, is Saudi Arabia, springboard for Operation Desert Storm and landfall for much of the drifting oil. Oddly absent from my list is Kuwait itself; the emirate is now a noncountry, its Washington embassy impotent, a visa meaningless. To enter Kuwait, I will somehow link up with one of the military convoys heading northward from Saudi Arabia. As one who normally carefully prearranges every hour of every day of every trip, I don't savor going halfway around the world to an uncertainty.

In the few days I have to prepare, I spend hours making international calls to potential contacts, to make arrangements with officials who can render my trip meaningful. With the guns of war still cooling and environmental disaster looming, Middle Eastern authorities have better things to do than accommodate one more clamoring journalist. Nevertheless, setting my alarm for one in the morning night after night to accommodate the eight-hour time difference between Maryland and the Persian Gulf, I pursue harried environmental ministers until—yielding to their good manners and the *Geographic's* luster—they promise access to themselves or their staffs. These promises will prove to be solid gold.

When possible in packing for assignment, I cram everything into a carry-on case and shoulder bag to avoid a schedule-busting luggage loss. Not this trip. Steve McCurry has asked for medical supplies, particularly surgical masks for lung protection in the flaming oil fields. I'm also taking Geographic atlases, as gifts to important contacts, and a pair of waders for exploring Gulf shallows blackened by the slick. Susan also stuffs in old pants and shirts she's been urging me to retire: "Wear them once in the oil, then chuck them."

M Y PLANE CANNOT LAND in Dhahran, the Saudi Arabian city that serves as Desert Storm's jumping-off point for Kuwait; the airport is dedicated to military traffic. I touch down in Bahrain, the low-lying island nation in the Persian Gulf off the Saudi coast. Low-lying, but not flat. Shallow domes dot Bahrain—domes that hinted to early oilmen of immense deposits trapped beneath. In the early 1930s they tapped the first gushers of what would grow into the vast river of Middle East petroleum exports. Today Bahrain's oil is all but gone, and resourceful Bahrainis have moved adroitly into finance and industry—and to succoring parched Saudis, whose puritanical government sternly forbids alcohol in the Kingdom.

The sky over Bahrain is strangely gray, even at high noon; opalescent, as if the sun were in partial eclipse. And the steely air is cold, disagreeable. The local climate reflects the sun-blocking work of a dense smoke plume from the flaming oil wells in Kuwait, 250 miles to the northwest. The hotel doorman is bundled in a long coat as he sees me into a taxi that will take me along the twenty-mile causeway that links Bahrain with Saudi Arabia. My driver, Abdullah Selman, is cheerful, chatty, even while a brisk Saudi customs agent thoroughly searches my bags for whiskey. I haven't smuggled any in a shaving lotion bottle, as do my nervier colleagues; the horror stories about Saudi jails have been persuasive. Now we are through customs, and Abdullah talks on, about his father the farmer, his father's three wives, his twenty-two brothers and sisters.

My ear follows Abdullah, but my eye probes the Gulf waters glinting outside the car window. The surface is clear, as sparkly as allowed by the pewter sky. Three weeks will elapse before the slick's southern fringe soils Bahrain.

But Dhahran and its sister city, the port of Dammam, wear the stamp of war. Not of destruction—Saddam's SCUD missiles have struck only one important target, a U.S. Army barracks, where twenty-seven died, the largest single loss of Desert Storm. Instead the cities attest a vast military presence. Three-quarters of a million foreign troops have massed in Saudi Arabia, most of them here on the Gulf. Trucks laden with tanks and other tracked vehicles lumber between camps and depots; military aircraft boil in and out like hornets at a nest. In early evening, off-duty troops throng the curio shops, the only entertainment. Most numerous are the Americans, soldiers of both sexes. Unveiled women in army blouses are a shocking sight in the Saudi culture, which until now has been almost completely insulated from Western influences. Years ago Saudi Arabia had closed its borders to tourists, as well as journalists, and had made sure that women were completely covered and attended by a male. "Culturally, this corner of the Kingdom is blown wide open," observed a bemused Australian familiar with the earlier, closed society.

This corner of the Kingdom has also been overrun with Kuwaiti refugees. Days before the invasion, thousands of families streamed down the coastal road connecting Kuwait City with Dhahran/Dammam, the closest Saudi sanctuary. More followed as the occupation wore on and Iraqi cruelties multiplied. Most seem to be crowded into my hotel, the Al-Gossaibi; refugees fill the rooms, overflow into the corridors, and camp in the lobby. But the hotel management is coping. In the chaos of check-in, the desk clerk coolly hands me a message from Steve McCurry in Kuwait. When I come, Steve urges, bring all the food and bottled water my car can carry, and those surgical masks for filtering the smoke-fouled air.

The first order of business is to obtain official permission to enter Kuwait. But who is "official" in this madhouse of a war zone? The nerve center for journalists is the International Hotel near the airport; its mezzanine now houses the information offices of Desert Storm's rainbow coalition. I pick up my rental car, a white Toyota Crown, large and eager, and follow the well-signed roads to airport and hotel. On the hotel's mezzanine I find scores of reporters milling among the information offices, swapping war stories, probing each other for leads, happy to explain the ropes to a new arrival. Quickly I zero in on a U.S. armed forces office as the place where I can arrange a trip to Kuwait. A Navy lieutenant commander checks my credentials, then tells me a small convoy for Kuwait will form at the hotel parking lot day after tomorrow, pulling out at 5:30 A.M. *sharp*. Three things, he stresses, are essential: passport, full gas tank, and empty bladder. It will be a six-hour drive.

My only chore before departure is stocking up on supplies, which gives me ample time to meet some of the Saudi officials I worked so hard to contact from the United States. Perhaps I'll even have a chance to scope out the slick on the Gulf.

I remount my white charger and make for the offices of the Meteorological and Environmental Protection Administration. MEPA is charged with orchestrating Saudi Arabia's response to the sea of floating oil that fouls its shores. A geometric network of modern highways leads me on. Taking my cue from fellow motorists, I drive faster than seems rational in this semiurban area, yet Saudi drivers rocket past at 100-plus.

The men at MEPA obviously are busy. But the courtly director, Dr. Nizar Tawfiq, expects me and interrupts his work; one of my calls from the States to his superior in distant Jiddah has helped open this door. He promises full access to his staff, and I present him with an atlas. Can I arrange a visit to the polluted shores of the Gulf? He reflects, then suggests that I drop in on an office at the end of the corridor, where emissaries of the U.S. Coast Guard have set up shop.

The Coast Guard is America's lead agency for coping with marine oil spills, and Uncle Sam has loaned the Saudis a high-level spill-response management team, including two sophisticated reconnaissance aircraft for monitoring the spread of the slick.

Other U.S. agencies have contributed a spill-trajectory analyst and a spill-response biologist. All are veterans of Alaska's *Exxon Valdez* spill and countless other accidents in American waters.

On the one hand, I'm delighted by the presence of Americans. It's almost always easier to work with one's countrymen than with persons of an entirely different culture and accompanying language difficulties. On the other, I'm also wary; a journalistic pitfall lurks here. To the extent that I rely on visiting Americans for information, even if at the Saudis' suggestion, I risk losing Saudi confidence that I can view their very serious problems through their eyes. Further, however selflessly and tactfully outside advisers proceed, their presence implies superiority and invites condescension toward the hosts, and eventually stirs resentment. I do not want those feelings to transfer to the *Geographic* and color my hosts' confidence and candor.

Mulling these lofty ethical matters, I march down the corridor. The Coast Guard team is headed by Captain Robert E. Luchun, conscientious and very mindful of the sensitivity of being a foreign adviser. Luchun has seen his share of spills, and the magnitude of this one shocks him. He mentions that his second in command, Kenneth Keane, will head out next day to reconnoiter the damage and cleanup efforts to the north. I snap up an offer to tag along. After all, I reassure my ethical side, I can repeat the visit sometime later with Saudi officials.

"So far, we haven't been able to accomplish much," Keane explains as we drive toward the spill's southern reach, 75 miles north of Dhahran. "Aramco is protecting its coastal oil installations, a royal prince is doing good work along his part of the coast, and MEPA has deployed booms to keep oil out of the vital desalinization plants. But the 200 miles of shoreline that is important only for wildlife and fisheries is getting killed."

We pass a pair of enormous brick structures perched by the sea and sprouting high brick chimneys—the desalinization plant at Jubayl, one of the largest in the world. Incredibly costly to build and operate, the facility processes 70 percent of the drinking water for distant Riyadh, the Saudi capital, far inland. As yet the slick has not tested its floating fortification of booms. The parched Kingdom, burdened with three-quarters of a million thirsty military visitors, can ill afford to let the oil contaminate this or any of three other coastal desalinization plants.

We approach Abu Ali Island, which is connected by a short causeway to the mainland and thrusts out into the Gulf like a porpoise flipper. The air thickens with the stench of oil, signaling the nearness of the spill's temporary southern terminus. We round a bend, and the beach spreads before us—not dazzling white, as off Dammam, but inky black, as far as the eye can see, a smear hundreds of feet wide stretching northward to the horizon. Another wide smudge marches eastward along the northern shore of Abu Ali. Seaward, the water lies flat and subdued, reflecting the pigeon-neck tints of decaying floating oil.

I turn from the sweep of blackened beaches to the noxious oil lapping at our feet. What appear at first glance to be shapeless blobs of crude slowly grow recognizable as the oil-soaked bodies of dead creatures: cormorants, terns, fishes. While I watch, a fish blob feebly flaps its tail and then lies still. The air around us reeks of oil and death, a pungent introduction to Saddam's ecoterrorism.

Here where Abu Ali abuts the coast, two small teams have begun the cleanup. We watch their floating skimmers push aside dead birds to corral the oil and transfer it to ditches dug along shore; tank trucks then vacuum up the recovered oil and carry it inland to enormous pits scooped from the desert. Ken Keane looks at the minuscule effort and shakes his head. "In Alaska after *Exxon Valdez*, as many as 10,000 people were working at one time, many of them volunteers, often getting in each other's way, competing to clean the same rock. This spill is accessible and would be simple to clean up, if the Saudis had the will."

We venture northward, past a large encampment of U.S. Marines recently returned from Kuwait, and come on an abandoned fishing operation, eleven steel trawlers rusting at an oil-stained pier. At this microsmudge on the tar-brushed coast, 180 local fishermen and families have lost their livelihoods to the slick, innocent victims of an unjust war in another land.

The beaches grow more shallow, and the blackened tidal zone stretches wider, in places spanning a mile. For weeks high tides have floated oil across the expanse, with each ebb leaving their burdens on the beach. Ordinarily pulsing with animal and plant life, the tidal zone lies stilled beneath a suffocating blanket. It's as if an invisible volcano has spewed a sheet of lava along the coast. Earlier reading has told me that oil breaks down over time and life springs forth anew, but for now those comforting words ring hollow.

In normal times these wide Gulf shallows and the sunlight beating down on them power an extraordinary ecosystem. Here, where descending air brands the planet with deserts, the terrestrial world is almost barren and the seas that lap those deserts provide the womb and way of most life.

Averaging only 110 feet deep and as large as Indiana, the Persian Gulf tirelessly converts solar energy into biological profusion. The shallowness admits sunlight to vast areas of the bottom, nourishing algae and meadows of sea grasses that provide food and habitat for marine species in staggering numbers. At the northern end, nutrients flow in from the Tigris and Euphrates Rivers, which drain the ancient Mesopotamia, home of the biblical Eden and cradle of civilization. Before oil achieved supremacy, the region's economy rode on the Gulf's generous yields of finfish, shellfish, and pearls.

The shallows nurture other life. Two million birds belonging to more than a hundred species winter in the Gulf; a hundred more species visit its wetlands during migrations between Africa and Eurasia. A chain of small islands off the Saudi coast is vital to two species of cormorants in vast numbers; here also green turtles and endangered hawksbill turtles crawl ashore to plant their eggs. Some of the world's northernmost corals border the islands and much of the shore. In the southern half of the Gulf dwells a prized population of dugongs, bulbous cousins to the Florida manatee.

Today the Gulf is the hub and highway of the world petroleum industry—and pays dearly for it. Thirty-seven oil and gas fields tap the Gulf floor itself; these are dwarfed by the megafields spewing forth across the land. To distribute this colossal flow of hydrocarbons, 30,000 tankers a year thread the Strait of Hormuz to load at Gulf terminals. Their spillage compels disbelief. A hundred tankers a day may discharge oil-tainted ballast; accidental spills are a daily routine. Every year the tortured Gulf digests more oil than escaped from the *Exxon Valdez*. War adds more. When Iraqis assaulted Iran's Noruz drilling platform in 1983, an eight-month blowout gushed half a million barrels, coating Gulf beaches and littering them with the corpses of sea turtles, dolphins, and dugongs.

Against this onslaught, the Gulf's defenses appear feeble. Unlike Alaska's choppy Prince William Sound, which flushes twice daily with the tides, the sluggish Persian Gulf requires five years to flush through the strait. On other coasts, crashing seas can help clean stained shorelines, as around the British Isles, but the short fetch of Gulf waves cleanses little.

A doomed ecology? Defying all reason, the Gulf ecosystem persists as nature triumphant. The searing sun quickly volatilizes much of the floating oil and sucks it into the atmosphere. Desert sand, blowing onto the water at a rate of a hundred tons per acre per month, binds to floating oil and weights it to the bottom, sparing waterfowl. Blowing across land, the sand falls onto the fouled beaches, where it deposits a new biological surface over the black veneer. Oil-eating bacteria, which evolved in the many oil seeps oozing naturally into the Gulf, help break down the offending spills. Like a giant petri dish, warm and incredibly nutrient-rich, the Gulf stubbornly flourishes. Often, when reading of global environmental threats such as ozone depletion and greenhouse warming, I pray that planet Earth possesses the Gulf's resilience.

Still, the Gulf has never before experienced despoliation on such a scale. Can it survive? For the moment I must return to Dhahran, to join the convoy heading to the flaming hell of Kuwait. Then I will return to these fouled shores and try to foretell their future.

I find a Safeway—yes, a Safeway—in Americanized Dhahran, and load three pushcarts to capacity with juices, milk, fruits, cereal, canned meats, candy bars, bottled water. I stop for two five-gallon cans of gasoline. The surgical masks are already in hand, along with decongestants, eye drops, and other smoke-protection medications dispensed by the Geographic nurses' station. My white-charger Toyota is sagging about the hindquarters, but I have faith in that steed.

Our convoy of eleven vehicles musters on schedule next morning at the International—two humbees with an officer and enlisted driver in each, a few cars carrying civilians recognizable as journalists, two vehicles manned by Europeans of undetermined origin, and several driven by Saudis or Kuwaitis. As the rising sun struggles to elbow its way through the smoke plume pressing down from Kuwait, we file out of awakening Dhahran and head north.

As quickly as urban Arabia falls behind us, the desert reasserts its hold on the land, and time slips backward a century. Tents replace modern masonry homes; herds of camels, sheep, and goats graze the sparse grass, watched by herdsmen wearing the flowing *thobe* and astride saddled camels. These people are Bedouins, many of them following the greening of the grass as their ancestors have done for millennia.

Periodically the clangor of wartime shatters this pastoral landscape as a military convoy rumbles south out of Kuwait, heading for Dammam. In the lead roll the armored vehicles, followed by huge flatbed trucks carrying tanks and earth movers of every description. With the war won, their job done, these weary soldiers are the ebb tide of the mighty buildup. Now they're ready to board ships for Egypt, France, the United Kingdom, Canada, and, primarily, the United States.

The sky darkens and the air chills as we push north, penetrating farther under the shadow of the smoke plume. Every five or ten miles we pass an enormous military camp set back from the road. In each, hundreds and sometimes thousands of vehicles are parked in perfect order, front to back and side to side. Rows of tents mirror their geometric precision. I feel a bit contemptuous of this fixation for order, until I reflect on the epidemic of disorder they would spawn if placed haphazardly.

The desert itself begins to grow greener, softer. We pull in at a grungy truck stop, and I meet one of the Europeans in our convoy, a Belgian scientist here to study the effects of the smoke cloud on vegetation. The greening of the desert, he explains, springs from a cloud-seeding effect of soot and other particulates borne by the plume and providing nuclei for the formation of raindrops; ironically, war has made the desert bloom. Black rains have fallen everywhere the plume has reached. Soot particles have ridden the winds like feathers, and black snow has greeted skiers in Kashmir, more than 1,500 miles east of Kuwait.

We pass through the Saudi seaside town of Khafji, near the Kuwait border, and see the first wreckage of war. Six weeks ago Iraqi troops crossed the border and assaulted the town, already abandoned by its Saudi residents. Though driven back, the Iraqis have left behind shell-pocked houses and ruptured oil storage tanks whose contents have flowed into the Gulf—the first freshet of the great slick to come.

Beside the ruins of a once-elaborate customs and immigration facility, we stop at a military checkpoint at the Kuwaiti border. With little delay our convoy officer sees us through. A checkpoint is not needed to announce that we're in Kuwait. Craters from shells and bombs pothole the single-lane road, and I groan for my laden white Toyota.

The cold increases—time to fish out sweater and jacket, compliments of my packer, Susan. Outside in the murk beneath the darkening plume, vegetation grows shiny black from a patter of falling oil droplets.

More southbound convoys growl past, until vehicles trail one another like links of an endless chain. The number of military camps also increases, their acres of vehicles underlining the overwhelming might amassed by the coalition to crush the Iraqis. Desert Storm was not to be a Bay of Pigs.

Far ahead, where Kuwait City should lie, the horizon shines with shafts of sunlight. Easterly winds are carrying the smoke inland, away from the city, temporarily lifting the cold and darkness. As we approach, the angular skyline slowly rises before us, pressed between desert and sea.

A modern freeway, one of many lacing Kuwait City, carries our little convoy toward the downtown. Sunlight dances on rows of attractive homes and apartments, high-rise offices and hotels. In peacetime the city was the pleasure dome of a million Kuwaitis; now it is dead. Residents who haven't fled are huddled in their houses: no businesses to tend, no wares to sell, all currency confiscated. No cars race on the modern freeways; Iraqis have stolen them, or their tires. Countless windows are boarded, many walls blown away. The city's sparkle is utterly deceptive, like light refracting through a terribly flawed diamond.

As we approach the International Hotel, we see the first signs of life. Cars bearing Saudi plates fill the street outside. Journalists throng the lobby and bunch before impromptu information offices—makeshift copies of those at the International in Dhahran. Impatient roomers, many holding boxes of food and drink, wait for the lone operating elevator. I tune in to the talk buzzing everywhere; much is about the threat of land mines and booby traps left behind by the Iraqis in large numbers. Land mines . . . bad news . . . and I'll be heading their way.

I locate Steve McCurry in the confusion, and we lock left hands—fingers of his right were misshapen in a childhood accident. Yes, I've brought much food, much water, many surgical masks, some gas. Yes, I've brought the film and batteries he requested of the picture editor (writers, with their relatively quick forays afield, traditionally relay equipment to photographers).

A third person hovers impatiently while we talk. "This is Mohammed Dashti," says Steve. "He's showing me around—one of the Kuwaiti volunteers helping the press." Of average height and compact build and charged with nervous energy, Mohammed Dashti speaks a slangy Americanese acquired while attending the

University of Tennessee. He remained in Kuwait during the brutal Iraqi occupation, was tortured by the Iraqis, hates them deeply, and has, I'll learn, killed his share of them.

We go to my car, and I dig out Steve's camera equipment. Eagerly he and Mohammed load up with milk, cereal, fruit, and juice, and both help themselves to face masks. "Smoke from the fires fills my apartment," Mohammed complains. "I get little sleep." He exhales luxuriously from his cigarette and pockets his masks.

The International is filled; I'll bed down in the war-damaged Holiday Inn. It has no power or running water, and Iraqis burned out its lobby, but it has a room and maybe food. We'll meet next morning at 7:30 and go into the burning oil field.

On the way to the hotel I spy an open gas station and swing in. A youthful Kuwaiti is pumping—a well-mannered fellow with perfect English, obviously overqualified. He recognizes the need to explain his job. "During the occupation the Iraqis drove out most of the Palestinians, who pumped gas and did other manual work. We don't need Palestinians; we can do the work. Good riddance." Really? Here's a product of petrodollar pampering if ever I've seen it; he'll grow to miss those working Palestinians.

At 7:30 that morning we are heading into the towering wall of smoke. Steve is at the wheel of his Land Cruiser; Mohammed is beside him, scouting our way; and I am crammed into the back seat with a jumble of jackets, rain gear, foods, juices, water bottles, gas cans, and a second spare tire. Mohammed has offered to ride in back, but Steve and I demur. We want no appearance of Americans ganging up.

The temperature plummets as we near the oil field, the air grows murky and foul, and the ambient light wanes to twilight, as if dawn were running on rewind. We reach Ahmadi, a housing enclave of the Kuwait Oil Company. Brick bungalows and duplexes line winding streets, obviously once choice housing; now, largely deserted and damaged by gunfire, they skulk inhospitably in the chill gloom. We see a man and woman in a dark doorway, looking out at us as if for help. "This is their hell," says Mohammed. I think about what it would be like to wake up every morning to such a scene.

We cap a slight rise, pass burned and twisted oil storage tanks, and drive a narrow macadam service road into the field itself. Since the Iraqi demolition teams departed, virtually no one has entered this hellish place.

The sky before us is pitch black and presses in close—we can see for only a few hundred yards. Within this short horizon blaze about six oil wells, each a volcano hurling fire 250 feet into the air. Suddenly I am swept by an editorial euphoria: I know beyond a doubt that we are driving into the lead of my article. A breeze stirs, and the fountains of fire twist and writhe. Now they resemble flaming tornadoes, each tethered to its wellhead. The subterranean pressures that send them leaping so high also cause them to scream maniacally—the final taunts of Saddam Hussein. Though he's lost a war, his malevolence triumphs in this awesome display of unharnessed energy.

We follow the service road toward the closest blazing wellhead. The headlights drill narrow holes through the blackness and glint in a drizzle of soot and unburned oil droplets. Near the wellhead the heat becomes fierce. A pool of oil on the ground is afire, as is part of the macadam road itself. McCurry, at the wheel, must make a decision. "Either we leave the road and take a chance with mines," he shouts, "or we stay on the road and blow our tires and gas tank." He veers off into the sand where—who knows where?— the Iraqis have planted the mines. I hold my breath, terrified, yet strangely thrilled.

The inferno cooks the side of our Land Cruiser as we whip past. Quickly we return to the macadam. Another well burns ahead. Its fire twists vertically in the wind, but it does not sit in a flaming puddle. This time McCurry stays on the macadam and guns the Land Cruiser into the slippery oil. Skidding as if on ice, we fishtail within feet of the screaming monster. I am able to see the blasted pipe and valves of the wellhead, or "Christmas tree," and the chain-link fence that surrounds this and every well. The fence reminds me of the small family cemeteries on farms back home, and the comparison is not amiss: After we leave Kuwait, a carload of Indian journalists and another of Brits will attempt to speed past blazing wells and skid into them, and all will be incinerated.

We come upon an abandoned farm, laid out among the wells, and get out to explore. Grasses and trees glisten black, oily to the touch. Oil droplets build up on my slicker and fleck my notebook pages. My feet grow heavy with sticky oil-soaked sand that steadily builds on my shoe soles. In this sad wasteland, I try to forget my personal fear of mines, but fail: I want no explosion ripping upward through feet and groin.

Ahead the darkness moves, and the faltering specter of a horse approaches. Once it was a fine white Arabian mare. Now it is a gaunt ghost, pitiably stained and matted with oil. It nuzzles our headlamps oddly, as if craving light, then reaches for our offering of apples and water. We know it will soon die in this befouled land. Its memory will haunt us. Could we have led it out?

The darkness precludes taking pictures, and we head across the sand toward a thin line of light hugging the horizon. This involves dodging Iraqi bunkers that dot the oil field by the thousands. Most are one-man and elaborate, dug four feet down, seven feet to a side, lined with heavy vinyl sheeting, roofed with corrugated metal, and often sprouting a small TV antenna. At every opportunity Mohammed disappears into one of the foxholes, vainly hoping the hastily departing owner left a pistol or object of similar value.

We finally reach a vantage point where the smoke cloud has lifted from the surface, and sufficient light seeps in for photography. While Steve shoots the violent panorama, I take a count of the flaming wells surrounding us. Sixty-eight geysers hurl flame and smoke into the black canopy overhead. It is a spectacle never before seen on the planet, yet it encompasses only a tenth of the total of burning Kuwaiti wells.

I reach into a bag for an orange and begin peeling it. A shape materializes at my open window, and suddenly a camel thrusts its head inside, inches from my face. With slobbering lips and ugly brown teeth the animal plucks the orange from my fingers and withdraws its head to chew. I look out and see three more camels—another female and two young, their emaciated bodies slick with oil.

We retrace our tracks to stricken Ahmadi. I hail a man entering his duplex home. Yes, he has time to talk, all the time in the world. Yes, he observed the Iraqis spilling the oil, firing the wells. From his ringside seat, Hammad Butti saw it all.

In the halting English gleaned during his stint in Houston, Butti tells of the release of the oil into the Gulf; of the staccato drumroll of wellhead dynamitings that engulfed his world in darkness, cold, and filth. As this decent man speaks in measured tones, members of his family slowly gather round—a staircase of boys, one as tall as the father; veiled girls; wife Fatima, mother of six and holding the newest; wife Saada, mother of eleven and once more pregnant.

A film of grimy oil coats the house, the landscape, the boys, and Hammad Butti. The girls are cleaner. Only the infant in Fatima's arms is spotless. Fatima follows my eyes. "We are always scrubbing and never clean," she says.

I ask Butti about food. "A city truck comes by but leaves only enough for a small family. We are always hungry." What will he do? "We have nowhere to go," he says. "I hear they will start putting out the fires in a week." He speaks as if they'll be extinguished quickly. And, true, Red Adair and other firefighters already are on the scene. I cannot tell Butti that the most optimistic experts estimate at least a year to snuff the fires.

We walk the few hundred yards to the oil field control room, where Butti worked before the Iraqis threw the Kuwaitis out and pushed the buttons that fed the slick. "My chair was in that corner," he points. *Was.* The retreating Iraqis have blown the room with its computerized controls to smithereens.

Steve points the Land Cruiser north, and we drive past Kuwait City on the main road to Basra in Iraq—the road by which the Iraqis retreated.

About twenty-five miles north of the city we top a slight rise and look across a broad valley. On the far side, the road climbs a gentle slope through what has become the graveyard of Desert Storm. At the start of the land war, loot-laden Iraqis by the tens of thousands fled Kuwait City and raced toward Basra. At Mutla'a allied aircraft screamed in and raked them again and again with bombs and rockets. The flaming wreckage choked off vehicles that were following, and they too were shattered, their occupants destroyed.

In the days following the war, allied troops removed the bodies and buried them in a mass grave a few hundred yards east of the road. Kuwaitis whose vehicles, shops, and homes had been plundered by the Iraqis came to Mutla'a and ransacked the wreckage. Finally army earthmovers pushed the hulks to the side of the road in great dunes of twisted metal.

Steve, Mohammed, and I strike east and pick up another escape route of panicked Iraqis. The aircraft picked them off mercilessly. Shattered vehicles scatter the roadside. Armor proved defenseless against air-to-ground missiles; heavy tanks sit askew, often with turrets blasted yards away.

We come upon remains of a convoy of about thirty vehicles, all destroyed, many by fire. Several personnel carriers still bear their loads of fleeing troops, clothes burned away, bodies totally blackened. Many remain fixed in the frantic poses they held at death, suggesting sculptures carved in black basalt and designed to depict the horror of war. Some have lost a chunk of flesh from a thigh or a whole limb—the work of wild dogs that feast on the convoy at night. A ghastly stench creeps from the lurid scene. I have never before smelled rotting human flesh, never wish to again.

McCurry works his way among the tangled wrecks, camera drive whirring. Mohammed darts from one vehicle to the next; the isolated microbattle has attracted few human scavengers, and pickings for pistols may be good. Neither seems to worry about the hundreds of gray-green plastic personnel mines scattered everywhere. As I tiptoe around I ponder a question I'm not certain I want answered: Are they reckless, or am I cowardly?

As at Mutla'a, these Iraqi troops were loaded with loot that now strews the scene: blankets, oriental rugs, typewriters, dress shirts, an unopened box of German Blue Puma shoes. Near one man's body lies a snapshot of his wife and two daughters; near another, a small book of phone numbers. Unused gas masks spill from vehicles. I gather up enough for souvenirs for my sons, and for Steve, Mohammed, and me to use in the flaming oil fields.

Events at the convoy have animated Mohammed, and on the way back to Kuwait City he talks of the Iraqi occupation and his work with the Kuwaiti underground.

"The Iraqis loved to torture. We formed the Resistance. My group specialized in going hunting for Iraqi officers. They had seized homes in the nicer parts of the city. We would go after them at night in teams of three automobiles, two persons to an auto. We looked for officers walking along the streets. Our first car would pick up an Iraqi in its headlights, so the second car—my car—could be ready. I would swerve and hit him with the right front fender. If he wasn't dead, the third car would stop and finish him off with a pistol—if we had a pistol.

"One day the Iraqi soldiers came to my apartment and seized me. They accused me of hunting down Iraqi officers. I denied it—told them I was an Iranian. My mother was Iranian, and I speak perfect Persian. They tortured me—burned my body with cigarettes. Finally they let me go.

"A month and a half before Desert Storm began, civilians poured down from Iraq and looted everything the soldiers hadn't taken. They emptied the shops, the houses. They took the good cars, and stripped the tires off cars they didn't steal. We went hunting for looters, tossing Molotov cocktails."

We reach the parking lot at the International. Every day is bringing more journalists, health officials, environmental scientists, businessmen, and government types to help put the city back together—and perhaps seize a few opportunities in the process. "Come," says Mohammed. He leads us between rows of cars and stops at a big brown Chevy, covered like the others with soot. He pats the right front fender, badly dented. "This is what I got them with."

My Holiday Inn is outdoing itself. Iraqis stole the ornate wood reception desk, and the receptionists have relocated in makeshift quarters in the huge, fire-blackened lobby, where they conduct business on plywood sheets resting on sawhorses. Each evening I'm given short fat candles to illuminate my pitch-dark room. Fortunately, the hotel kitchen is still functioning, so meals—the only ones available in the city—are served in the lobby to a growing clientele that soon includes McCurry and Mohammed. Each night a land breeze fills the lobby with a cloud of oil-fire smoke, reminding me at breakfast of the environment outside.

I want to explore the extent of Iraqi destruction. McCurry's interests lie elsewhere, and he'll need Mohammed. I go to the Kuwaiti desk in the International to recruit another guide. One man is available, a solemn, ascetic-looking individual, forty-ish, with good English, Ahmed Mansoor by name. Ahmed goes to collect a jacket, and a bystander speaks confidentially: "He's a very religious man, a sort of mullah." Different from Mohammed, the Iraqi hunter, but one who inspires equal confidence. For reasons I never ascertain, he will address me throughout as "Uncle Tom."

When the Iraqis first invaded, they called Kuwait the nineteenth province of Iraq and preserved much of its infrastructure for their own eventual use. As the relentless allied buildup raised the likelihood of defeat, Saddam Hussein adopted a new policy: What could not be stolen and trucked north to Iraq would be destroyed.

The resulting barbarism, inflicted largely on civilians, left a wake of rubble and shame that included even the destruction of hospitals and shooting of terminally ill patients in their beds.

Ahmed and I drive to the Kuwait Institute for Scientific Research, whose work I've read of as science editor. Once a gleaming laboratory for transmuting petrodollars into knowledge and technology, the building before us has been stripped to the walls and dynamited. In a minor victory for decency, Iraqi scientists directing the looting risked punishment by their military overseers in order to signal their shame to watching Kuwaiti counterparts, many of whom they knew as colleagues. Once the institute was plundered, Iraqi troops gave their familiar final insult by defecating on the floor.

We go to the Doha Power Station and Desalinization Plant, one of the world's most advanced—major supplier of electricity and drinking water. Hot on the heels of their victorious troops, Iraqi engineers dismantled Doha's prized reverse osmosis desalinator and trucked it north. Then they planted dynamite charges and linked them with detonator wire. With the start of the ground war they activated the switch, reducing the distillation plant and control room to rubble.

At the Kuwait Zoo, Iraqi riflemen shot caged animals for food and fun; Iraqi plunderers kidnaped choice portable creatures for pens back home. Now the once-numerous menagerie is reduced to three lean bears, three wolves, two tigers, five lions, two water buffalo, a Highland cow, seven assorted monkeys, a sick hippo, and an emaciated elephant with an Iraqi bullet in its shoulder. More pathetic noncombatants victimized by war.

We move on to the Agricultural Experiment Station, which was used as an Iraqi command and control center. Iraqi troops ate livestock that Kuwaiti geneticists had selectively adapted to the desert for as many as ten generations: fine dairy cattle, sheep, goats, camels, poultry, horses. At the end the soldiers shot most of what they had not eaten; now the reek of rotting bodies vies with that of the oil fires. During the air war the Kuwaiti resistance secretly guided allied fighter-bombers, and now the control center is a crater. But booby traps still lurk in Xerox machines and computers, and returning staffers move gingerly.

A station microbiologist, a wiry older man who was taken to Basra as a hostage, wants to talk. "They kept me there fifteen days, 326 of us in a room twelve feet by ninety feet. We got a half cup of filthy water a day, and one hard sandwich for every four people. There was no toilet, only a room we had to wait two hours to get into. I went to the bathroom three times in those fifteen days. I learned how tough people are."

After five days in Kuwait, it's time to return to Saudi Arabia and the oil slick. I join the long line of vehicles waiting for gas at my old station. My youthful friend is there, but in scarcely recognizable form. The novelty of work has worn off; repetition and tedium have extinguished postwar euphoria. Obviously a few Palestinians would now be welcome back.

One more quick stop in Kuwait. The meals served at my plucky hotel have left a surplus of food in my Toyota trunk. I drive to Ahmadi, to the oil-stained duplex of Hammad Butti. "Yes, I would be grateful," he says with dignity. "It hurts to see my children hungry." Butti's children materialize like magic as we unload, their eyes as large as their shrunken stomachs. This gratifying deed will require a little ingenuity in filling out my *Geographic* expense account, but expense accounts breed ingenuity.

M<small>Y OLD HOTEL</small> in Dhahran is still packed with refugees; they will delay their return home until food, water, and electrical power flow again in liberated Kuwait City. I point my once-white Toyota—now a hopeless oil-soot gray—to the office of MEPA, to see how it's coping with the oil slick.

Not well, judging by the atmosphere that pervades the agency. The Saudis appear harried and misunderstood; the foreign advisers radiate frustration, which they comically believe they are successfully masking. Matters are not helped by the onset of Ramadan, the Islamic month of daytime fasting that ennobles its devotees but also renders them testy.

The American advisers inform me the wind is pushing the oil slick relentlessly southward. Worse, the slick is growing, fed by untraced discharges from Iraq and Kuwait. This latest revelation shreds the first rule of pollution response: Plug a spill at its source. Never has so much oil coated a sea surface. Layers eight to twelve inches thick commonly ride the tides onto beaches; in places the oil measures an unbelievable three feet deep. MEPA's protective booms still guard the water intakes of the vital desalinization plants. But the countless embayments unused by man and left to nature grow blacker with every tide.

These bays, the foreign experts know, could easily be closed by booms, skimmed of their floating oil, and left to heal. That's why a dozen nations have sent experts and/or committed funds to aid in the cleanup, and why many private contractors hover around MEPA. These consultants have reconnoitered the fouled beaches and drawn up protection and cleanup strategies. But no high-ranking Saudis have viewed the disaster firsthand, or even flown over the coast in reconnaissance planes. Unlike the war itself, which involved the collaboration of many countries, tactical control of the postwar cleanup rests by agreement in Saudi hands, out of respect for Saudi sovereignty. Yet MEPA appears powerless to exercise its authority.

Why are the Saudis dragging their feet? Part of the problem, confide the international advisers in uneasy *sotto voce*, traces to turf battles between MEPA and all-powerful Aramco and has nothing to do with the spill. In voices even lower, the advisers question the Saudis' environmental ethic. After all, why should desert people value a coastal habitat that, no matter how fecund, begins beyond the cherished grasses for grazing Bedouin goats and camels? A tanker runs aground in remote Alaska, and 10,000 Americans flock to the affected shores. Here 300 miles of coast cry out for help, and not a volunteer responds. True, goodly numbers of young Saudis are helping at a bird-cleaning center in Jubayl, under the jurisdiction of a Saudi director. But when I visit, the men cleaning an oil-soaked cormorant are a Royal Highland Fusilier and a U.S. marine, and the hundreds of recovering waterfowl are being pampered not by Saudis but by some of the 900 British nurses, whose enormous Desert Storm hospital has treated only nine ground-war casualties and who gratefully nurse ailing birds.

I pursue the question of environmental ethic. The Kingdom does indeed possess one—more likely the embryo of an ethic, per-

haps early in its first trimester. Unlike the American environmental experience, in which public consciousness percolated upward
from an aroused citizenry, in authoritarian Saudi Arabia environmentalism has germinated at the top, with the royal family's passion
for falconry.

Virtually any picture archive containing photos of a Saudi
prince (of whom there are scores) will have images of a young man
posed with wrist extended and on it perched his favorite falcon.
From the love of falcons (and the desire to protect the habitat
of their preferred species of prey) has come the creation of the
National Commission for Wildlife Conservation and Development
and the designation of wildlife areas.

Certainly such an ethic motivates Dr. Nezar Tawfiq, the local
head of MEPA. Each evening he chairs a meeting of MEPA's spill-
response team. The press is barred from these meetings—all but
National Geographic. Each evening a Saudi reconnaissance observer
reports on the slick's movement, a meteorologist forecasts where
the winds will push the slick, and the few active contractors tally
the day's oil recovery—often a respectable 20,000 or 30,000 barrels.
But Tawfiq knows these are drops in the bucket. "Let's do something to save the mangroves, the turtles," he implores. But little
happens.

Late in March my month on the Gulf is ending, and I visit two
key Saudis whom I most admire, Dr. Tawfiq of MEPA and Dr.
Abdallah Dabbagh, head of the Research Institute at King Fahd
University in Dhahran. I ask them to talk about environmentalism
in Saudi Arabia. They ably defend the response of government and
citizenry to the massive oil slick: The affected beaches are outside
the cities and therefore invisible to most Saudis, they explain, and
many have been restricted since the war's outbreak. They remind
me that many think of the oil kingdom as rich, but war and the
enormous foreign presence have drained Saudi resources, and post-
war aid has not compensated. Their cleanup strategy was to collect
the floating oil first, then remediate the beaches. Why, I ask, was
there so little volunteer response? Tawfiq replies: If the people had

been asked to participate they would have, as they did at the bird-cleaning center. Why, I ask, weren't they asked . . . ?

Leaving Tawfiq's office, I reflect on the access I've enjoyed to Saudi officials, and its ramifications. My success has undoubtedly resulted in part from my nocturnal calls before leaving home. A larger factor is probably the magazine's reputation for positive reporting of whatever prevails—the rose-colored-glasses syndrome. But times have changed; the magazine now routinely reports failures in areas of its special expertise and concern, especially the environment. Peering down the editorial road, I know that the men of MEPA will feel betrayed by what I must write.

Meanwhile, good news arrives out of smoke-choked Kuwait. Teams of tough Texans and Canadians have arrived to squelch those shrieking oil well fires, and the fires are winking out.

Initially only four companies do battle against the legions of infernos: Wild Well Control, Boots and Coots, Safety Boss of Canada, and of course Red Adair, whose legendary triumphs include quenching the colossal Algerian gas fire known as the Devil's Cigarette Lighter. Working amid a nightmare of unexploded mines, grenades, bombs, artillery shells, and rocket charges, they confront wells that often are surrounded by blazing lakes of oil and encrusted in hardened masses of coke and sand that must be blasted away before capping. Until now, firefighters have faced at most half a dozen wells burning simultaneously. Kuwait holds 640.

It is dawn, and an assault on a well begins. Drenched with crude and battling fierce temperatures, a demolition crew carefully neutralizes the live ordinance. Bulldozers snort into action, excavating a huge lagoon, which is filled with water from the Gulf. Gingerly a boom reaches into the wellhead with 100-plus pounds of dynamite to shatter the coke mass. Operating behind heat shields, the bulldozers push desert soil over the blazing lake to give firefighters access to the site. Now four hoses fire streams of water like cannons, permitting a boom to reach into the "Christmas tree" and rip off metal mangled by the Iraqi explosions. At last the *coup de* grâce: The boom's long arm thrusts a nozzle over the center pipe and drives down tons of mudlike material to seal it. Long after the fire is out, the ground around the wellhead will be hot enough to boil water.

Kuwaitis themselves soon form a firefighting team; within months others arrive, from Iran, China, Britain, France, Romania, the USSR, Argentina. A Hungarian unit brings the most innovative technology: a jet engine named Big Wind powerful enough to blow out some fires.

Bolstered by reinforcements, by midsummer some 15,000 oilfield combatants and support troops are snuffing an average of four wells a day. On November 6, 1991, the last fiery dragon expires. The men have completed in seven months a stupendous task that many believed would drag on for years. More than Kuwait has been saved. While the fires raged, oil droplets borne aloft by updrafts rained down on the Gulf, contaminating it more than the record-smashing spills themselves.

One very large question remains to be answered: What will be my report to Geographic readers about the environmental effects of the fires and the slick?

In Kuwait and Saudi Arabia I've talked with U.S. scientists sent to measure air quality in Kuwait City and other areas under the plume. They've found surprisingly little danger from combustion products such as carbon monoxide, hydrogen sulfide, and polycyclic aromatic hydrocarbons. Questions still exist about possible effects on the lungs of atmospheric particulates occurring downwind of the fires, but these could take years to answer.

To gauge the effects of the oil slick, I ply the corridors of the prestigious Research Institute in Dhahran. Almost without exception the scientists foresee damage to marine life populations because of the oil's destruction of nursery habitat in intertidal shallows. None, however, prophesies the collapse of the ecosystem itself. All shake their heads in dismay that by his actions Saddam has stained not only the regional environment but also the human soul itself.

As do I; as does the entire world. The shrieking oil fires, the fish dying beneath the oil, the blackened Iraqi bodies in the desert, the cigarette burns on Mohammed Dashti's back, the quiet suffering of the Hammad Butti family—these are ample war experience for me, proof positive of war's horror. I will find it difficult to write this article without anger.

Chapter 10

BAGSFUL OF BUGS

I can understand why my colleagues sometimes look at me these days with sympathy. We all know each other's story assignments, and mine is microbes. The other writers are working on typical *Geographic* glamour assignments, and I'm stuck with a bunch of single-cell organisms too small even to see, much less to interview.

I don't pity myself—far from it. This is a powerful subject. Not only are microbes essential to life—all life—on Earth, they also are our obedient servants in countless ways. For example, microbes are the superstars of the burgeoning biotech industry. They are shining hopes in the struggle to clean up our ubiquitous toxic wastes. Cleverly manipulated microbes are making snow for ski resorts, manufacturing plastics and pharmaceuticals, processing ores, fermenting our beer and wine and cheese. In addition, the subject offers another, personal payoff. If I do this article right, there's an excellent chance it will stimulate the interest of young readers, who may decide to become microbiologists, bacteriologists, or biochemists. This possibility is one of the many rewards of writing science articles, as opposed to the more geographically oriented stories of most of my colleagues.

At the moment I'm deskbound for a spell, catching up on the mail, returning calls, and—most important—submitting proposals for science articles. As science editor, I'm responsible for keeping abreast of developments in science and technology and recommending what the magazine should present to its readers—a lot of ground to cover.

I do it partly by scanning the science sections of the *New York Times* and the many good science magazines. This is a treasured luxury: being paid a salary to read and learn.

I get a lot of skilled help from my staff of three science writers. But the most prolific source is *Geographic* readers themselves. Their suggestions pour in; surely the entire membership out there is busy dreaming up ideas for articles or even entire issues. Most filter through the office of Research Correspondence, whose sensitive and articulate chief, Joe Blanton, tactfully responds in the negative. Occasionally he rings me up, always with a tone of apology for what we both know is probably a foredoomed effort: "Tom, a pretty good science idea came in. I'm going to forward it, just in case." The great bulk of serious suggestions fail because they overlook the basic requirement of any *Geographic* subject: It must be photographable. After all, and to the chagrin of us wordsmiths, three pages of four in every issue of the magazine are illustrations.

No single subject dominates these outside suggestions, but one crops up consistently: fascination with events and places relating to stories of the Old Testament. Many overstrain credulity: the Pennsylvanian who calls about excavating a slate formation whose foliated slabs each bear likenesses of one of the prophets. Other intriguing biblical proposals come from established scientists—archaeologists and geologists. One geologist has uncovered evidence of ancient earthquakes that explain the parting of the Red Sea or the falling walls of Jericho. Another documents the refilling of the Black Sea following the melting of Ice Age glaciers to explain the Flood.

My phone jangles.

"Canby? Schneeberger." It's my friend Jon the picture editor, at times a man of few words, at times grandiloquent. "I have a visitor you might be interested in. Okay if we drop by?"

In they stride, Schneeberger in the fore, behind him an impressive man—sixtyish, well-built, radiating spirit but wearing a pallor and looking vaguely familiar.

"Tom, meet Jim Irwin, astronaut, lunar module pilot on *Apollo 15*. Jim's got some space pictures to show you."

No wonder Jim Irwin looks familiar. He is one of my heroes. With mission commander Dave Scott he explored the moon's Hadley Mountains in 1971, collecting the Apollo program's geologically most precious cargo of moon rocks. During three days of exhausting lunar geology, both men experienced heart irregularities. Irwin, always religious, acquired a new spiritual intensity during the mission; soon after returning, the onetime test pilot retired from the Astronaut Corps and founded a ministry he called High Flight. He spoke of his experiences before audiences and congregations around the world and became known as the "moon missionary." In 1982 he nearly died in a fall on Turkey's Mount Ararat while seeking the remains of Noah's Ark. A few years later he suffered a serious heart attack. Thus the pallor.

Schneeberger spreads out some colorful satellite images. They show a rugged mountainside. "Ararat," explains Jon. "Taken from Landsat." His finger points to a specific feature. "Jim believes that's the Ark."

Gradually my eyes focus. The feature *does* look like a ship, or at least most of one. As if a large vessel without a superstructure had run aground there, thousands of feet above present sea level, then transmuted into rock and soil. It is hypnotizing . . . but . . .

I know what Jon is doing. He enjoys friendships with many of the Apollo astronauts that are easy, bantering, warm. But today Jon is a little tense, his voice pitched a shade high. He is confronted by someone he knows and deeply respects, whose astronaut pedigree he vastly admires—but to whom he must ultimately say no, without hurting feelings. Jon would like some help, just as I have come to him for help in similar situations.

I ask, "Do we have any more pictures?" Jon proffers a space shot of the entire mountain, lording over easternmost Turkey. "Anything else we could use?" There isn't. "Jon, Jim, this is remarkable stuff but not nearly enough. We haven't a chance of conjuring up a story. Not a prayer." I immediately regret that final word, but Jim Irwin is accustomed to klutzes. He graciously accepts a failed mission—that we cannot share his conviction that this is really the Ark—and we shift the conversation.

The microbes article will be my last as a *Geographic* staff writer and editor. The Society has put together an attractive early retirement package for ten of us in the editorial and business departments who have served for long periods and rank as senior assistant editors or vice presidents. I've accepted the offer, sorry indeed to leave what for me has been the perfect job but glad at age sixty-one to have the vigor and desire to pursue my own ends.

Retirement will deliver me from work's only unpleasantness, the necessity of a long daily commute. Susan and I live at the edge of the Maryland countryside, some twenty-three miles north of Washington, near the Patuxent River. But enjoying this fair haven translates into an hour's combative drive each way. On one hand, I calculate that I have spent several years inside an auto's padded cage and driven nearly as far as the moon and back. On the other hand, my carpool-mate since remarriage has been Susan, and we have enjoyed this time together.

Another factor makes the timing of my departure appropriate. The photographer for the microbes article will be Charles O'Rear, with whom I collaborated two years ago on the article, "Advanced Materials—Shaping Our Lives." On our round-the-world itinerary, Chuck was the best of traveling companions—resourceful, even-tempered, fine company. With this article, his eighteenth, Chuck is nearing a record for most prolific free-lance photographer in *Geographic* history. There'll be no writer/photographer tensions on this assignment.

The story on microbes, known in the trade as "bugs," was my idea. My main selling point was the growing role of bacteria in cleaning up oil spills and industrial wastes, a technology known as bioremediation. Numerous field tests, including those at Alaska's *Exxon Valdez* oil spill, had shown the microbes' value. The Environmental Protection Agency was increasingly using them at Superfund sites around the nation. Large bioremediation companies were thriving and new ones springing up. Of course the article would also delve into the many other high-tech uses that microbiologists were finding for the versatile bugs.

My fellow editors on the Planning Council, which passes judgment on story suggestions, had doubts. After all, microbes are invisible and therefore not especially photogenic. But the editors also knew that my minuscule science department had a track record for pulling off successful articles on unlikely but important subjects. And they also knew that the ingenuity of *Geographic* photographers was virtually limitless. Further, the environmental angle had strong appeal. The council went along. And so did then-editor Bill Garrett, who had a fondness for challenging subjects on the cutting edge.

There will be no lack of material for my article. Microbes thrive from the stratosphere to the abysses of the sea to the bowels of the earth, in steaming hot springs and arctic cold and noxious acids and alkalis. A teaspoonful of garden soil holds more than a billion of them—the yeasts that do our fermenting, the fungi known as molds that break down our compost, the protozoans that prey on other microbes, and—by far the most abundant—the bacteria, who reign as Earth's oldest, most abundant, and most useful creatures.

Among those teeming legions lurk some bad actors, of course. Certain fungi can cause cancer. A protozoan inflicts the scourge of malaria. The deadliest poison known on this planet lurks in the swamp-dwelling botulism bacterium. However, only one in a thousand microbes is a germ; the vast majority are beneficial.

THE PHONE RINGS AGAIN, and the message it bears this time is sheer mortification. A reader has spotted a very embarrassing mistake in my recent "Advanced Materials." I've been proud of this difficult presentation of important advances in new ceramics, plastics, composites, high-performance alloys, and high-temperature superconductors.

The article's error concerns the most attention-grabbing feature—a foldout black silhouette of a human male figure, gleaming with three dozen artificial body parts, or prostheses, all incorporating advanced materials. Because the body is a grueling environment for implants—hot, wet, salty, always in motion, and defended by an immune system alert to reject what is foreign—tough new materials are always welcome.

The picture editor, realizing the complexity of putting together such an illustration, declined involvement. Because I'd strongly believed in the picture's informational value and editorial appeal, I persuaded the editor to let me take responsibility for the image.

I assigned the task to my willing and able assistant, Marie Barnes. She faced a formidable task. Each manufacturer—of the artificial heart, the nose implant, the penile prosthesis, the great toe joint—required reassurance of the use to which the part would be put. In addition, the suppliers worried about safeguarding their treasures: Many of the implants were worth thousands of dollars. Marie had to coordinate both players and props.

Soon her office resembled a Hollywood special-effects studio for assembling bionic humans. Periodically a specialist from the Food and Drug Administration visited to check on her growing inventory, suggest sources for more, and set each part in its proper orientation.

Right on schedule, the FDA put in place the final implant. The result, shot by photographic intern Ted Tamburo, was a riveting tribute to materials science and modern medicine. Artificial organs of every shape, emplaced on the ebony silhouette, gave the photograph the Cubist look of an early Picasso. Even the doubting picture editor graciously declared it a winner.

A winner until now. An alert reader has notified the *Geographic* that the penile prosthesis—the penis implant—is shown upside-down. At least it's not a harmful error, barring the extreme unlikelihood that someone will prefer to consult our image instead of the manufacturer's installation manual. Far worse is the humiliation of having produced an error in the *Geographic*—and the ribbing I'll have to endure from snickering colleagues about anatomical ignorance.

Lunchtime, and I'm off to the new office building next to headquarters. The brick structure, its ascending floors stepped back like a Maya temple, contains the Gilbert H. Grosvenor Auditorium, used for Society lectures. It also houses the Society's single, large, democratized cafeteria; no longer is there an elitist masthead dining room with waiters and red carpet.

Loading a tray, I scan the immense dining area for friends. Two former photographers are sitting at an isolated table. I head for them with pleasure.

These are great men. The brilliant careers of Volkmar Kurt Wentzel and Luis Marden define half a century of *Geographic* photography, a century of combined experience. Both are innovative artists who shaped their own photographic playing fields. They personify the romance of the *Geographic* of an earlier era, and their work epitomizes an excellence that Jane Livingston, chief curator of the Corcoran Gallery of Art, characterized as "a prolonged, quiet unfolding of genius."

Refined in features, manner, and dress, unassuming Volkmar Wentzel recorded a world radically changing before his lens, from European colonies in Asia and Africa to struggling would-be republics.

Wentzel won his first photographic assignment—to "do India"—in 1946 after returning from military service in World War II. He set off in true *Geographic* fashion at a time when expeditions abroad were lavish and laborious undertakings. Estimating that his coverage would require two years, Wentzel packed fourteen trunks with clothes, reading material, three types of bulky cameras, masses of flash bulbs and lenses, color and black-and-white film, and developing tanks, chemicals, and processing equipment for setting up a darkroom in the field. With this cargo he boarded a Swedish freighter for a monthlong voyage across the Atlantic, through the Strait of Gibraltar, across the Mediterranean, through the Suez Canal, and across the Indian Ocean to the port of Bombay. During this time Wentzel devoured books on India's heroic past, its great religious epics, its complex system of castes, its colonial history, and the political struggles of Mahatma Gandhi. He of course read E. M. Forster's A *Passage to India* and studied maps to plan his coverage. He noted that a Royal Geographical Society guidebook suggested that visiting European sahibs wear sun helmets in the Curzon style, pith helmets for shooting, and formal evening wear.

Wentzel traveled to Delhi only to discover that destitute post-war India offered no vehicles to transport his fourteen trunks. Following a tip, he made his way to an immense junkyard in Calcutta, the end of the line for thousands of battered U.S. Army vehicles that had seen service on Stilwell's road to China. For $400 and a gift membership to the *Geographic* he obtained an old ambulance. Then, on a diet of tea and tinned biscuits and sleeping at night on a stretcher, he drove a thousand miles over the dusty Grand Trunk Road to Delhi, where he had left his gear. In Delhi he engaged a sign painter to paint out the red crosses and to emblazon in their place, in *Geographic* yellow, a large map of India beneath the words NATIONAL GEOGRAPHIC SOCIETY, PHOTO-SURVEY OF INDIA in English, Hindi, and Urdu. On both doors were painted American and Geographic flags.

Wentzel drove his laden ambulance over the 9,000-foot Banihal Pass to the emerald Vale of Kashmir. A month's delay while a fanbelt was replaced gave him time to travel on foot, by yak, and by pony over the Himalaya into Tibetan Ladakh, a land of prayer wheels and stone lamaseries perched on lofty cliffs. He completed coverage of Delhi, saw it become the capital of the newly independent India, and visited little-known Nepal. At last he reached his most cherished goal, the caves of Ajanta and Ellora, great chambers carved into living rock 2,000 years ago with frescoes depicting the life of the Buddha and magnificently sculpted statues—"voluptuous guardians, wrapped in gossamer saris." To gain access to Ajanta's least vandalized frescoes, Wentzel built scaffoldings, then photographed them from dawn to dusk in almost unbearable heat. At night he developed his film in eleven stainless-steel tanks cooled by ice brought from sixty miles away. Wentzel's classic India photographs, like his other work, have been praised for their "painterly sense . . . refinement, and literary discipline."

Luis Marden, now in his seventies, is trim, courtly and charming, and a spellbinding raconteur. Like Wentzel he is a master of his medium, renowned equally for his epic accomplishments in the field and for forcing progress on a Society reluctant to change.

Growing up in Boston with a camera as a third eye, by age nineteen the self-taught journalist had written the book *Color Photography with the Miniature Camera*, the first treatise on the subject. By "miniature" he meant his 35-millimeter Leica, in contrast to the cumbersome glass-plate-and-tripod equipment then employed by almost every professional photographer, including those at the *Geographic*. The usual product was the then-standard black-and-white image, which when enlarged became disagreeably grainy.

Learning that the Society was seeking photographers, in 1935 Marden wrote that he was "experimenting with color" and won an invitation to visit Washington. The aging and autocratic illustrations editor was not overly impressed with the young Bostonian and his puny Leica. Marden settled for a job in the photographic lab.

Within a year he moved up to become a full-time photographer. At the same time Kodak was introducing its new Kodachrome film for the 35-millimeter camera. To Marden, the film's revolutionary promise was obvious: a grainlessness permitting limitless enlargement; a faster shutter speed allowing action "snapshots"; the miracle of color; and, at long last, freedom from carrying tripod, glass plates, and large camera. "It'll be a photographer's liberation, like being let out of prison," Marden exulted.

His enthusiasm failed to ignite the staid Illustrations Department. Not until 1938, when a veteran field photographer brought back Kodachromes capturing Viennese dancers in colorful, swirling motion, did the magazine embark on the new course Marden had been urging. Surprisingly, for a decade the *Geographic* was alone among magazines publishing Kodachrome.

Marden's pioneering exploits were just beginning. Diving in the Indian Ocean in 1955 with marine explorer Jacques-Yves Cousteau, he illustrated virtually an entire article with color photographs of reef fishes—a milestone in the development of underwater photography.

The lure of diving called him to Pitcairn Island in the Pacific, refuge of the mutineers who had cast off Captain William Bligh from H.M.S. *Bounty*, sailed her to the island in 1790, and burned her in Bounty Bay. Marden searched for her remains for six weeks, then photographed them. His gripping article, "I Found the Bones of the *Bounty*," made headlines worldwide.

Marden's sensational discovery, like his innovativeness in photography, set the Society on a totally new course. Editor Melville Grosvenor, struck by the *Bounty*'s popularity on an NBC television program and as a lecture film, became persuaded that the Society itself should produce television shows. He initiated an unprecedented series of prize-winning Geographic "specials" and other programs that today attract some 40 million viewers monthly.

Unusual distinctions came to Marden. Preparing an article on orchids that appeared in April 1971, he discovered a new species later named *E. mardeni*. Diving in the Atlantic, he recovered a new species of sand flea, adding *D. mardeni* to his namesakes. In 1986 Luis set sail from Spain's Canary Islands with his wife, Ethel, a mathematician, and again made world headlines. Performing exacting mathematical calculations and using navigation computers, they accurately determined the track of Columbus in discovering the New World.

An article in the *Washington Post* called Marden "one of the last old-time adventurers, the epitome of the phenomenon once known as 'the *Geographic* man.'"

Leaving these Geographic giants, I return to my microbes. By now Dave Arnold, my collaborator on the "First Americans" article, has been assigned as picture editor to work with Chuck O'Rear, filling out the core team for our story.

To GET AN OVERVIEW, a one-stop briefing on what is happening and where in the vast arena of microbes, Dave, Chuck, and I head to the University of Wisconsin in Madison, where the world's largest biotechnology center supports more than 300 faculty research groups. Small wonder that bacteria are of interest in the Dairy State, where microbiologists toil to keep bacteria out of the milk, keep them fermenting the cheese, and control their proliferation in the bacterial bouillabaisse we call yogurt.

And so we three pilgrims find ourselves on the shores of Lake Mendota, deep in the labs of the university, contemplating the stomach of a cow, which our researcher/guides are striving to understand.

A cow's stomach, we learn, is a microbe megalopolis; inside those four chambers some 500 trillion microorganisms live and work a microbial paradise. Their efficiency as digesters of the tough cellulose in grasses explains the success of the animals known as ruminants—the cattle, camels, sheep, goats, antelopes, and other grazers that provide much of the world's milk and meat.

The researchers wish to replicate the miracle of the cow's stomach in cleaning up polluting industries such as papermaking. Today, pulp mills break down cellulose in wood by using vast amounts of sulfuric acid and energy. Far better to avoid this environmentally undesirable process by "biopulping" the wood in bacteria-filled fermenters patterned after the cow's stomach. This is the good news of cow bellies.

The bad relates to cows and the environment. The microbes in a cow's stomach expel methane instead of the carbon dioxide given off by air-living microbes. The methane issues from both ends of cattle, though primarily from the front. The scientists are concerned not about manners but about methane's role as a green-house gas in global warming.

How can scientists hope to modify bovine behavior to limit the release of methane? They think termites, which also break down cellulose, may point to a solution. Termites, like all cellulose eaters, house anaerobic microbes in their gut, but this strain produces not methane but harmless acetic acid. It turns out that cattle, too, harbor acid-producing microbes in their stomachs, but the latter are suppressed by the dominant methane producers. The scientists hope to find a way to alter the microbial balance in a cow's stomach, to tip the scales in favor of the acid producers.

We move on to the domain of Dr. Jo Handelsman, a rising star among microbe hunters. Screening 1,200 microbes in lab cultures, she discovered that a strain of the familiar bacterium B. cereus can help control a fungus that kills soybean and alfalfa plants during wet spells. Her bug will become a biological substitute for fungicides, some of which are virulent carcinogens.

Now Handelsman is grooming microbes for a higher goal: to help crops fix nitrogen in the soil, one of the great dreams of world agriculture. Farmers rich and poor around the world spread immense amounts of costly nitrogen fertilizer on crops. An estimated half of what is applied washes away with runoff, polluting waterways like Chesapeake Bay. Handelsman has identified *Rhizobia* bacteria that willingly fix nitrogen in roots. However, they don't compete with species already occupying that niche. Handelsman hopes to introduce a competitiveness gene into her nitrogen fixers.

Our guides parade us past a large and venerable fermenter now preserved as a medical shrine: In it, scientists first created the demanding environment for producing penicillin in bulk, in time to save lives during the Korean War.

We pause at the microscope facility, where electronic magnifiers three stories tall bring scientists and microbes face to face. I seize the opportunity for an epochal study. We all know money is filthy, passed from hand to dirty hand. I dig out my most stained dollar and stick it into a scanning electron microscope. Myth exploded! The magnified area contains only one lone bacterium, small and lethargic.

On to a lab where scientists study the role of bacteria in making snow and ice; much basic research on this strange phenomenon unfolded here at Wisconsin. We focus on a test tube of distilled water, chilled to nearly zero degrees Farenheit but still unfrozen because lacking nuclei for forming ice. Now a technician injects the bodies of dead bacteria. *Zap!*—water becomes ice crystals, formed around the bacteria and demonstrating the principle used by snowmakers at ski resorts.

And here we meet the celebrated microbe hunter Tom Brock, whose talent-scouting has lifted many bugs to stardom. They include bacteria that thrive in scalding springs of Yellowstone National Park, and whose enzymes are vital to the forensic miracle of DNA fingerprinting.

Like its counterparts elsewhere, the university has attracted satellite businesses that enjoy a symbiotic relationship with its academic departments, including biotech. We visit a dynamic firm called Agracetus that uses a specialized bacterium to introduce genes into plants, giving them resistance to insects and diseases and dramatically reducing pesticide use. At Promega, another booming biotech business, biochemists transfer genes for snipping DNA into "factory" bacteria that are reproduced by the billions for use by genetic researchers.

Flying back to Washington, I carry the usual overload of scientific papers acquired on such a foray. I resist the urge to pull out a novel, and instead obey a self-imposed rule: Read or at least scan all the material I carry home; the press of events back in the office will make later study unlikely.

On my desk lies a welcome message from Dr. Harry Roberts of Louisiana State University. It has to do with bacteria that make rock, such as the travertine used in the Roman Coliseum. Roberts and a team of scientists will soon be going out into the Gulf of Mexico to study its floor—including colonies of bacteria making rock. The *Geographic* is welcome to come along.

Now Roberts and I are tucked in the submersible *Johnson Sealink I*, descending 530 feet into the dark waters of the Gulf of Mexico. The *Sealink* resembles a tiny helicopter without a rotor. Pilot Don Liberatore is pressed against my left shoulder, and Roberts is scrunched into the stern. Although we're confined and at depth, I feel none of the apprehension that attended my scuba diving; this is more like the days when my carpool riders crowded into my Volkswagen Beetle. My only concern has been to limit pre-dive coffee drinking: Restrooms are nonexistent in this cramped conveyance. Anchored above us on the surface rolls our parent research vessel, *Seward Johnson*, on charter by LSU to study the rich Gulf basin, which provides so much of the nation's petroleum and natural gas.

I focus ahead, in the beam of *Sealink's* headlights. "There they are," says Roberts, "bacteria converting basic elements of seawater into the rocks that pave the planet." These jumbo bacteria *are* visible—members of the genus *Beggiatoa*, among the largest species known. Resembling angel-hair spaghetti, they cover the bottom with a fuzzy white mat nearly as large as a basketball court and now aglow in our lights. "Looks like a night city seen from the air," observes Roberts. "Our little Atlantis."

"The bacteria generate energy chemically," explains Roberts, "using hydrogen and sulfur. They built much of the environment down here. See that rock ahead? That's calcium carbonate, good old limestone, made by the chemical reactions of these and other Gulf floor bacteria. You're seeing rock born from living creatures." Some thirty of these dense bacterial colonies have been found on the Gulf floor, centered on seeps of petroleum and natural gas escaping from oil-rich sediments below.

It's an amazing world, the bottom of this colossal embayment. From small craters pocking the mat of *Beggiatoa*, two jets of natural gas spasmodically erupt bubbles into the sea. Rubbly rocks strew the seascape, sheltering small fishes in their crevices. A school of foot-long fish glides over a fronded gorgonian coral. Ahead looms a sheer limestone wall, a ledge of which holds a lone sea urchin. A red snapper lazes past. Though we move in near darkness, daylight glimmers palely overhead, like an early dawn on a distant horizon.

Shining eyes of a sea monster break the gloom above us. Boldly it approaches. It is a remote camera vehicle lowered from *Seward Johnson* by my colleague Emory Kristof, the Society's specialist in underwater technology and frequent partner of ocean explorer Robert D. Ballard, discoverer of the lost *Titanic*. We watch, hypnotized, as the robot, strobe lights flashing like lightning bolts, photographs the rock and the microbes that make it. Once finished, it silently turns and stares at us in our bubble, then eerily rises at the end of its snakelike umbilical cord.

We collect bottom samples, then ascend into the brilliant Gulf sunlight and onto the fantail of *Seward Johnson*. I join Kristof on deck. He's monitored the robot's picture-taking through an attached video camera, and he wears a concerned look. "We see the bacteria down there, and we see some rocks, but the setting lacks drama." No towering boulders or strange sea life; static. Though scientifically significant, these scenes may look insipid against the thousands of exposures flowing in from Chuck O'Rear. This hurts. Both the *Geographic* and Roberts have gone to much trouble and expense, and not to show this generous scientist's worthwhile work would be an injustice.

Yet that is what happens; our bacteria-made rocks fail to make the final picture cut. It is a problem that occurs all too frequently and causes bitter disappointment: Expectant interviewees give time, effort, and information, only to see no mention of them or their work in the final article. When this happened in my articles, I sometimes had the time and decency to write an apology, but not nearly often enough. Years later I was able to describe the dive and Roberts' work in the Geographic book *Our Changing Earth*—not magazine coverage, but the best I could do.

To board *Seward Johnson* I've driven south from New Orleans to the delta port of Grand Isle, a casting-off point for Gulf fishing boats and craft servicing offshore oil rigs. Now I need to depart. The research vessel will remain at sea, but there's an oil platform not far from our anchorage. It will send a barge and put me up for the night. Tomorrow a helicopter will carry me and another passenger back to Grand Isle, weather permitting.

From the direction of the oil rig, a large motorized barge cautiously closes on our starboard quarter in rolling seas. A swell slams the bow against our fenders. "Leap!" shouts a ship's officer, and I leap, while a deckhand tosses my bag. Instantly the barge churns full astern to put distance between it and the ship, and we slap waves toward the oil rig.

The platform grows awesomely as we approach, into a towering Tinkertoy island of steel nearly twenty stories tall. The barge ties up at the base, and a crane perched far overhead lowers a waist-high steel cage. I climb in. "Hold on to the cable—hard!" shouts the barge pilot. A motor hums, and I rise, as if wafting into heaven, then come to rest softly on steel grillwork 160 feet above the sea. A crewman escorts me to the comfortable guest bunkroom, and next day on schedule the copter whisks me to Grand Isle. All part of the magic that unfolds during the preparation of a *Geographic* story.

From New Orleans I drive alongside the Mississippi River toward Baton Rouge. The river itself is invisible, a matter of faith, hidden by levees that rise from the flatland like a giant earthen tsunami. Occasionally I spot the superstructure of a ship gliding past, its hull obscured by the berm.

Along this stretch of river lies a chain of huge petrochemical plants—formidable snarls of pipes, tanks, buildings, and stacks, each gulping Gulf oil and natural gas and transmuting them into bulk "intermediate" compounds. These will be barged upriver into America's heartland and processed into plastics and consumer items for Kmarts and grocery stores and gas stations and dry cleaners.

This potent corridor fuels American industrial strength. It also is sorely fouled by toxic wastes, now being cleaned up. A principal player in the cleanup is microbiologist Ralph Portier of LSU. His billions of helpers are specialized bacteria, which he has bred to feed on things toxic to humans. He and they are pioneers in the burgeoning business of bioremediation.

I track down Portier in a basement lab at the Baton Rouge campus. Tall, heavyset, purposeful, he wastes no time in introducing his microbe minions: hundreds of species and strains of bacteria, coddled in cultures and immobilized in freezers, each one computer-labeled as to the type of contaminant it feeds on. These dietary preferences are chilling: benzene, xylene, phenols, PCBs, TCE, triazine.

In healing sore spots that line the river, Portier and his microbial legions have achieved many firsts: first EPA-approved bioremediation of a Superfund site; first to remove PCBs under the Toxic Substance Control Act; first toxic site rehabilitation under the Resource Conservation Recovery Act. The state of Louisiana strongly supports Portier's handiwork. Dirty plants that can be cleaned up instead of forced to close down can expand and create more jobs.

Portier takes me to a Superfund project at the Old Inger Oil Refinery. This odious facility once reprocessed crankcase oil and the like, and left the surrounding soil black with contaminants. Portier found more than 200 toxic compounds here.

The daunting task of cleansing Old Inger illumines a schism that still divides EPA and others coping with toxic wastes.

The traditional approach to such sites is to incinerate the contaminants or haul away the contaminated soil to a safe landfill. Bioremediation lacks acceptance among traditional engineers. To clean up Old Inger, EPA wanted to excavate and truck the poisoned soil to a Texas landfill, at a cost of 25 million dollars. But the site sits at the foot of the levee holding back the mighty Mississippi; the U.S. Army Corps of Engineers rejected a plan that might undermine the levee. Thus Old Inger became the first Superfund site approved for bioremediation, at a cost of 10 million dollars. Since the success of Old Inger, bioremediation has taken to the field at numerous other Superfund sites.

I visit some of those other sites, depressing scenes one and all: a Florida nightmare where a plume of creosote in groundwater is poisoning wells, a Utah Air Force base where almost every shovelful of earth turns up contaminants, a Michigan Coast Guard station where leaking jet fuel is fouling residents' tapwater. Depressing places, yes; but each also is a showcase for the uncanny powers of bacteria in delivering us from past environmental sins.

Long before we humans began rearranging our environment, bacteria were busy shaping our world. At Harvard University, in the office of paleontologist Andrew Knoll, I learn how they went about it.

"Paleontology" stirs visions of ancient dinosaur bones, but not in Knoll's office. Many of the fossils in the rocks crowding his sagging shelves are invisible to the eye: microscopic traces of Earth's oldest life-forms, the paleobacteria.

These ancient organisms date back astonishingly far. Sedimentary rocks from South Africa and Australia hold fossil bacteria that lived 3.5 *billion* years ago. Rock found in Greenland hints of life-forms 3.8 billion years old, though the distortions of metamorphism blur the record. "Either way," says Knoll, "the dates are impressive when you recall that the Earth was under intense bombardment by meteorites until 3.9 billion years ago." He believes that even during the bombardment, life at times might have flickered and been snuffed on the still-hot Earth.

For 2 billion years, until the dawn of the Cambrian era 500 million years ago, bacteria not only ruled the Earth but also did much to mold its oceans, air, and rock. Soon after forming, they developed photosynthesis, the ability to convert sunlight and carbon dioxide into carbohydrates, the basis of all higher life. Quickly they mastered the chemistry of stripping nitrogen from the atmosphere—nitrogen fixing—essential for making proteins and nucleic acids; not until World War I would humans catch up. Hungering for hydrogen, bacteria invented a new kind of photosynthesis that used the sun's energy to split hydrogen from oxygen in water molecules. They excreted the oxygen as waste, into an atmosphere then devoid of gaseous oxygen.

Bacteria's cast-off oxygen, bubbling up from the mud and slime where they dwelled, enveloped the planet in a slow burn that created today's oxides. By 2 billion years ago bacteria had produced enough oxygen for the element to begin accumulating in the atmosphere. Some wafted into the stratosphere, where oxygen atoms clumped to form ozone. Gradually these large molecules created the shield that blocks most ultraviolet radiation. This shield, it is believed, permitted Cambrian life-forms to leave protective waters and invade the land.

The bacterial gift of atmospheric oxygen also allowed the evolution of the respirers, the breathers—creatures that could take oxygen into their bodies, use it to combust sugars as takes place in our blood, and generate vast energy. The Earth's stage was set for advanced life-forms, including *Homo sapiens*.

I push on, to the University of Massachusetts, to learn of one of bacteria's earliest and most bizarre accomplishments—one I still find hard to believe. In his laboratory professor R. Clinton Fuller is making a convincing case that bacteria make polyester plastic almost exactly like that in our fabrics—and have done so for 3.5 billion years.

In Fuller's lab my interest fastens on electron-microscope pictures showing weird-looking microbes. Their tiny bodies bulge with whitish lipids, or fatty acids. Chemically and practically speaking, these fats are polymers, virtually identical with today's polyesters. The only difference between them is that bacterial polymer is biodegradable, while synthetic is not—thus the plastic litter that lingers along our roadways and in our full-to-bursting landfills.

Why, I muse, don't we get bacteria to make our plastics, and avoid the undesirable chemicals and litter of synthetics? The British chemical giant ICI makes a limited volume of natural-plastic containers, today expensive and afforded only by those intensely committed to a clean environment. Still, many experts, including Clint Fuller, believe that before long the world will turn to polymer-making bugs.

JANUARY 1991. Washington is blustery, but a warm occasion is spreading its glow. The Society has a tradition of celebrating the twenty-fifth and thirtieth anniversaries of senior employees. My thirtieth is at hand—luncheon in Hubbard Hall, in the dining room I've visited so often after meetings of the Planning Council and Research Committee.

Wine flows and toasts ring, embracing both Susan and me. My guests are writers, editors, researchers, photographers, picture editors, and administrative assistants whom I have long known and loved. With many, like Jon Schneeberger, Don Belt, and the Rogerses, working relationships have grown into warm, lifetime friendships. This is particularly so with personnel director Adrian Loftin, my old carpool-mate whose family has been especially close to ours. Many, like Carolyn Patterson, Len Grant, Ralph Gray, and Ken Weaver, have helped me immensely. I miss Joe Judge and Bill Garrett, who also meant so much.

The room accommodates only twenty-five or so, and in deference to closer friends I have not invited Gil Grosvenor. But he has come anyway, unfazed by my omission. Graciously he pins on the thirty-year emblem.

Heading back to my office, I am waylaid by more nostalgia, high in the rotunda of the Maya-temple-like building dedicated by President Reagan in 1983. From the domed black ceiling glimmer lights representing stars positioned as they were on the evening of January 13, 1888, when thirty-three men met at the Cosmos Club and launched the National Geographic Society.

THERE IS MORE MICROBE WORK to be done. Chuck O'Rear and I converge on Japan, land of canny bacteria users. As my All Nippon jet circles Tokyo International, I fondly reread my customs declaration, which asks if I have brought my sword.

In this ancient Asian culture, specialized microbes enjoy pampered lives and high status. In Tokyo, at the headquarters of the Kikkoman Corporation, our hosts have laid out the ingredients of their illustrious soy sauce: soybeans, wheat, salt, and the cherished mold *Aspergillus* for fermenting it all. Five hundred years have gone into the perfection of this condiment, and Kikkoman has been fermenting for 350 of them. "At our plant," says an official, alluding to Japanese reverence for forefathers, "they call the mold *Gosenzo-sama*—Ancestor."

I hop the J-13 train, to the suburban Tokyo lab of Japan's celebrated microbe hunter Koki Horikoshi. Hospitable, informal, fluent in English, Horikoshi has pursued intriguing and useful bacteria around the world, most often in extreme environments of heat, salinity, and alkalinity. He and Tom Brock of the University of Wisconsin are mutual admirers, and he jokes that neither trespasses on the other's hunting grounds. Horikoshi's finds include a unique triangle-shaped bacterium, a donut-shaped species, and bacteria with magnetic properties. Household products made from his discoveries have earned billions of dollars—and he knows he will find more.

At times, on these trips to technology's frontiers abroad, I come away concerned that America is lagging in an important or promising area. And so it is when Chuck and I visit biotechnologist Isao Karube at immense Tokyo University. The U.S.-educated innovator is marrying microbes with electronics to develop a variety of clever sensors. One of these submerges in a patient's toilet in a hospital or nursing home to record automatically the chemistries of urine and feces for instant analysis by computer. My travels have shown me no comparably advanced research in the States. And Karube's sensors could be big-ticket technology.

Back home, my microbe coverage is winding down. But I still must address a pervasive public fear—of genetically engineered microbes being released into the environment and proliferating out of control. This fear flared two decades ago when microbiologist Ananda Chakrabarty used ultraviolet radiation to create a mutant bacterium designed for cleaning up oil spills; in a landmark decision the U.S. Supreme Court held that Chakrabarty could patent this new life-form. Alarm escalated into hysteria in the 1980s when California scientists field-tested genetically engineered bacteria for controlling frost. When I visit Ananda Chakrabarty at the University of Illinois in Chicago, he is still engineering microbes to cleanse the environment of toxic wastes. But now he will treat wastes not with living bugs but with the cleansing enzymes they manufacture, mass-produced in fermenters. The public's fear has prevailed.

A last foray awaits—a visit to the happiest, most numerous microbes in the state of Maryland. They thrive at the Back River Waste Water Treatment Plant in Baltimore, the city's sewage works.

It's only right that my formal *Geographic* career end thus; after all, one of my earliest assignments, on rats, took me to the vaulted sewers of the Vatican. Furthermore, the Back River plant is a neglected urban treasure—460 acres boasting a woodland, a stream with frogs and minnows, a nature trail, and a golf practice area, all on Chesapeake Bay and in a no-smell environment.

Back River's task is formidable. Every day 180 million gallons of sewage, industrial wastes, and society's most loathsome other excretions surge into its treatment tanks.

Plant manager Gerry Slattery does not flinch. His microbes are deployed, uncountable hordes of them, ten pounds of bacteria for every pound of arriving sludge. "They're lean, they're hungry, and they grab," he boasts. He adds philosophically, "Sometimes I wonder who is working for whom."

Slattery's confidence is well placed. I look at the river of treated, cleansed effluent cascading out of the plant, picking up oxygen before entering the bay. It runs as clear as a piedmont stream. Fishermen congregate along a concrete pier jutting into the bay, catching white perch and stripers. Seven great blue heron nests cluster here. Golden tributes to bugs well used.

Now, after months of travel, I must repay the *Geographic* with an article. As usual, conjuring up a lead is the biggest challenge. I settle on the heroic role of microbes at the Homestake Mine in South Dakota.

For a hundred years the Homestake, biggest gold producer in the Americas, discharged lethal cyanide from its gold-processing plant into Whitewood Creek, along with mercury, arsenic, and sewage. The toxic flow left a wake of sterility through the Black Hills and stained waterways halfway across the state.

Environmental pressures in the 1970s forced the company to act. To neutralize the gushing cyanide, biochemist Jim Whitlock isolated bacteria that lived in the toxic water, feeding on the cyanide's carbon and nitrogen. Growing them by the billions in massive treatment tanks, he channeled the cyanide effluent slowly past the feeding bacteria. When I visited Homestake's discharge outlet, the effluent ran clean, and creel-size brown and brook trout swirled in the rushing flow. Whitlock's achievement won worldwide acclaim. It becomes the natural lead for my article: "Like venom squirting from a fang, lethal cyanide poured daily . . ."

IT'S A FRIDAY EVENING in October 1991, and the Society is hosting its ten retirees at a lavish fête at the Chevy Chase Country Club. Following an elegant dinner Gil Grosvenor pays tribute to the group's cumulative three centuries of service, service that has paralleled his own. A slide presentation, using snapshots retrieved from film archives and secretly obtained from our spouses, portrays each of us in the various stages of our careers. Group pictures are taken, small presents received. It is a heartfelt and heartwarming farewell.

Back to the office, to the inevitable clearing out of three decades of pack-ratting. Marie Barnes and I box up assorted memorabilia of twenty-plus article assignments—the vertebral disk of a whale from my trip to the Bering Sea, a corn-grinding stone from an article about the Anasazi Indians, the rat-shaped liqueur bottle from Hamelin, a brick of salt from a Saharan salt caravan, my Inuit harpoon and fish spear, a ceramic catalytic converter from my advanced materials article. We pack the Peruvian wall hangings, the books and science papers unneeded by the library. Special care goes to gathering up the 200 or so small spiral-bound notebooks that rode in my hip pocket during assignments. Only one is missing, from my travels in India on the food/famine assignment.

The ritual of packing is astonishingly painless. I wonder if this is because I am coldly unsentimental, unmoved at leaving the most rewarding career I can imagine. I don't think so. Instead, I'm turning a page we all must turn, and the next page, too, appears rewarding.

In this sense I am fortunate to be a writer. A writer's venue is not fixed to any one place, or to physical needs beyond some paper, a pen, and perhaps a PC. If no assignments send one forth to exotic lands, the writer can draw on memory's vast inventory of experiences and on matters closer at hand—family, home, and community. Already pushing forward from the back of my mind are my own long-dreamed-of books, ideas now urging me to bring them to light.

And there is so much beyond writing. For this ardent amateur landscaper there are azaleas to plant, stone walls to build, and ponds to dig. There are the many rewards of being a father and now a grandfather. And there are years ahead with Susan, years that grew out of the Golden Age of the *Geographic* and continue so for both of us. I am indeed blessed.

Many more friends have since left the *Geographic*, some through predictable retirement, some as the result of a paroxysm of downsizing in the early 1990s. But the magazine arriving in my mail looks better every month: skillfully written and photographed, beautifully designed, packed with short articles wisely geared to varied interests and attention spans. In a few years Gil Grosvenor will step down as chairman of the board; eventually the family name may vanish from the masthead, and with it a century-long publishing dynasty. Will the magazine with the yellow border also fade below the horizon? Although nothing is permanent, I think not and fervently hope not.

Index

Following is a comprehensive list of the articles contributed by Thomas Y. Canby to *National Geographic* magazine:

California's San Andreas Fault   *January 1973*
Pioneers in Man's Search for the Universe   *May 1974*
Skylab, Outpost on the Frontier of Space   *October 1974*
Can the World Feed Its People?   *July 1975*
Apollo-Soyuz: Handclasp in Space   *February 1976*
Can We Predict Quakes?   *June 1976*
The Rat, Lapdog of the Devil   *July 1977*
The Year the Weather Went Wild   *December 1977*
Aluminum, the Magic Metal   *August 1978*
The Search for the First Americans   *September 1979*
Our Most Precious Resource: Water   *August 1980*
Synfuels: Fill'er Up? With What?   *February 1981*
The Anasazi—Riddles in the Ruins   *November 1982*
Satellites That Serve Us   *September 1983*
El Niño's Ill Wind   *February 1984*
Soviets in Space: Are They Ahead?   *October 1986*
Advanced Materials—Reshaping Our Lives   *December 1989*
Earthquake—Prelude to the Big One   *May 1990*
The Persian Gulf—After the Storm   *August 1991*
Satellite Rescue   *November 1991*
Bacteria: Teaching Old Bugs New Tricks   *August 1993*